Stay

MINDFUL

How to Deepen Your Experience of Mindfulness and Appreciate Your Life

Annee Griffiths

Staying Mindful
How to Deepen Your Experience of Mindfulness and Appreciate Your Life

© Pavilion Publishing & Media

Published by:
Pavilion Publishing and Media Ltd
Blue Sky Offices
25 Cecil Pashley Way
Shoreham-by-Sea
West Sussex
BN43 5FF

Tel: 01273 434 943
Email: info@pavpub.com
Web: www.pavpub.com

Published 2020

ISBN: 978-1-913414-23-8

Pavilion Publishing and Media is a leading publisher of books, training materials and digital content in mental health, social care and allied fields. Pavilion and its imprints offer must-have knowledge and innovative learning solutions underpinned by sound research and professional values.

Author: Annee Griffiths
Production editor: Ruth Chalmers, Pavilion Publishing & Media Ltd
Cover design: Phil Morash, Pavilion Publishing & Media Ltd
Page layout and typesetting: Phil Morash, Pavilion Publishing & Media Ltd
Printing: Print2Demand

"This timely, important and skilfully written book is clearly borne out of decades of experience. At a surface level it is eminently practical, offering sensible guidance, structure and encouragement. At a deeper level it is infused with wisdom and compassion. As a whole it will support and inspire readers to develop and sustain their mindfulness practice. This is not surprising as Annee Griffiths has lived every word she writes in her own mindfulness practice and teaching. This book is a timely gift that will become a mainstay go-to resource for anyone looking for ways to develop a lifelong mindfulness practice."

Willem Kuyken, Ritblat Professor of Mindfulness and Psychological Science, University of Oxford

"Designed to support on-going meditation practice after an eight-week introductory course, this book provides an easy read for practitioners using it on their own and for teachers wanting to run follow-up courses. With a collection of poems, guidance on practices and personal stories, Annee has brought this book together beautifully. I imagine it will become a popular resource for those wanting to maintain their practice."

Sharon Hadley, Chief Executive Officer, Oxford Mindfulness Centre

"Staying Mindful is a wonderful introduction to mindfulness practices. It is full of useful advice and meditational practices that clearly demonstrate the importance of being mindful in the bustle of the contemporary world. Annee Griffiths writes with a wealth of personal experience in teaching mindfulness, and this is clearly shown in the accessible style, depth of knowledge and practical wisdom to be found within these pages."

John Peacock, former Associate Director, Oxford Mindfulness Centre

Contents

To

John, Hannah, Esther, Tom, Joe, Iola, Cai, Robyn and Sylvie

Permissions

Cover Photo by Sarah Holyfield with kind permission.

Thank you also Sarah Holyfield for the photographs beginning Chapters 1,2,3,4,7,8, and 11

Balthazar Serreau for his heart photo for Ruth in Chapter 6 and to Esther Griffiths and Matt Wharton.

John Griffiths for his photos in the Introduction, Chapters 5, 9, and 10.

With kind permission from John Peacock for the translation of the Metta Sutra and other quotations.

Lesley Conran for her kind permission for the late Tony Conran's poem 'Purpose' from 'The Three Symphonies' published by Agenda Editions.

David Rynick for kind permission for poems and blog extract..

With Kind permission from Melissa Blacker for a quotation from The Book of Mu edited by James Ishmael Ford and Melissa Myozen Blacker, © 2011 James Ishmael Ford, Melissa Myozen Blacker. Reprinted by permission of Wisdom Publications, www.wisdomexperience.org.

From Welsh poets: Fiona Owen for her kind permission of her poem 'Present' from Screen of Brightness pub-lished by Cinnamon Press.

And Lloyd Jones, Trish Bartley, Meilyr Wyn Jones, Jody Mardula, Lindsey Tossell, Emma L. Lloyd, and Vicki Thomas for kindly allowing me to use their poems Also for permission from Emma Gibson Illustrator for her diagram: the seven attitudes.

Sarah Silverton and Vanessa Hope with kind permission for an extract from The Mindfulness Breakthrough, published by Watkins

With kind permission from Paul Gilbert for the Emotional Affect Regulation diagram and theory.

Coleman Barks for his kind permission for 'The Guest House', 'Bird Wings', and extracts from 'Childhood Friends' and 'Music Master' reprinted from Maypop Books Athens, Georgia.

With kind permission from Welsh publisher 'Gomer' for Pa Beth Yw Dyn from The Peacemakers by Waldo Williams translated by Tony Conran

Thanks to Kristen Neff for the Self-Compassion Break widely used on Mindfulness Self-Compassion courses.

Acknowledgements

To John Griffiths and David Shannon for their unfailing patience and generosity when proofreading, and especially to Hannah Griffiths for her insightful comments and tireless re-reading of all chapters to maximise their potential and to ensure their authenticity and accessibility.

For all at Pavilion Publishing and Media for their work and generosity. Especially to Darren Reed for having faith in publishing me. To Ruth Chalmers for her kind and thoughtful guidance and the team at Pavilion Publishing for their care.

I would like to thank John Griffiths, Sarah Holyfield and Balthazar Serreau for their wonderful photographs, included at the beginning of each chapter; Sarah Holyfield for her photograph and inspiration for the book cover. I am lucky to be friends with such talented people. And not forgetting Emma Gibson for her illustration.

I am grateful to friends and students who contributed poems: Jody Mardula, Trish Bartley, Lloyd Jones, Fiona Owen, Meilyr Wyn Jones, Emma Lloyd, Lindsey Tossell and Vicki Thomas. Thank you.

To my former colleagues at the Centre for Mindfulness, Research and Practice (CMRP) for their generosity in sharing their wisdom with me. Especially to the initial team in 2001, Mark Williams who set up the CMRP, the director Rebecca Crane for her kind Foreword and Eluned Gold and Sharon Hadley who supported the development of the 'Staying Mindful' course. Much gratitude and love to my team of special friends and colleagues: Judith Soulsby, Jody Mardula, Sarah Silverton, Mariel Jones, David Elias, Vanessa Hope, Trish Bartley, David Shannon and the late Cindy Cooper.

To all my teachers, especially Melissa Blacker and David Rynick whose friendship and wisdom have warmed and inspired me. To John Peacock who is a good friend with an abundance of knowledge. To Mark Williams, Jon Kabat-Zinn and Pam Erdman who inspired me to do this work. And of course to all my former students and supervisees – without you it would not have been possible. I loved our time together.

To my good friends who supported me through this, especially Pauline Williams for more than 50 years of generous friendship; Sarah Holyfield for the inspiration of her art works and whose artistic career grew alongside this book; Tim Clark for conversations; and my meditation group – Mary McIntyre, Alison Pearson, Jani Evans and Hugh Knott. To Barbara Gaskin for early adventures into the unknown, Sheila Brooke for joy and the singing Bluebelles. Also Sarah Millband for teaching alongside me at the Staying Mindful Retreat and inspiring me with her resilience and love.

I also need to mention my walking group (particularly leaders Oliver Knowles, Sue Carter and John Charles) who have kept me physically fit and emotionally warm throughout. I may have finished this book earlier but missed many mountain and coastal walks.

Thanks to my parents Frances and Guy Matthews and my siblings John Matthews, Ali Williams and Mike Matthews for their past support.

To my wonderful children, the Griffiths: Hannah, your wisdom has inspired me; Esther, your good company has cheered me; Tom, with your great sense of fun and bravery; and Joe with your ready wit, warm humour and considered life view. You are all amazing and I love you all. And Taz Serreau, Matt Wharton and Kelly MacDonald for making us all happy.

To my beautiful and brave grandchildren: Iola and Cai Serreau, Robyn and Sylvie Wharton-Griffiths, all of whom have been my most profound teachers and are the light of my life.

To John, words fail me! For your support and belief in me beyond my own belief, for your deepest teaching on the meaning of acceptance, kindness and – most of all – love, and for your unfailing generosity and regard for improving the environment and other people's lives.

Foreword

by Rebecca Crane

Sustaining a meditative practice over time is a great challenge. Even though we may be deeply committed to engaging regularly in practice there can be significant resistance, and a lot that takes us in other directions.

Annee recognises these challenges, and also knows the ways in which building mindfulness practice into everyday life brings great benefit for ourselves and the world. She has been thinking about the issue of what happens after the eight-week course for many years. Annee was one of our first students on Bangor University's Master's programme in mindfulness-based approaches. For her thesis, she conducted research on participants' experiences of their mindfulness practice after the eight-week course, and through this become convinced that something more structured was needed. Her study and subsequent studies found that the monthly follow-up course offered by the University was a useful support to graduates of the eight-week mindfulness course but it had its limitations. Participants expressed a need for a follow-up course that gave them the opportunity to explore more deeply their practice and share the experience in a supportive environment.

Over the years, she has gradually developed and refined a follow-up course that she offers both in weekly sessions and as a residential retreat. Now this beautiful curriculum is available also in the book you are holding in your hands; a book that will be a useful guide and companion to you as you engage in the ongoing exploration of being human – and the ways your mindfulness practice can be a central support to this exploration.

Annee brings a depth of experience of personal mindfulness practice, of teaching and of training teachers. All this accumulated wisdom unfolds wonderfully in this book. I commend it to you.

Rebecca Crane PhD

Director, Centre for Mindfulness Research and Practice, Bangor University

Introduction

Why meditate? What is it about? How do you do it? What motivates you? How do you continue to practise mindfulness? Do you have an intention around the practice or do you think it might help to have an intention to stay motivated, to stay interested?

I have found that all these questions are worth revisiting time and time again if we wish to live mindfully and nurture our wellbeing. Not everyone needs a formal practice to be mindful, but in my case (and that of millions of others) a formal practice of meditation helps to cultivate mindful awareness and compassion; to be more awake in the present moment rather than preoccupied with worries and difficulties. This book aims to explore mindfulness practice and indeed life itself.

This book was finished just before our world was shaken to the core with the spread of the Covid-19 in early 2020. Before we were all required to lock down, to socially distance ourselves. Before the real threat to us all when the news told us that we were in a potentially life-or-death situation. While the book was going through the editing process with Pavilion Publishing & Media, the publisher, I thought it necessary to take the book back and insert some reflections on my experience of the phenomenon. When the book is released most of us will have lived through a time that has transformed the world. I do not know how this world will look. I do know that being in the moment alive to all my senses has helped me with my own anxiety and coping mechanisms through an extremely challenging time. I know that living through this time has fostered a sense of connection to others and a deeper understanding of acceptance.

Mindfulness practice has been essential for my mental health throughout my life and particularly in these difficult times. The commitment to remember to bring awareness into my life, with the breath, the body and sounds in the present moment, has encouraged me to realise with gratitude all the good things in my life. To realise in spite of danger that I am still alive now, as are my loved ones.

This book is an aide memoir for practice. Its aim is to ignite or reignite an interest in mindfulness and to share how others use mindfulness, so that we can realise that we are not alone and isolated but connected in myriad ways.

I first started practising in 1975 when I took a gap year or two to journey to India and Japan in search of inspiration and authentic meditation teachers. My initial motivation for this journey was a disappointed and disrupted love life. I knew I had to find another way of being. My early teachers included Christopher Titmus who ran retreats in India before setting up the retreat centre Gaia House; Moringa Soko Roshi, a Zen Master of Daisho-in Kyoto; and Nisargadatta Maharaj in Mumbai. I visited the Dalai Lama's small palace in India and was blessed by him. When I came home I found it difficult to maintain a practice. I attended retreats at Gaia House and read many meditation books. But I felt lonely. It was hard maintaining a regular meditation practice in isolation.

Imagine my delight when I discovered there were other mindfulness practitioners in the remote area of North Wales where I was now living and that my local university was researching into the benefits of mindfulness for depression. Consequently, under Mark Williams and Rebecca Crane, Bangor University set up a Centre for Mindfulness, Research and Practice (CMRP) and invited world-famous teachers to North Wales. This centre was the first in Britain and I was privileged to be part of the initial team. The CMRP was followed swiftly by a number of centres for mindfulness at other UK universities, including Oxford, Exeter and Aberdeen. And in the Republic of Ireland Dublin and Cork. Some of the teachers on these other universities studied at Bangor University first.

Now we don't have to go to the East to seek out mindfulness teachers. We have our own home-grown teachers on our doorstep.

Mindfulness has become a mainstream word in Western civilisation. Many people have had contact with some aspect of mindfulness. It is now a familiar aspect in our culture to hold moments of silence. The two-minute silence in vigils for disasters and terrorist attacks. The minute's silence held in Britain on Armistice Day on the eleventh hour, the eleventh day, the eleventh month in remembrance of those who died in the world wars, and to foster peace. The surprising compliance of a noisy football crowd to hush into a minute's silence for the death of football colleagues or recent victims of terrorism. This has meant that there is a recognition of the importance of 'quiet time', of the practice of being in silence.

At this time in our history we are aware that more children and adults are suffering from stress, anxiety and mental health problems than ever before. One way to alleviate this suffering is through mindfulness meditation, which has been useful in helping people understand and improve their mental health. Many people say their lives have been transformed by mindful awareness and acknowledge that it is a contributory element to their sense of wellbeing and happiness. They affirm that it has been of benefit and often compare their lives before and after they studied mindfulness.

Certainly, being mindless is unpleasant, from feeling ungrounded and scatty to being quite overwhelmed by irritation, anxiety, stress, sadness or other emotions. While these emotions don't necessarily go away, a mindfulness practice gives us a place to stand, a way to be with and in the world. For me, when I am in doubt around the worth of my mindfulness practice, I find it is useful to remember that many people whom I respect have sustained a practice and assert that it is essential for their life. This is an affirmation for me and helps to sustain my own practice.

I have a strong belief that as I become more intimate with my own mind and feelings I can become more understanding of how the experiences of other people might affect them. As I become aware of the facets of feeling different emotions, and of their effect on the body and mind, with the spiralling consequences of reaction, I have the possibility of realising the intricacies of what it is to be a human being.

Meditation exists in many spiritual traditions and mindfulness practice in its current popular form is not a new-fangled fashion but has survived and flourished in many cultures for over 2,500 years. The eight-week Mindfulness-Based Stress Reduction (MBSR) course was developed by Jon Kabat-Zinn in 1979 in Massachusetts for hospital patients who had chronic pain conditions. This widened the access to mindfulness as people from many walks of life discovered a new way to be with their life.

In the early 90s, two psychologists from Britain, Mark Williams and John Teasdale, collaborated with Zindal Segal from Canada to test this approach for people with depression. They set up an eight-week course specifically designed for people suffering from depression. They called it Mindfulness-Based Cognitive Therapy (MBCT). Their subsequent research results (Williams et al, 2000) (Crane et al, 2014) led to many people training to be mindfulness teachers to facilitate health and wellbeing in the National Health Service (NICE, 2004) and in schools, workplaces, prisons and for the general public.

I trained as a mindfulness teacher at Bangor University and was privileged to teach on Bangor University's Master's degree course in Mindfulness Approaches and to train mindfulness teachers. The Foundation module of the Master's degree fosters a deep exploration of personal practice. I experienced this both as a student and as a teacher. This model of deepening into the themes of mindfulness practice originally inspired this book.

I have been teaching the eight-week MBSR course since 2001 and I have met many people in North Wales who have completed the course. This experience and research evidence informed me that eight weeks of a practice is barely enough. People need support and stimulation after the course to maximise the benefits that they originally realised. My Master's dissertation was a study of the long-term effects of mindfulness practice and investigated whether people needed support to continue practising. Research (Griffiths, 2008) (Lambie, 2016) has shown that indeed most people need support to continue a practice.

My results encouraged me to develop a follow-up course and I have been running these follow-up courses for 10 years now. Random, drop-in follow-up sessions, rather than a themed course, are often disappointing for people who have experienced the intensity of group support in an eight-week mindfulness course. A study on follow-up support by Hopkins and Kuyken (2012) showed that participants appreciated the safety of a closed group in order to share in depth. Knowing this from my own experience and research I set up a six-week follow-up course to integrate, support and expand on earlier learning, to instil a habit of practice and to help people realise the relevance of the practice for their life. The success of these courses encouraged me to write this book both for practitioners using it on their own and teachers wanting to run follow-up courses.

The Staying Mindful course has proved to be useful for many graduates of the eight-week course. It has helped people develop a regular mindfulness practice thus enabling them to manage anxiety, depression, chronic pain and other difficulties, while enhancing their wellbeing and happiness. One participant wrote that the course has 'enabled me to embrace mindfulness and is helping me to transform my personal wellbeing and better manage life's pressures'.

This book can be used as a self-help book, taking in one chapter for a period of time and focusing on the themes therein. Or it can be used as a resource to dip into the relevant concern of the moment. It can also be used as a resource for teachers who wish to run follow-on courses for people who have started this journey. The final chapter outlines session plans for running a mindfulness follow-up course. All the chapters are illustrated by poems and stories from mindfulness practitioners about how they work with practice in their lives.

I am a magpie, taking the jewels of wisdom from wherever I find them. My treasures are from Buddhist and other spiritual traditions, psychological knowledge, research, quotes from people steeped in wisdom, published poems and, for originality, poems and stories from my community, including my own poems and personal stories. I hope you will enjoy the journey.

A brief summary of the contents of this book

Mindfulness is paying attention in a particular way, on purpose,
in the present moment and non-judgementally.

This definition by Jon Kabat-Zinn (1994) holds all the elements necessary for mindfulness practice. This book, *Staying Mindful*, aims to expand on elements of this definition and reiterate and develop the themes that were helpful in the courses for beginners. It will also introduce new aspects of mindfulness practice not necessarily revealed in the initial MBSR course.

Chapter 1: Intention is an exploration of *'on purpose'*. This is the intention we bring to a mindfulness practice and how to sustain practice. What is it we long for? What is our motivation to practise and how can we purposely cultivate motivation and intention? What do we want for our lives?

Chapter 2: Paying Attention is at the heart of practice. What we intend to pay attention to affects our experience of life. Meditation is a honing of this attention. This chapter looks in more depth at paying attention, what it means and what pulls us away from paying attention in the present moment. It investigates obstacles to and in meditation and how being aware of our barriers can support a regular practice.

Chapter 3: Practising with Attitude In this chapter we consider 'in a particular way' the importance of cultivating specific attitudes in practice. Qualities that enhance your experience in practice and in life are highlighted. Non-judgement is one of the seven attitudinal foundations described by Jon Kabat-Zinn (1990). The self-critic is particularly prevalent in our culture. The attitudinal foundations of mindfulness considered in this chapter are also profoundly relevant. These are: Patience, Trust, Non-Striving, Acceptance, Letting Go or Letting Be and Beginner's Mind.

The themes of the above chapters – intention, attention and attitude – are described as the three axioms of mindfulness (Shapiro *et al*, 2006).

Chapter 4: Working with Difficulty elaborates upon three main types of emotional regulation systems that work together to regulate emotions – the approach, avoidance and soothing systems (Gilbert, 2009). The chapter contains practices to work with difficulties, including the RAIN practice and personal stories that illustrate how mindfulness has helped people in times of emotional upheaval.

Chapter 5: Working with Anxiety is included because so many people come to mindfulness classes with stress and anxiety. The chapter gives some national statistics defining the extent of the predicament in Britain. There are some practices specific to anxiety or fearfulness. The chapter is enlivened by relevant personal stories and poems.

Chapter 6: Basic Friendliness and Self-Compassion emphasises how compassion starts with self-compassion. Although an essential component of mindfulness practice, kindness and compassion has been implicit in the previous chapters. Now it is explored and practised explicitly with meditations that focus on generating friendliness and self-compassion. It includes a pointer towards the growing research in this area and people's reactions to the practices.

Chapter 7: Interconnection covers early conditioning and how it impacts on relationships. It also includes seven steps for mindful communications and provides exercises to help us with communications. There are practices working with anger, forgiveness, equanimity and tolerance. 'Healer, heal thy self' is the first step in being congruent with implementing useful action in the world. Peace and reconciliation work and other ways to be active in the world are touched on in this chapter.

Chapter 8: Gratitude looks at nurturing gratitude and includes meditations on appreciation. It explores counting our blessings and reflects on the possible negative aspects of gratitude practice. It also considers research studies on gratitude including the growing popularity of keeping a gratitude journal.

Chapter 9: Continuing to Practise – Keeping it Alive suggests ways to keep the practice alive. Finding sources of support through meditating with like-minded groups, reading inspirational books and using mindfulness apps are highlighted, as well as the advantages of going on retreat. This chapter also includes helpful short practices to keep the thread going. A description of the Zen practice of Koan study is also included.

Chapter 10: Personal Stories celebrates six stories that describe how mindfulness practice has helped people with chronic and terminal illness, addictive behaviours, anxiety, depression and ordinary life. One of these stories celebrates Cindy Cooper, a well-known and well-loved teacher in the mindfulness world. Her touching interview with Becca Crane, the Director of the Centre for Mindfulness Research and Practice, is inspirational and a remarkable tribute to her work.

Chapter 11: Course Session Plans contains session plans and notes for teachers of mindfulness. These are guidelines for a six-week course following the themes of the book. Several sessions offer alternative activities.

> In spring, numerous flowers;
>
> in autumn, the moon.
>
> In summer the cool breeze;
>
> in winter the snow.
>
> If you don't worry about other people's business,
>
> Exactly this is the best season of your life

– Wumen

Chapter 1:
The Power of Intention

Your intention is really important; it needs to be refreshed and examined regularly. We embody this intention to be awake.

– John Peacock

There is an old story attributed to a Native American elder about feeding wolves. It illustrates the power of where we place our deepest intention. In the story a grandmother tells her granddaughter: 'I have two wolves fighting in my heart. One wolf is full of hate – vengeful, fearful, envious, resentful and deceitful. The other wolf is loving, compassionate, generous, truthful, wise and calm.'

'But which one will win the fight, grandmother?' asks the granddaughter, nervously.

The grandmother answers, 'The one I feed.'

All our actions result from an intention which arises in the brain. They stem from an intention to move towards or away from something. Many of these initial intentions are not within our awareness. Thought and impulse may well be unconscious. However, we can deliberately forge intentions. It is possible to shape our lives with skilful intentions that ultimately lead to less suffering. 'Neurons that fire together, wire together' said brain neuroscientist, Donald Hebb, in 1949. An intention to be mindful, to be present in the present moment can become a habit of being mindful. A deep practice. An intention to practise being attentive 'in a particular way, on purpose, in the present moment and non-judgementally' (Kabat-Zinn, 1994).

An intention to notice things we normally take for granted or ignore, to be alive to our senses – here for our moments, like noticing the smile of a child or the rays of the sun arriving at the window after three days of rain (a reality in North Wales where I live). An intention to encourage within ourselves attitudes that promote mental health, for example to be more self-compassionate.

Intention in our practice has two aspects. One is for our whole life. Let's call this our over-arching intention. This is a lodestone. It is a guide star, our north star by which we navigate. This represents our deepest reasons for practising mindfulness. This is always individual and deeply personal. We are aware of the map and we know where we are on it. It is a heartfelt intention to keep up a mindfulness practice, to do it regularly. That is to find time and the necessary energy and inspiration which motivates us to practise.

The other is around setting an intention for a particular practice. Each meditation practice may have a different intention. This is a stake in the ground, a marker – 'I am here on this mountain, I know its name.' It is a locator, like knowing the street name of the territory we are exploring; one that grounds us in the knowledge that this is what we are doing for the next moments.

Over-arching intention

An intention to live our life as mindfully as possible may involve developing a habit of regular practice. This could be a lifelong resolution, a sense of direction. It is founded on remembering or reminding ourselves of the benefit of practising. A translation of mindfulness from the ancient language of Pali is 'remembering'. Remembering to be aware, remembering to be kind, to be compassionate. In the eastern languages 'mindfulness' and 'heartfulness' are often the same word. Our intention here is in remembering – remembering to keep in touch with our heart's desire, to consider what matters most in our lives.

It is a path to follow, to love. It is an intention to cultivate more awareness in our life, to live life as a 'good' person with values of care and consideration. It is to remember to be here for our moments, for our life. Our intention to practise means holding on to a vision.

What has kept me practising for more than 40 years has been a vision of freedom; freedom from the fetters of uncontrolled emotion, a spiritual calling which goes beyond limitations of mind and body. Poetry and music are part of the inspiration. I like William Blake's heartfelt intention:

> To see a World in a Grain of Sand
>
> And a Heaven in a wildflower
>
> Hold Infinity in the palm of your hand
>
> And Eternity in an hour.

Another long-term vision that motivates me to do a daily practice is Plato's maxim: 'Know thyself.' Or Socrates' adage: 'The unexamined life is not worth living'. Alexander Pope from our own literary tradition expanded this to: 'Know then thyself, presume not God to scan. The proper study of mankind is Man.' (From 'An Essay on Man, Epistle II', 1734.)

Why start a meditation practice? There are many reasons. Usually it is because life is unsatisfactory in some way. This could be because of a life-threatening or debilitating illness or disability, a devastating grief, too much uncomfortable stress, depression, anxiety, disappointment or a broken heart.

Why continue a meditation practice? It may be remembering that the practice benefitted you in the past. Or you feel the practice could lead to less suffering in your life now or in the future. Or maybe you remember moments of joy and peace.

In order to commit to a regular practice we need to remind ourselves why we practise, which may take us back to our original motivation. Commitment to a regular daily practice is central to cultivating mindfulness in daily life. The practice becomes a way of being and enables us to be more focused, more present in our lives rather than living an alternative life in our head. As we focus our attention in the present moment we also cultivate a self-compassionate attitude. This may involve being aware of layers of experience.

Plenty of people tell me that they are still practising mindfulness by being mindful in their daily lives. This informal practice is useful. However, although it is possible to be mindful without a daily formal practice it is hard for most of us. In order to be mindful in my life I have to set aside time to practise. Time to practise being patient, practise being non-reactive, practise being kind. If I don't do a formal practice I begin to feel like I haven't washed for a while – kind of scratchy; for me it's part of my mental, physical and spiritual cleanliness. One of my fellow teachers who teaches mindfulness to trainee nurses tells them that 'mental hygiene' is as essential in a hospital setting as physical hygiene, and this can be cultivated by practising mindfulness.

Forcing ourselves to practise is counter-productive. We can feel restless and frustrated with our busy minds, our restless bodies. If this is the case choose a shorter practice, say 10 minutes, and work up to a longer practice or begin with some mindful movement or a walk. Even a very short 'formal' practice is useful. A regular place to practise can be helpful. A place to simply sit down for a few seconds. That simple acknowledgement may keep the intention to practise alive.

Many teachers talk about mindfulness as a training and, like regular visits to the gym or any physical fitness regime, the training eventually pays off. With commitment and determination it becomes easier. Ruby Wax comments in her book and show 'Frazzled' that many of us are committed to going to the gym for physical exercise but we are resistant to the mental exercise that ensues with a mindfulness practice: 'We need to exercise what's in our heads just like any other muscle'.

What happens when you think about practising meditation? Do you just think of all the jobs you have to do? Too busy to practise? The to-do list ever beckons and is often prioritised over meditation practice. What thoughts go through your mind? What excuses do you make to yourself? Might you see that as soon as you think about practising there is a moment of volition, of decision, of making a choice? These moments are key moments.

Ask yourself at this point: 'Why practise?'

Or ask yourself any of the following questions:

'How can I best take care of myself?'

'Do I not want to practise because I am feeling sad or angry, restless or worried?'

'Am I afraid of being bored?'

'Do I feel too tired or sleepy?'

The reasons we give for not practising could be: 'I get impatient and edgy.' 'It's a waste of time.' 'I am not achieving anything.' 'I don't believe in it.' 'I'll do it later after I've done…'

Or maybe we want to do something more pleasurable with this time? A walk, read a book, watch a film or TV, talk on the phone, or go on social media or other computer options. We need to make a wise choice without building up a resistance and this may differ from day to day. 'Just do it.' Do it in spite of your excuses. Remember your intention, remind yourself of your commitment. Just do it. (We will look again at barriers to practise in the next chapter.)

We may find it hard to sustain a meditation practice for some of the above reasons and others. I asked people who attended the Staying Mindful course why they had come on the course. Here are some of the reasons people gave:

'When I was meditating regularly I was managing my anxiety much better – I need a regular practice.'

'I suffer from depression and the eight-week course helped me. I am concerned that I will get depressed again as I have not been doing the practice and I notice I am beginning to ruminate again.'

'I find that I am still identifying with my thoughts and get carried away by them. One thought follows another and I am taken over, sucked in.'

'I have been so busy that I have made excuses not to practise. When I do practise I feel calmer and less anxious. Things don't get to me so much.'

'I would like to live more simply and not be in my head so much ruminating over the past. I just want to go for a walk without a particular purpose and feel the wind on my face and be in the moment.'

'On the eight-week MBSR course I just started to discover what meditation is and want to learn more. I just touched the surface.'

'My partner died recently and I feel the practice helps me come to terms with it.'

We may go back on our intention to practise regularly many times. That's ok. We tell ourselves we will get back to formal practice when the time is right. We have not failed or broken our commitment. For me, having a demanding baby resulted in me being too tired to practise. However, when I finally caught up with my sleep I needed to practise in order to cope with toddler tantrums. We can return to our intention to have a meditation practice no matter how long we have strayed from it:

> Wanderer, worshiper, lover of leaving,
>
> it doesn't matter.
>
> Ours is not a caravan of despair.
>
> Come, even if you have broken your vow a hundred times.
>
> Come, come again, come.

– Rumi

ANNA, with a small child and a demanding job, was too busy to practise. However, a back injury that left her unable to even read for a period of time meant that she had nothing to do but practise. Lying there for long hours meant she could do the body scan, she could be aware of her breathing and be alive to her senses. When she was well again she continued to find time to practise.

DEEPTA had moved to a new house and she was surrounded by boxes that needed to be sorted. She felt that she couldn't practise in this chaos. Her house was disorganised and so was her mind. She meditated with the follow-up group which shifted her perspective. She realised that although her mind 'was all over the place' there were a few moments of peace, of space. She went home and found that in spite of all the clutter she could create some space for herself by keeping up with her meditation practice.

LUKA said that he had not been able to practise because he couldn't do 45 minutes. He discovered that if he sat down to practise with the idea of just doing five or ten minutes he enjoyed it more. He felt less agitated and anxious. Gradually he was able to build up his practice to 30 minutes a day.

LAURA turned to meditation as a way through her problems. When her boyfriend wanted to see less of her, she experienced a crisis, an identity crisis. She was not the centre of the universe, or at least not his universe, and this shattered her. She had relied on his admiration and approval in order to shine. She needed to discover some other baseline for existence. Mindfulness meditation with its emphasis on the moment enabled her to do this. In fact, the practice brought her a kind of independence and freedom previously unimagined in her ego-led hedonistic life.

'What is my own over-arching intention? What is my motivation to practise?'

I ask myself this regularly and sometimes it is answered by a body sensation, a warmth in my heart area. Sometimes the words 'freedom' or 'love' arise. Freedom is the signpost, love is the lodestone. My ex-colleague and teacher, Cindy Cooper, always asked me: 'What does your heart say?'

Sometimes we have to be very quiet before we know what our heart is saying. The Dalai Lama says, 'My religion is kindness'. Inspired by this and influenced by my own mother, I would like to be kind whenever I can. All religious traditions emphasise the importance of community, of looking out for one another.

My concrete day-by-day do-able intention? Is to notice judgement, to work with that inner critic who says, 'You can't', 'You're not good enough', 'You should have done this', 'You shouldn't have done that', and to bring some kindness to myself as well as others as best I can.

I have found it useful when working with intention to acknowledge that this time spent with myself will benefit me even if it doesn't feel like it at the time and has the potentiality of benefitting others. This may sound grandiose; nevertheless, it helps me to consider that this time spent quietly is not harming others, not consuming anything and may have a positive effect on the world. This may lead to denunciations of magical thinking, so I will qualify this statement by saying that I trust it will prepare me to be more effective in this world.

It can be hard to practise on your own. It may be possible to find a group in your area or even set one up with like-minded friends. This strongly supports your intention to practise.

Steps to set up a regular practice

A five-minute practice

Step 1   Set an intention to practise regularly.

Step 2   Find a way to remind yourself of your intention.

It may be useful to set a phone reminder or a daily note on your computer or paper calendar. Or maybe set up Post-it notes to yourself and leave them in strategic places.

It is helpful to have a particular place to practise. A cushion in a corner, or your meditation chair strategically placed. This is not always possible in our busy households but carving out a space that is a reminder to meditate can be useful.

Step 3   On awakening, reconnect to your over-arching intention for the practice in your life. Intend to fit in a practice that day.

Step 4   Review the day ahead and decide on a time. Some people set an alarm to practise early in the morning before the business of the day gets going. However, many people, including myself, find this difficult. If you are very busy you could decide on a short practice or even mark out a practice as the walk to work or from the car to the workplace and make up for it with a longer practice the next day. As you do this, say to yourself: 'This is my meditation practice'.

Step 5   When you get to the time you have allocated, decide on the nature of the practice. Will it be silent or guided (i.e. a recording)? Decide on a practice: a body scan, a movement practice, a walking practice (slow or faster) or a sitting practice.

Pebble in the well contemplation

The purpose of this short meditation is to find your deep intention or motivation for practice.

Choose a quiet place to sit, stand or lie down. Close your eyes if that feels comfortable.

Feeling your feet on the floor and your bottom on the seat, noticing the sensation of touch and support as you make contact with whatever is supporting you – floor, seat, and beneath it all, the earth itself. Taking a few breaths and, as best you can, being really present for each in-breath and each out-breath.

Now ask yourself the question: *'What do I really want from my practice?'*

You can imagine you are dropping a stone into a deep well (it's a wishing well!) Or this can be any body of water, perhaps a lake.

As the stone falls repeat the question silently to yourself. Allow whatever answer arises to come to you. No need to force this. This pebble is going to take some time before it finally comes to rest at the bottom.

At a certain point, allow the deep well/body of water to 'merge' with your own body, so that the water becomes a metaphor for yourself.

In your 'mind's eye' see the stone gently falling deeper through the water and asking yourself the question again: *'What do I really want from my practice?'* Accept whatever arises in your body-mind in response to this question.

The stone hits the bottom and as it wriggles deeper into the mud ask yourself again. *'What do I really, really want in my heart for this practice?'* You can focus on your heart area, even if you wish, bringing your hand to your heart.

The answer may not be in words but a feeling, a body sensation, a strong sense of intention. Whatever your experience, intend to stay open to the feelings or thoughts that arrive, even if you experience it as a sense of resistance. Be curious about whatever arises. It may surprise you.

Bringing your attention now back to your breath. After a few breaths, again be aware of your bottom on the seat and your feet on the floor.

Comments from the Staying Mindful course

'I want to change some unhelpful behaviour. I know I am not going to change habits I have had for 40 or more years overnight, but I need to keep practising and I need all the encouragement I can get.'

'I first thought that I had come to the course to develop my practice and become more concentrated, but as the stone fell through the water and touched the bottom I felt in my guts my deep longing for something, for connection, for truth.'

'I too felt a deep longing. It was a feeling in here [touches her chest] *my heart, the word for it is love.'*

'To deepen my practice, particularly learning to live in and appreciate the moment.'

'To be more relaxed and to discover the origin of my fear and to gain more control over-anxious thoughts'

'To be more compassionate to myself'.

'To stay mindful in the face of illness'

'Coming home.'

One word often arises for people when talking about what they want out of practice: 'Peace'. 'Calming' is another word often used. We could translate this as a strong desire to be free from the worries, cares, self-judgements, recriminations and ruminations of our lives. This genuine yearning for freedom from suffering is often the principal call to a practice. As we practise being present with our life as it is, we find we can't escape from life's vicissitudes and the recognition of this may lead us to be more accepting of our life, more free within it and feel a greater peace.

Setting an intention for a particular practice

Setting an intention is placing a stake in the ground and deciding on what the focus of the practice is. Intention depends on our heart's wish. What do we really, really want? As we sit down to practise we may intend simply to be present. We may be interested in noticing self-judgement without judging ourselves for being judgemental. The intention could be to be less harsh or more gentle with ourselves, to bring kindness or compassion to ourselves or others at this time.

A practice intention could be to cultivate certain attitudes such as patience or trust or acceptance or Beginner's Mind (more on these attitudes in Chapter 3). It could be to sit with a difficulty in our life or a barrier to the practice. The intention might be merely to be with the body, honouring sensations, even when they are painful. Or it could be simply an intention to feel your life just as it is right now.

Exploring intention in practice includes finding the time, finding a place, setting a time (i.e. 5 or 10 minutes or 30–45 minutes), deciding what form the practice will take and what we are going to focus on. It may also include an attitude to the practice that feels relevant at the time.

At the beginning of a meditation I set an intention. It is usually something simple. When I lead a meditation I usually invite participants to quietly set their own intention or at the very least suggest that the posture is, in itself, an intention to be aware in the present moment. As I take my seat I am resolved to put energy into being present at least for some of the time. Each time I sit down to practise I am linked to all the experience and faith in the practice that has gone before.

First choose whether to sit, lie, or move. Some people find it very useful to combine two practices. For example, to do mindful movement or walking practice just before a sitting practice. They might do 10 minutes of movement and 20 minutes of sitting. Or 20 minutes of movement and 10 minutes of sitting.

Another choice is to do a mindfulness meditation and start or finish with a befriending or compassion practice.

To help remain motivated some variety in meditation may be needed in order to keep it fresh and alive. You could read something inspirational before you start or occasionally find a new recording or a new meditation from a book or the Internet. Sometimes, counting your blessings or simply taking time to notice the freshness of the day or the shadows in the night before you start will give you a moment of awareness that could affect your whole practice. Or perhaps you could take a fresh look at a loved one and see him or her as if for the first time and this could give you a sense of purpose which awakens your attention.

At first SIMON was falling asleep in the body scan and his initial reaction was a harsh one. 'You are not doing this right, try harder, it's not good enough.' Then he realised the distress he was causing himself and how it led to his lack of motivation to do the practice. He deliberately set an intention to be kinder to himself, to accept whatever happened, even if it was falling asleep. His intention at the start of the practice was to bring compassion to his experience.

Later he felt that as he was setting aside this time he didn't want to be sleeping through it. Neither did he wish to return to a judgement of failure, to being critical of himself. He made a deliberate intention to be aware of his experience, noting where it was in the body that he drifted off to sleep (at the right leg where there were no sensations) and noted what his thoughts were during the body scan. He felt pleased that now he had more awareness of drowsiness and more awareness of the preoccupations of his mind. He could track back and remember some of his thought trails. He was curious and attentive to the whole of his experience and the practice became alive and worthwhile.

Simon had changed his intention from 'doing it right' – that is, having perfect concentration – to being alert to what was really happening, which was being aware of drowsiness. Where in the body did it happen? Did it always happen at a particular place in the body, at a particular time? His project was to study it, how it felt. As his intention shifted so did his attitude to his practice and eventually to himself. The need to be perfect in whatever he did was highlighted in the body scan. This harsh driving force and need for perfection was present in other places in his life. As he became more aware of this, he was able to modify his perfectionism substantially and consequently had greater mental ease in his life.

Intention and the brain

Science is now revealing that pathways in neural circuits become strengthened by intention. If our drive is towards selfishness and fighting for what we want, or our inclination is towards negative thinking about ourselves and others, these pathways can become habitual. If our thoughts are harsh towards either ourselves or others we are reinforcing harshness in our thinking and this is habit-forming. The brain's neural pathways towards negativity are strengthened. The hypothalamus is activated by thoughts of rage and fear. The amygdala is activated by a sense of threat and the pre-frontal cortex moves us into a plan for action.

However, wholesome intentions around kindness, generosity and insight strengthen positive responses in the brain and progressively weaken habits of negative and harmful impulses. The Anterior Cingulate Cortex (ACC) hub and the amygdala hub work together in a system that is involved in all motivated activity. The ACC is the rational centre for the integration of thought and feeling and is involved in any effort of will. The amygdala is involved in more passionate motivation (liking, disliking, opportunity and threat). Intention in meditation reflects a neural coherence between the two.

The intention for a regular practice becomes part of our experience, normalising it, making it part of our routine. We are cultivating a good habit that will help us recognise our helpful and unhelpful habitual patterns. If we are not too attached to a goal or become judgemental around our progress then we do not get caught up in the old adage, 'The road to hell is paved with good intentions'. We just lighten up a little and come back to our original wholesome intention knowing that we are forging or strengthening new neural pathways in our brain. (See Rick Hanson's *Buddha's Brain* (2009) for more in-depth information on how the brain works.)

I shall finish this chapter with four over-arching intentions, from others and from myself.

An intention from a staying mindful student:

Hedwig used this quote from Herman Hesse to talk about her experience *'I'm now aware of the spot – deep inside myself – where there is always silence and a place to rest with myself*. She said she hoped to visit this place every day. She continued: *'I hope to remember the little mantra that comes to me during kind and unkind times*: "This is a moment of suffering, let's embrace it. Let's soothe it with compassion. This is a moment of happiness, let's cherish it. Let's enjoy it fully".'

Why I Cry for the Moon

May what I do flow from me like a river
Sometimes flooding
Sometimes barely moving.

Why rush when the moment is languid?
Why long for stillness when the rushing is current?
Why cry for the moon when the sky is black?

– Trish Bartley

Grace

*Grace
'What is it?' You ask.
As we stand on a great plain
At Abermenai

Skylarks above.
And all around us space.
At our feet violets and violas,
Purple and white, yellow and white
And more white from the burnet roses.

On the sea plain beyond acres of sedum.
Far in the distance- the sea
And beyond the Menai Straits
On the horizon
Misty mountains.

High so high sounds above
Heard not seen
The trilling,
Skylarks soaring.

'Hail to thee, blithe spirit!
Bird thou never wert.*

This is grace
I say.
This call to happiness.
This space

Wide and free.

*Percy Bysshe Shelley

Purpose

Is there a reason
For us?
Like a hiraeth*
For the one shy kiss

Of first love, the question's
Beyond our imagining –
The first what-must-have-been –
The first love song –

The first time I was shown
The cherry tree
Of the world
Bending, flowering insanely

White around us
Like a blockade of stars,
My mother's canopy
And me in her arms.

– Tony Conran

*Hiraeth: loosely translated from Welsh as 'a longing for home'

Chapter 2:
Paying Attention

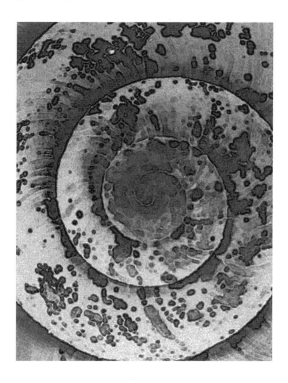

*My experience is what I agree to attend to. Only those items which
I notice shape my mind.*

– William James

In the Greek myth of Eros and Psyche, Psyche is given an impossible task.
She is asked to sort out an enormous pile of different seeds into separate
piles. She is confronted with a large granary of seeds and grains. Like many
of us, particularly early on in the practice, she despairs at this task of paying
attention for a long time. Interestingly, she feels that she can't do it and
yet it gets done. In her case she is helped by ants that sort out the seeds
overnight. The ants show her that, step by step, the task can be completed.
In meditation we need this resolve to keep going. To take stock, to pay
attention to the minutiae of what is happening in our experience, so that we
can learn about our life. This comes back to motivation but it is useful to
know what we are up against; when we realise what the common obstacles

to meditation are, we can gain some courage. It is doable but we may need the support of others to stick with it.

KANE said: 'I wasn't really practising after I did the eight-week course. I felt that when I couldn't do the 45 minutes practice every day I was a failure and so I gave up. However, making it my own and deciding to do shorter practices and/or mixing and matching the guided recordings or sometimes doing my own practice without guidance, has been a way forward, and has given me new impetus. I am not so hard on myself now. Working on intention has really helped me to establish a practice routine that works for me.'

What is paying attention in meditation?

In school 'Pay attention!' was often a reprimand for not paying attention. In meditation we sometimes use this strict voice as a stick to beat ourselves up with. We can get angry or frustrated with ourselves because we find it hard to keep our attention focused.

We sit down with the intention to be present and within a short time the mind wanders off. When we see this happening we bring the mind back to be in the present moment. When we do this with gentleness and kindness it is meditation. It's not perfect, it's practice. We are practising being in the present moment and we forget over and over again that's what we are doing.

In popular parlance meditation is about having no thoughts, as in 'emptying the mind'. But this is not our aim. Our intention is to cultivate awareness. By bringing more attention to our thoughts, and by skilfully seeing them as thoughts, we are loosening our identification with the thoughts as 'me' or 'mine'. We can have a very narrow view of who we are when we cling to an identity that is fed by thoughts. We are not who we think we are, we are more than our limited thinking. Our thoughts can contradict each other so it is important to remember that 'thought is not fact'.

Our meditation practice is a dance of awareness that moves in and out of the spotlight of attention. In our practice we are able to notice how attention moves from one place to another. Sometimes we shine the spotlight of attention on the present moment and at other times we are somewhere else, not fully aware of our experience, distracted by this or that. Sometimes our distractions are quite trivial, a stream of consciousness about everyday concerns or flights of fantasy. Sometimes our distractions may be painful recriminations or ruminations, replays from the past or anxious thoughts about the future. These thoughts may be so powerful that they affect our whole nervous system and cause physical sensations of stress.

'Paying attention is a platform for leaving suffering', says Kathleen Dowling Singh (2017). We get caught up in our own preoccupations. We are so hooked up to our own story that we don't see the bigger picture. This is a case of inattentional blindness. A study called 'Gorillas in our midst' (Simons and Chabris, 1999) had surprising results. Two small teams, one in red and one in blue, pass the ball to teammates and the viewers of the video are asked to count the number of times the red team catch the ball. Our attention is so fixed on this task that more than 50% of viewers don't see the appearance of a gorilla wandering about in the middle of the game. Jon Kabat-Zinn showed this video at a Bangor University mindfulness conference. Most of the audience of over 100 people, except for two or three, did not see the gorilla in the midst of the game. Although I had an accurate score of the counted balls I didn't see the gorilla. I was shocked when we watched the video again to see how obvious he was. How much more am I missing? I still wonder. As we fixate on our own preoccupations, what are we missing? The awareness that we are more than our story, our ego, is indeed liberating.

Choosing where we can place our attention

1. Concentration meditation

We may choose to work with a **narrow focus of attention** by concentrating on one thing. For example, either the breath, body sensations, sounds, sight or the words of a befriending or compassion meditation. When we notice our mind wandering, we acknowledge where it has gone and then simply come back to the focus. In the body scan we practise using the narrow focus when we focus on our toes and the wide focus when we focus on the whole body.

2. Mindfulness meditation

We may choose to practise with a **wide focus of attention**, simply being in open awareness with whatever arises, moment by moment. This could be an awareness of the whole of the body rather than a specific part. Or all the sounds rather than one sound. This wider focus allows us to work with mind, emotion and bodily sensations almost simultaneously. Or we focus on 'choiceless awareness' and take in whatever arises in the moment.

3. Focused meditation

We may choose **mindfully to explore a particular issue**. This could be one that we are acutely aware of, either mentally or physically. This exploration is not merely analysis or rumination but includes awareness of the full range of our experience. It may be a narrow focus of awareness on one area which widens out to awareness of thoughts, emotional feelings and related body sensations. When we pay attention we might notice what stories take over our minds and how they affect us physically. Being with our experience in this way may be unpleasant but as we practise we realise that moments – whether unpleasant, pleasant or neutral – are transitory, and we become more resilient. We develop the courage to be curious. Working with pain or working with difficulty meditations have this focus.

4. Cultivating particular attitudes

Cultivating particular attitudes in our practice, such as courage and curiosity, reinforces these qualities in our life. Attention shapes the brain's neural circuits and if we cultivate some of the attitudinal foundations of mindfulness, such as compassion, these neural networks become stronger too. More about this in Chapter 3.

> *To pay attention means we care, which means we really love.*

– J. Krishnamurti

It may help the quality of our attention when we remember this quotation. When we are with another person we can give them our full attention, which means we care. When we are with ourselves we aspire to give our full attention to ourselves, showing a deep care for ourselves by practising mindfulness.

The five hindrances or obstacles to practice – what stops us practising?

Mindfulness meditation has existed for more than 2,500 years. There is guidance from the Buddhist tradition on what stops us meditating or hinders us while we are practising meditation. What is it that pulls us away from and stops us paying attention to the present moment? When you do your meditation practice you can make a mental note of which hindrance is most prevalent:

1. Wanting or clinging to pleasant experience – wanting your experience to be different (sensory desire)

2. Focusing on or avoiding the unpleasant – again, wanting your experience to be different (aversion)

3. Feeling dull or sleepy: 'Too tired', 'numbed out'

4. Feeling restless or bored: 'I haven't time', 'no space', 'I am interrupted by the demands of others'

5. Doubting the practice, or self-doubt (sceptical doubt): 'Does it really work?' 'I can't do it', 'It's not working'.

1. Wanting pleasant experience

Wanting pleasant experience and clinging to it is a major force in our life. Our meditation practice may not be very satisfactory and we may put it off for a more rewarding experience.

During the practice we might spend time fantasising about our favourite food, planning the meal we will cook, thinking over pleasant experience or thinking fondly of a loved one. We could have a strong sensual desire, be it craving a piece of food, like chocolate, alcohol, tobacco or a sexual experience. Most of us experience the urge to move sometimes, the wanting to be somewhere else, to do something else, even if it is a chore that 'must be done'.

All these urges can be very strong. The practice is to be with the urge, 'surfing it'. We can watch it arise, grow in intensity and then eventually fade away. Seeking the pleasant has a subtle grasping element. If we attend to the body sensations while having the thoughts that accompany grasping, we can experience this grasping physically.

Grasping after things, states or people is a deep drive. We become entranced or obsessed with the object of desire and seduced by the anticipation or momentary good feeling when we possess it. This doesn't last and we find ourselves clinging to thoughts and fantasies that build up our attachment to the desired. We are seeking pleasant feelings but often they may fall short or be short-lived. In meditation we can notice this tendency. We have time and space to step back and observe, to notice how the body feels without acting on this strong impulse. We can also notice the relief when we let it go and to see its impermanence. A sense of freedom occurs when we realise we are not bound.

Another obstacle that prevents us from truly experiencing the present moment is wanting a special state in meditation. Peace, light, love, bliss, happiness. We want to experience the deep peace promised by our idea of what meditation is. A special state. Our culture has led us to believe that there is a 'zone', and we may buy into this modern myth: 'I just want to get in the zone'. We could be clinging to a pleasant meditation experience we have had in the past and wanting this again. Maybe we want to be 'nice and relaxed' and again we are disappointed with our experience. These expectations are also a barrier to being in the present moment and accepting what is here now. These are very much part of the theme of wanting things to be different.

This wanting gets in the way of feeling peaceful. Rather than pursuing a special state, we might explore the uniqueness of this moment. It may sharpen our experience to recognize how precious our life is. We can realise the newness of every breath, each breath a new breath.

Sometimes in my meditation I feel myself really wanting, grasping after a 'deeper experience'. It is goal-orientated and has the tension of striving within it. Sometimes when I realise that I am feeling dissatisfied or bored with this moment and wanting a special feeling I focus on the sensations I can feel in my heart area, the yearning, the wanting.

We can focus on this wanting, this longing, and let that be the object of our attention and see it as a form of love. Or we can focus on this wanting as a feeling of dissatisfaction, noticing what the grasping feeling is like. This assumption about how the practice should be gets in the way of just simply being with what is here in the moment. Mindfulness meditation is counter-intuitive in our culture. Our consumerism, our achievement orientation, our wish for constant entertainment, is possibly greater than ever before in our history. Nevertheless, people everywhere and in every time have experienced this wanting or grasping.

JOY had a 'lovely meditation' the first few times she did the body scan. Her body felt very light – in fact, filled with light – and all her cares vanished. She felt complete and happy. She felt 'at one with the world'.

'This is what meditation is about,' she thought and for weeks and months afterwards she sought to regain this experience. The wanting was very strong but it didn't make any difference, in fact it made meditation an unpleasant experience as it was filled with disappointment, boredom, dullness and restlessness. She began to doubt herself.

Sometimes having a 'wonderful experience' in meditation is the greatest hindrance of all, because we continually strive to 'achieve' this again.

2. Aversion: focusing on or avoiding the unpleasant

For many of us the present moment is not enough. We are distracted by our preoccupations, maybe planning or rehearsing something for the future or dwelling on a past occurrence that is still hanging over us. We may be trying with both future and past concerns to shore up our safety in subtle ways.

Over-planning is a form of anxiety; is this future planning and anxiety a usual place to go in our meditation? If so, might we examine how this feels in the body? What does this looking forward feel like somatically? Does it feel like a leaning into the future? Check out the face, the belly, chest and shoulders. Maybe we can notice some tightening around these thoughts. We are trying to be in control even in the future – a time we have not reached yet.

To muse over the past might be a regretting or resenting past actions or interactions. Perhaps we ruminate over past events as a way of trying to understand and somehow control them in hindsight. Sometimes, in meditation, we can notice this as a wanting state. Notice that we are blocked from being in the present moment because we want things to be different. We want the pain or difficulty in our life to go away or we want the moment to be special. How can we be with pain when experiencing it in the moment is painful? How to be with our wanting heart when we feel we are just not good enough or the meditation is not good enough? If we can be with whatever is here in the moment, staying with it a while and exploring, inevitably it changes and shifts. Sometimes clarity emerges, sometimes we wake up. Sometimes we discover that the pain is bearable or different to how we thought it was.

Another reason we stop practising is when we are suffering in some way. We are in pain or too sad or too anxious, too angry or irritated. It is unpleasant to stay with this distress. We resist it. However, what we resist persists. Often this distress is based on a story about ourselves. We are not good enough, a failure, we are not loved or other stories we tell ourselves. Sometimes within the stories we are justifying ourselves and trying to make ourselves comfortable; sometimes we are avoiding really feeling our experience for what it is.

If we are thinking rather than feeling, we can find ourselves living mainly in our heads and we continue to construct an identity based on our story. Maybe we are not that fixed self we imagine ourselves to be? We have many conditioned reflexes – it's the human condition. By investigating our feeling in the present moment we are more able to fully experience it, to face whatever is in front of us.

When we fully acknowledge them, we are more able to work with our difficulties. One way of working is to label the emotions present: 'Here is anxiety'. 'This is anger.' Then we can choose to go a little deeper, to allow ourselves to feel the emotion more fully. Maybe we are aware of bodily sensations around this strong emotion. It may be possible to befriend the feeling and, as best we can, bring some kindness to ourselves for this suffering and in the process let go of judgemental thoughts. Practising when we are experiencing intense feelings can be very rewarding. We may be able to acknowledge our suffering and while the purpose of the practice is not to resolve it, or make it go away, we often find we change our relationship to it.

Physical discomfort may be a significant distraction compounding our lack of attention. However, how we relate to pain or tension in our mind amplifies the problem. We will often add extra discomfort by layering our experience with the dislike of the physical pain and wanting it to be different – adding resistance or avoidance.

A story from the Buddha tells of the man who was wounded by the dart of an arrow. He was in agony; this is the first dart, the dart of physical pain, the actual pain he was experiencing. That was bad enough, but he added a second dart himself, one of mental suffering. *Will I die? Who did it? Will I be able to revenge myself? This shouldn't happen to me. I hate this.* And so on. He had more to deal with as the brain and body were stressed by these painful thoughts. If we can become aware of this second dart our awareness lessens our suffering and reduces the effect. The self-critical voice is also a second dart.

There is the initial experience, which we then elaborate upon, and before we know it we have built a story around it. The mind may elaborate around anxiety, despair, self-judgement. All these are avoidance modes of mind that we look at in more detail in Chapter 4.

Sometimes, we can be caught up in a state of aversion: anger, judgement, fear, resentment or confusion. If we say, 'I shouldn't be like this' and try to push it away it often gets worse. Experiment with this. Try pushing it away or avoiding these feeling – see what happens. Does it go or does it get worse? Then what happens? It often results in another layer of judgement. Then we might add yet another layer by saying 'I shouldn't be judging'!

Anger, irritation, ill-will to others or yourself (self-judgement), hurt or resentment cause an agitation that disturbs the mind and affects the body. This state has been compared with a turbulent lake where the water is whipped into waves and there is no clarity, no possibility of seeing a reflection. It is not possible to be present with the whole of your experience – the ill-will may dominate your perception and your world.

Aversion shows us what we are attached to and what holds us back, where we are stuck. It has a tight hold on us. We could allow this uncomfortable feeling to be there and notice the thoughts, emotions and body sensations that arise with this. As we turn towards it with curiosity, we could explore how this 'stressor' constricts or excites the body. As well as this curious noticing we might bring a sense of kindness to this suffering self, caught up in unpleasant feelings. We could cultivate some self-compassion.

Viktor Frankl, a psychiatrist and author, was a survivor from a Nazi concentration camp. His book, *Man's Search for Meaning* (1959), is an inspirational discourse about how to survive amid absolute horror. He refused to be pulled into anger or despair about the terror to which he was subjected. *'What is to become light must endure burning'*, he said. He held on to a firm belief that his mind was his own, seeing the good in others, noticing the sunset and enjoying the occasional humour that broke through the blackness. Although he didn't call this way of being 'mindfulness', these words show that he was practising in a similar way:

> *Between stimulus and response there is a space. In that space is our power to choose our response. In our response lies our growth and our freedom.*

– Viktor Frankl

To sum up, there are two ways of working here: the first way of being with this aversion is to connect and feel the suffering in the body; the second is to wish ourselves well and befriend ourselves in the moment of suffering.

3. Sleepiness or dullness

Yes, you may well be tired, it's been a hard week or a difficult day, but what if you always feel sleepy when you come to a quiet place with yourself? There are various reasons for this. It could be:

- Avoidance – it could it be a way of not being with yourself in the present moment
- There is emotional pain or old wounds or hurts deep beneath the surface that you are not ready to be with yet
- Sometimes a habitually busy mind will shut down and go to sleep when it isn't busy, problem solving or striving.

We work with this by bringing mindfulness to sleepiness, observing how the body feels, the limbs, the eyes. Are we feeling heaviness, drooping, nodding? We can intend to notice how and when it begins, the middle of it, how, where, when it ends. Make a project of studying it.

Sometimes this curiosity brings its own energy. Sometimes we are able to discover an emotion lurking under the sleepiness. We make an intention to be curious about our experience. Perhaps it is boredom, which also falls under this hindrance, although I include in 'restlessness' a need for entertainment. Boredom can be a generator of drowsiness or sleepiness.

We can practise with our eyes open, or splash water on our face, or stand up, put one hand in the air or do a walking or movement meditation. If it's really bad, you could do what meditation teacher Jack Kornfield did and practise on the edge of a well (or cliff top)! Perhaps not!

The Victorians translated dullness and sleepiness as 'sloth and torpor'. I can relate to these words sometimes. Sometimes my meditation practice can feel like wading through treacle or porridge. This kind of meditation practice can be compared to a muddy pond. We can't see into it nor can we see our reflection. We need to be determined and committed and this will bring the needed energy and clarity.

4. Restlessness, boredom or worry

This is so familiar to most of us. Impatience with meditation that seems to go on forever, the 'to do lists' repeating themselves, the desire to get up immediately after we have sat down to meditate, and worst of all, anxiety manifesting as restlessness. Restlessness can be so strong that it is almost unbearable. The urge to jump up and attend to something else may be just the everyday cluttered mind thinking this, thinking that and finding it difficult to settle on the moment. However, restlessness may be a desire to avoid whatever is here, it might be impatience with the moment. Often this impatience is a familiar pattern reflected in our everyday life.

How to be with this restlessness? First we acknowledge and name the feeling: 'Restlessness is here; it won't kill me'. Then explore with curiosity the physical sensations it engenders and bring self-compassion to mind and heart. We can tell ourselves 'this too will pass', that it is only transitory and acknowledge that it is uncomfortable.

Working with this obstacle to practice is very similar to the work with aversion, noticing and being curious around the sensations and deliberately bringing a feeling of kindness to this suffering self.

Sometimes, we might steady the mind (and body) with concentration on the breath, counting the breath up to 10, starting with one on the in-breath, two on the out-breath, three on the next in-breath and so on. Sometimes, extending the exhalation will steady us in the moment. This has an impact on the parasympathetic nervous system, which has a calming effect.

If restlessness is truly unbearable choose to do some mindful movement or walking within your allocated meditation time. It's fine to do this for a while and then come back to exploring all the different meditation focuses and work with barriers to practice.

AMIR found he was too restless to do the sitting meditation. He found doing 10 minutes of yoga before he did a sitting practice helped him to sit for longer. He found the combination of the two practices served him well.

Sometimes it is hard to sit still. So how can we work with this? On one hand we really want to do the practice. We pay for the course, we sign up, we call ourselves a meditator. But another part of our self doesn't want to do it. 'I just can't stand it' or the sun is shining outside or we have a to-do list that's calling out. Then we are springing out of the chair, up off the cushion and finished.

This is where intention is so important. Just like in the practice, when we have an intense body sensation we have a choice of whether to move or not. We can make a conscious decision. 'I will stay with this feeling of restlessness for one minute, two minutes, five minutes.' Then notice what happens to the body; any tension, any leaning forward and what happens in the mind. Maybe do a three-step breathing space and then get up and go. This is how we honour our commitment or intention.

It is important not to make the practice another place where we feel forced. There may have been times, particularly in our childhood, with parents, carers or teachers when we felt coerced or forced and we withdrew or rebelled. So we need to find a way to be compassionate and also honour our commitment to working with ourselves.

Is boredom restlessness? A need for entertainment. When we pay attention and look at our experience there are subtle changes, something happens all the time. However, in our fast-paced culture, we look for entertainment and our boredom threshold is low. We are immersed in excitement from an early age: TV with dramatic stories, the endless entertainment of the Internet and social media, the coming and going of all our jobs and interactions. We long for the significant, the peak experience and forget to live our moments fully. A body scan or slow yoga is not very exciting.

AME said that she would sometimes find herself catapulting out of her seat and moving on to the next task apparently without warning. She said it was when she was feeling busy, pressurised or excited about the need to do something. She would also react like this if she was feeling down, unhappy or dwelling on unpleasant thoughts.

'Recently I have really paid attention to my desire to move. If I can catch this before the action/reaction I might be able to explore the feeling that is so compelling. I have given myself a time limit, saying to myself: "OK, I will stay sitting for another five minutes and explore how this feels in my body".'

'It's been very interesting. The twitchy jumpy feeling has felt quite alive, tingly. Staying with this feeling no matter how subtle has kept my interest. There is a feeling of being alive, a vibration of aliveness in the body akin to a gentle yellow flame. The experience is pleasant. How long can I stay with this sensation before something else comes in? Sometimes the focus on the body will move to a hearing focus to sounds of the spring chorus of birds outside or maybe the shrill cry of the cock pheasant who wonders around the garden. This too is very pleasant. Then my desire to move dissolves and I am able to stay much longer.'

5. Sceptical doubt

This is either doubting the practice: 'Mindfulness practice is no good', 'Will this really benefit me?' Or self-doubt: 'I can't do this', 'I'm useless', 'I'm not good enough'. Again, we are adding extra, telling ourselves stories that are based in negativity. We live the stories by believing them, repeating them to ourselves and getting stuck.

Doubt is a form of rumination. It is an aversion and avoidance mentality. Doubt can be compared to a pond covered in weeds or a bog. We cannot see our reflection in the water. We cannot see all experience when beset by doubt. Doubt is like walking through the desert with no food and only a little water. There is danger lurking all around and we have no road map. Not a very attractive state to be in!

First, we need to recognise the pattern of thoughts and emotional reactions, and any consequential feeling in the body. Then we need to question the truth of these thoughts – are they true? Are these thoughts facts? We need to realise their fleetingness, their impermanence, and not give them credibility. We need to be especially careful that we are not adding another layer by being judgemental: *'I shouldn't be experiencing this'*. Maybe some humour or some kindness would be appropriate here.

We could be aware of how we continually reconstruct our notion of ourselves and see ourselves in a wider container than just our skin; maybe sensing the space in the room or outside. Maybe we can envisage that we are a part of a greater whole and this will help us not be so caught up in identifying with 'me' and 'mine'. The small self ...sitting in the centre of the universe.

If we are half hearted about our practice, not really being able to commit ourselves to it, doubt will inevitably arise. Sometimes we have to wait out this dry time, which seems barren. We have to keep going with the practice and with ourselves no matter what the doubting voice is saying to us. Remembering that the practice did bring us some peace, some joy. Speaking to others about their faith in the practice could be helpful. Acknowledging and exploring this state with curiosity is an essential way forward.

Curiosity is an integral part of the practice. What matters to me? What do I really want from my practice? This questioning may bring us back to intention and keep us on track. Remembering why we practise or reminding ourselves that we did feel the benefits at some point is a helpful spur to establishing a regular practice. People remember that they felt less anxious when they practised. They were able to be less reactive and often kinder to themselves and others.

An antidote to doubt about the practice is to mindfully come into the moment, to hear the sounds of the moment or to experience the breath. The truth of the present moment cannot be refuted. Another way to work with doubt is to practise with and talk to other meditators about their faith in the practice. Or talk with meditation teachers or read inspirational books to renew your interest and prevent a sense of isolation. Begin to or continue to cultivate a love for this work

In the spiritual tradition there is also the 'Great Doubt' which seeks 'the truth' of 'Who am I?' 'What is awareness?' 'What does it mean to be awake?' 'What is freedom?'. This questioning mind will lead to very rich practice.

'I should practise' exercise

This exercise is a useful way of noticing and working with the voice that says 'I should...' For example: I should be more active, I should have more energy, I should be giving more, should do more work, should fit more in, should not feel stressed, I should meditate, and so on.

Bring to mind 'the should' of the moment.

Stay with the sentence with 'should' in it and feel the energy.

Take a few minutes to allow the attention to drop beneath the words into the feeling in the body.

Where is it? How does it feel? Heavy? Light? Tightening up of chest, throat, guts, tummy?

Nausea? Or maybe very little sensation at all.... just stay with the body.

Listen to the voice. Does it belong to anybody? Perhaps one of your parents? A grandparent or carer? A sibling? A teacher?

Is the voice saying anything else? For example: 'Pull your socks up', 'You are weak'.

How does that feel? (Vulnerable, shameful, fear, irritation, anger, sadness?).

How does it feel in the body? Allow the feeling to be there, allow your posture to show how you feel, your facial expression.

Is there any other voice, any different view? For example: 'It's OK to be how you are at the moment', you are just a bit tired, you will be OK later'.

Ask yourself what is the purpose of the voice or voices? Do they contradict each other? For example, one is a call to action and the other a call for compassion?

Where are they in relation to the sides of the body? Perhaps one is on the right, one on the left.

Move your hands around so that they are in relation to each other; let them play, relate, dance together.

(Adapted from an exercise by Melissa Blacker)

GWEN didn't want to meditate. She felt strong resistance and just didn't do it. Then she felt guilty. Does this sound familiar? She felt she was letting herself down, breaking with that strong intention she had made to herself to meditate every day. Sometimes she did and it was so unsatisfactory she simply got up and did something else. She felt even more guilty because she had retired after a very busy work life and now had plenty of time. She said to me: 'I should practise but I don't want to'.

We did the 'should' exercise together. I asked her to say: 'I should meditate' and notice how her body felt. Just to stay with the 'should' sentence and feel into it. She said: 'I feel heavy and drained.' As she repeated the 'should' sentence to herself, did she recognise the voice? Gwen said, 'It's my mother'. I asked whether she saying anything else. Gwen said: 'She is telling me in a scolding voice to be more disciplined, not to be so lazy and weak. I am surprised – I thought it would be my father.'

I asked her if there was another voice with another view. 'Yes, it's me, I am about 20. I am saying "No! I won't do as you say. NO!"'

I went on to ask her if she could identify whether the voices have a purpose. She said that the strict voice wanted the best for her but she was trying to control her. Gwen's voice was saying: 'How would you know what's best for me? I will do what I want. I feel quite angry.' →

Gwen experienced her mother's voice on the left-hand side, and her 20-year-old self was on the right. She allowed her left and right hands to express this and after some pushing and pulling, she noticed that she was holding her hands together peacefully. She found the exercise interesting.

When I next spoke to her she said it had made such a difference. She had let go of the strict approach. She said: 'Discipline is not so important now, I have just been sitting and not timing myself and I am actually doing the practice for a longer time. I feel calm inside and feel that the practice is a gift rather than a "should do"'.

'When you guided me in that "should practice" last time I realised that I had avoided sitting with the feeling of not wanting to do it and saying "should" to myself. When you guided I realised that it was here and it was OK to feel it. After I could keep in touch with these feelings and thoughts and either sit with them or allow myself to not sit with intention. When I realised the "should" voice was my mother's voice I started to have a different relationship to it. Over the years I have sat with feelings of sadness and worry but I have never sat with this "should" even though it has been, as you know, a strong driver in my life.'

'This has spilled over into my life in general. I feel I have more trust now that my life will work out the way it needs to without me feeling I should be doing this. I have felt I should be working, helping people or teaching. But my heart is not saying "yes", my mind is saying "should"... "I should be useful, otherwise it is selfish." But now I trust that the work I need to do will come in its own time. And I have time for my friend who is sick, I have time for another friend whose husband has died, and I have time for nature.'

We don't always know what the best way forward is. We can listen to our mind and our deep family and cultural conditioning or we can listen to our heart and trust that our life is the way it needs to be just at the moment.

We talked about the importance of befriending rather than pushing away. How resistance persists. Gwen said 'I am thinking about the poem by Rumi, *The Guest House*... "The dark thought, the shame, the malice/meet them at the door laughing and invite them in". I do feel shame that I am now quite old and I am still fighting my mother. I'm a grown up!'

These patterns go deep and often they are under the radar, disguised as 'should' and 'ought'. More about this in Chapter 3.

Overcoming barriers

'Just do it'

Jon Kabat-Zinn's invitation to 'just do it' when people say they don't like the practice certainly works for some during the eight-week course. However, after the course many people's practice tends to scale down to nothing. Remembering the benefits and finding a practice that suits us individually seems to be the key in keeping a regular practice. If we sit or lie in stillness for some time we have an opportunity to look into our life in a different way. Insights occur, we become more robust around being with difficulty and sometimes realise how precious our life is as we practise living in the present moment.

A number of friends have told me that while they find meditation difficult and find they make any excuse not to practise, they acknowledge it does benefit them when they are having difficulties. They appreciate Jon Kabat-Zinn's encouragement 'to weave the parachute before you jump out of the plane' but they have many strategies for avoiding sitting in formal meditation. Nevertheless, many of them find it easy to sit simply with a cup of tea and watch the birds in the garden or people in the street out of the window. Watching clouds, a fast mountain stream, a slow river or waves lapping or bashing the shore are other prompts to anchor us into the present moment. This relaxed way of being does not register as meditation for most of us and yet it can give us a moment of awareness of the present and a necessary break from a mind that wishes to be busy, busy, busy.

There are many ways of working with barriers to practising. Sometimes it revitalises our practice to do a befriending meditation or compassion meditation (see Chapter 6). Or we can simply bring kindness or tenderness more into our practice by acknowledging that 'this is hard' and find a way to practise which is appropriate at the time.

Leisure

What is this life if, full of care,

We have no time to stand and stare? —

No time to stand beneath the boughs,

And stare as long as sheep and cows:

No time to see, when woods we pass,

Where squirrels hide their nuts in grass:

No time to see, in broad daylight,

Streams full of stars, like skies at night:

No time to turn at Beauty's glance,

And watch her feet, how they can dance:

No time to wait till her mouth can

Enrich that smile her eyes began?

– W.H. Davies

Exercises and practices

The following exercises are designed to encourage you to meditate and set up a regular practice.

What stops me practising?

Ask yourself the following questions:

What benefits do you get from meditation? Are you happier, calmer? Are you more relaxed, more aware? Are you more in touch with yourself?

1. How important is it to you to find time for yourself? How important is meditation in the time you have for yourself?

2. Do you feel you don't deserve this time set aside? If so, what are the feelings here, what are the thoughts behind them? Where are they coming from? Are they true?

3. What else do you do every day that needs discipline? Getting up in the morning, putting dinner on the table at night, feeding yourself regularly, walking the dog? Finding time for you is essential.

4. Why is finding the time or the space to practise so difficult?

How you physically set yourself up to meditate is important. This time for your practice needs to be acknowledged by you and your living companions. It needs to be ring-fenced so that demands from outside (including the phone) don't intrude. Maybe you are able to make a special place for your practice – a corner of a room or an outside spot in the summer.

Short practice for when you can't practise

When you think about or remember to do your practice and you think you can't, you could try doing the following:

Stand or sit. Become still. Feel your feet on the ground. (If you are sitting, feel your bottom on the seat.) Sense the contact of the ground and chair, feeling the pull of gravity, the earth's support.

Acknowledge how you are feeling. Perhaps you can say to yourself: 'Not now – I really can't do practice right now, I'm too…' and take a moment to feel how the body is in response to these words.

Any tension? Tightening or numbness?

Are you leaning forward or pulling back?

How is the breath? Is the breath held or quite short?

Do a quick scan of the body and check your belly, chest, shoulders and mouth. Can you feel tension anywhere here?

Saying to yourself, 'It's OK' and breathing deeply.

Take three purposeful breaths.

Now, breathe naturally and continue with your day, maybe with an intention to stop later for a 'breather' even if it is just a short one.

What stops you practising: a practical assignment

Spend some time in the next few weeks noticing what your thoughts are when you decide not to practise. Do you tell yourself that you haven't got time? Too busy? Is it that you are feeling too tired or too unhappy? Is it that the practice is boring, unsatisfying in some way? Is it fear of being uncomfortable?

Whatever the 'excuse' you give yourself can you just stop and, in that moment, do a short practice?

Come to the body. Are there any sensations? Where are they? Is it a tightening in the gut area? A squeeze around the chest area? A fizzing or clenching? A heavy feeling? Where is the heavy feeling? Hot or cold?

Allow this resistance to practice to be the practice.

Sea of reactions around barriers to practice

This is an exercise we do in class but can be done on your own too.

1. Take a pause and connect with the feelings you get when you think about fitting practice into that day. Connect with the excuses you make to yourself not to do it now, or how you react to the voice that says you 'should' do it.

Connect into the feeling in the body.

2. Write down on pieces of A4 paper the words that relate to the feelings or impulses that came up. For example: I feel too anxious, I'm tired, I have chores to do etc.

Then place the paper on the floor.

3. Walk through your own sea of reactions. Notice what draws you, what resonates.

4. Stand on the paper that seems to best capture your experience in this moment.*

Examples of this*

5. Do a three-step breathing space:

- Acknowledging how you are feeling, what emotions, body sensations and thoughts are here right now.
- Breathe: focusing on the in-breath and the out-breath.
- Staying with the sensation of breathing, expand your awareness to your body. Feel your feet on the floor, any sensations in the body, the space around the body, sounds.

6. What did you learn from the exploration? How does this holding, in a gentle awareness the particular barrier we have chosen, enable us to come to our practice from a different place?

7. Review and write down what you have learnt, if this is a useful learning tool.

Examples of how you could be feeling:

*Do you feel a kind of dread? A heavy dragging of your feet towards a sorry end kind of feeling?

Does it feel more like impatience? A restless, scratchy, anxious feeling? 'I've got so much to do. I'm too busy.'

Is it that my mood (sadness, anxiety, restlessness, anger, resentment) is too strong?

Are there emotional, negative thoughts that are unbearable? How does that feel in the body?

Is there physical discomfort that discourages you from practising?

Is it disappointment, irritation, shame, rejection, sadness, resentment, arrogance, insecurity, hopelessness, wild rebellion, indifference, apathy? Something else? And can you get a sense of this feeling in the body, or perhaps in your facial expression when you identify this emotion?

(Adapted from Bartley T (2012) *The Sea of Reactions in Mindfulness-Based Cognitive Therapy for Cancer*. Chichester: Wiley-Blackwell.)

Where does my mind go?

1. Meditate for a good length of time – at least 15–20 minutes – grounding and breathing; when you notice your mind has wandered, acknowledge where the mind went. Note it.

At the end of the meditation recollect what thoughts you had; see if there is a pattern. What thought or stimulus initiates the moment of arising of a thought? Do you keep getting pulled away by the same thoughts? You won't remember all of them; probably you will only remember one or two. That is fine. Notice if judgement or frustration comes up. Try to keep it light. It is just a snapshot of your mind in this instant, not who you are. It is important not to judge yourself on the preoccupations of the mind. These change over time.

2. Write down as many of these thoughts as you can.
3. When you look at your collection of thoughts, what hindrances can you identify?
4. Then look at the list below and seeing how many thoughts fit the different categories.

List of possible mind wanderings

- Planning or worrying about the future
- Rehearsing future moments
- Thinking or ruminating over the past
- Reworking the past (what you should have said or done)
- Analysing a situation or a person
- Problem-solving
- Thinking about something you like or dislike
- Day-dreaming or fantasying
- Judging
- Procrastinating
- Making up stories
- Calculating
- Rambling randomly
- Nonsensical thoughts (maybe close to sleep)
- Are any of the hindrances involved?
- How many of the thoughts involve 'me', 'my', 'mine'?
- Is the thinking process involved with our own survival, is it designed to strengthen our identity?
- Is it a mixed bag?

Top 10 favourite thoughts

Do meditation practice for a week and see if there are any thoughts that come up every practice. Write them down in a journal. Again, they could be past or future based. They could be self-critical or self-justifying. You might always have a thought about food or where to go on your next holiday. You could have a pet bugbear, your partner, boss, friend or child that you worry about or criticise.

Do this again in a month and write the thoughts down. Compare. Are you preoccupied with the same kind of thoughts?

Back-tracking a thought

Grounding and breathing. When you notice your mind has wandered, acknowledging where the mind went at the moment of noticing. Then see if you can back-track to the thought before it and all the way back to the initial thought.

After back-tracking a thought, coming back to the breath and focusing on the breath again until you notice that you have gone off on a train of thought again.

At the end of the meditation remembering all the thoughts and seeing if there is a pattern.

What thought or stimulus initiates the moment of arising of a thought? Do we keep getting pulled away by the same thoughts? Are we planning or worrying about the future or thinking or ruminating over the past? Is it a mixed bag? Are any of the hindrances involved? How many of the thoughts involve 'me', 'my', 'mine'? Is the thinking process designed to strengthen our identity?

Back-tracking needs some practice but you will see how far the mind can travel. It is like a train travelling through many stations and arriving in another country. Sometimes we can even perceive what set us off, a smell or a sound.

Reflection on your practice

Some hints for keeping the practice alive.

Do you vary your practice? Do you always listen to a recording, a guided practice? Do you do the same practice every time? Do you just do mindfulness of breathing? Varying your practice can be very helpful. Try doing a different practice for a while. There are plenty of meditations on the Internet that you may find helpful. Centre for Mindfulness, Research and Practice (CMRP) have free audio downloads at https://www.bangor.ac.uk/mindfulness.

Oxford Mindfulness Centre also have an app for practices: https://oxfordmindfulness.org/news/oxford-mbct-app/

For one week or for a few weeks choose to do a specific practice.

What's your intention when you start the practice? Can you set an intention to meet whatever is here with openness and kindness? Are you able to meet yourself and your experience with basic friendliness?

What's the feeling in your heart towards your practice when you start the practice and when you finish?

When is the best time to practise? Explore different times of the day to practise. We can feel more sleepy or restless at different times in our day. Sometimes you may like to have a nap before practice so that the practice isn't simply sleep. Or you might do some movement before a sitting practice if that is an antidote to your restlessness.

Be flexible.

Some people find it useful to allocate the same time and space for practice.

What do you do if you are just too busy, with work commitments, family, etc? Even the days when you have no time to do a practice you can try to find time to do a very quick breathing space. Experiment with different lengths and times of day.

Gates

for John Griffiths

This you should know about me – that
when I come to an attractive gate
I like to rest on it, adopting a reflective
performing elephant pose:
one foot up on the crossbar,
arms athwart the frigid metal
and hands splices together
in an impromptu alfresco prayer.

At this portal between two worlds
I wait for nothing to happen
over long periods of time;
I wish for neither a famous face to appear
Nor an explosion of camera clicks...

Rather, give me the sameness of reeds
unmoving on the bed of ice
or winter willows frozen bare
against the windless sky; call me
counter-dramatist, contra-paparazzi
or a country hick without a brain,
but that's how it stands:
forever expecting the great non-event,
gripped slowly by iron,
I practise stillness to perfection
And observe, calm as a corn stook,
The frieze of my non-existence.

– Lloyd Jones

Slow Time

For Gerry

'Life is so short, we must move very slowly'
Ancient Thai saying

World whirls so fast
Quick, quick, slow is a way to go.
Yet with the spinning earth's ricochet
Slow, slow, quick maybe more so.
Otherwise I am dizzy in the flow.

All by my very self
I couldn't plant a wood
A great company gathered
With friends I could.
The thin twigs of oak and birch
Moving in slow time
Shall inherit the speeding earth
Growing beside the Scot's Pine.

We plant for squirrels
Hazel for the red.
We plant for the children
Or their children instead.

The earth spins on its axis
revolving around the sun.
Moving faster anchored to this star
We rush around the galaxy.
Far out, moving far, far.

Travelling through time
Around the Milky Way
All through the night
And all through the day.

And even speedier is light.
So just my sitting still
Is a whirling way.
No need to do a thing
On this particular day.

– Annee Griffiths

Chapter 3:
Practising with Attitude

Mindfulness is paying attention, in a particular way, on purpose,
in the present moment, non-judgementally.

– Jon Kabat-Zinn (1994)

Remember the story about the two wolves? A grandmother tells her granddaughter about a wolf full of hate and a loving and kind wolf which are fighting in her heart. When the little girl asks which wolf will win the fight, she answers: 'The one I feed'. We need to cultivate certain attitudes or qualities to feed the loving and kind wolf.

The greatest discovery of my generation is that a human being can
alter his life by altering his attitudes.

– William James

In a Zen story from ancient China, Layman Pang was struggling with his meditation one day and remarked to his family 'Ah difficult, difficult. It is like throwing sesame seeds on to the leaves in the garden and expecting them to stick.'

'Easy, easy, easy,' said his wife, Mrs Pang. 'It's like your feet touching the floor when you get out of bed.'

Their daughter, Lingzhou said 'Mum, Dad. No. No. Not hard, not easy. It's like the drops of dew shining on the hundred grass tips. Not hard. Not easy. A practice of the heart.'

How often do we approach our meditation with pre-conceived ideas. 'It's got to be like this, I need to get rid of that, it's not working if I don't have peaceful or pleasant feelings, I've got to become/should be a good meditator?' It's not surprising that we might have this attitude in meditation because we are often this way in life.

When I asked a class what qualities they would like in a good friend they offered: loyalty, empathy, sensitivity, a sense of humour, love, consistency, reliability, trust and faithfulness. These are all qualities we can cultivate as we befriend ourselves in meditation. What do you hope for in a good friend? Can you be this to yourself? Can you bring this attitude to your practice?

Exercise: what do you value in a good friend?

List the qualities you consider important in a good friend.

Have these changed over the years? For example, it may be that you used to think it was important that someone should be good fun, a good laugh or do crazy things but after experiencing some difficulties in your life you may value tolerance or loyalty more. It may be that you want a friend to be kind or forgiving.

Sometimes, it is easier to be more accepting of a friend's good qualities than it is our own. In the film Angel A, directed by Luc Besson, there is a touching scene where a young man looks into the mirror and can't find anything good about himself. He is instructed to look closely into his own eyes and notice what is there. After a good deal of resistance and denial he sees gentleness and kindness. How would it be to look into the mirror without self-critical judgement or an idealised way that you should look?

Exercise: mirror, mirror on the wall

Spend five minutes looking into your own eyes in the mirror. How does it feel? Note what goes on in your mind.

Attitudes to cultivate in meditation

Paying attention in meditation is not just about being focused in the present moment. It is also about cultivating certain attitudes or qualities. The attitudinal foundations are described by Jon Kabat-Zinn (1990). They are: Patience, Trust, Non-Striving, Acceptance, Letting Go or Letting Be, Beginner's Mind, and Non-judging. Also intrinsic to our meditation practice are kindness and self-compassion (see Chapter 6). Recently Jon has added three more attitudinal foundations: Gratitude, Generosity (Chapter 8) and Curiosity, which I have added to Beginner's Mind.

Beginner's Mind

> In the Beginner's Mind there are many possibilities;
> in the expert's mind there are few.

– Shunryu Suzuki

> The familiar, precisely because it is familiar, remains unknown.

– Hegel

Seeing things with fresh eyes or with Beginner's Mind is an essential element to bring to our meditation every time. The question here to ask ourselves is: How can I bring a new awareness to each moment, to see with fresh eyes, hear with fresh ears and so on through all the senses? Each moment is different. Can we notice that?

When I first started meditation I often wondered if I was doing it right. I still wonder! And then I let this thought go. How do I know if I am doing it right? When we are concerned with 'doing it right' it seems very hard. Sometimes it seems impossible to concentrate on the breath or bear the barrage of thoughts that can assail us when we sit down to practise. This is when Curiosity and Beginner's Mind is so helpful. Rather than striving to do it right we become interested, alive to our experience right now in the present moment. Open to what is here in the body, in sounds, thoughts, and the breath. Awake to this moment as the only moment we have to live.

> 'Most people think that to meditate, I should feel a particular, special something, and if I don't, then I must be doing something wrong. That is a common but incorrect view of meditation. Mindfulness is not about getting anywhere else – it's about being where you are and knowing it. We are talking about awareness itself; a whole repertoire of ways of knowing that virtually all come through the senses.'

– Kabat-Zinn (2006)

In the Zen tradition there is this story. The expert comes to learn about meditation, he thinks he knows a great deal. The teacher offers him a cup of tea and just keeps pouring the tea into the cup until it is overflowing. 'Stop, stop', says the expert, 'the cup is full'. 'So are you', says the teacher, 'before I can teach you, you will have to empty the cup of your prior knowledge of what you think meditation is'. This is Beginner's Mind.

Josephine had been practising mindfulness meditation for more than 20 years. She said she didn't want to do the meditation 'Working With Difficulty' because she would be dwelling on the negative and that would bring more negativity into her life. She had used her practice to safeguard against feeling emotion and felt she had transcended being emotional. She felt calm but very flat. She assumed that was the purpose of meditation; to become calm and unaffected. In fact she was frozen. At first she was very resistant to feeling anything as she felt her meditation practice had cured her from life's vicissitudes. Learning to have Beginner's Mind meant a new rather frightening but more alive practice. She learnt she had just closed down, become numb around her emotions.

How often do we take things for granted, assume we know? The secret here is to bring curiosity into the equation. What is this breath like... and this one? What sound does the rain make? Can you hear its different tones? Beginner's Mind stops us getting stuck in dullness and enables us to be more receptive and open to our lives. It opens us to the possibility of experiencing every moment as a new moment.

'Among the sixteen types of meditation the baby's practice is best.'

– Larry Rosenberg

Curiosity

Great questioning, great awakening. Small questioning small awakening; no questioning no awakening.

– Martine Batchelor

What can I learn now? What's new? What am I assuming about my experience my life? If we are curious about our experience we are open to the unknown. We may be able to foster courage rather than anxiety. In mindfulness approaches there is a strong emphasis on enquiry.

We look deeply into our experience and explore aspects that may not be so obvious to the conceptual mind, for instance being present with the impact of thoughts and emotions on the body and the assumption we often make that our thoughts are true. We assume that they are facts rather than a series of thoughts that are just passing through.

Enquiry can free us from being stuck in our own assumptions. Curiosity shores us up against ignorance. Ignorance is the absence of attention. A fog. We cannot see far. Curiosity can pierce the fog and give us insight. It can lead us to wonder, to wonder at our experience in the present moment.

When I was in India in 1978 I attended the teachings of an Indian teacher, Nisargadatta. He had a small upstairs room reached by a ladder. In this room in the middle of Bombay's red-light district he talked of freedom:

To see the universe as it is, you must step beyond the net. It is not hard to do so because the net is full of holes.

Patience

One moment of patience may ward off great disaster.
One moment of impatience may ruin a whole life.

– Chinese Proverb

When we remember that patience is part of the practice, it can help us step back from evaluating our experience as good or bad. Even the act of allowing ourselves to stop and practise develops our patience. With patience, if we continue to practise, our meditation practice will evolve in its own time, just as a butterfly unfolds slowly from its cocoon without need for any interference from outside. Our patience is challenged when we notice ourselves judging our experience. It is also sorely tested at times by restlessness, we want to get up and go, but the time drags on. 'When will it end?' we groan. Sometimes, we need to persuade ourselves gently to stay here with this moment knowing that the feeling is only transitory. When we recognise and notice how this urge to move feels in the body, allowing the feeling just to be there for a few moments without reacting to it, we are cultivating our patience.

How poor are they that hath not patience. What wound did ever heal but by degrees.

– William Shakespeare, Othello (Act 2, Scene 3)

Last spring I noticed two pairs of Greylag geese at the lake near my house. I followed them with interest all through the spring. One pair had three goslings, the other seven! I visited them daily and usually I came upon them grazing with their broods waddling on the shore of the lake. As soon as they saw me they would take to the water honking. How marvellous it was to see a couple of pairs turn into a flock. I watched them grow and one amazing day heard them fly over my house, the sound of their wings and goose cries indeed 'harsh and exciting' as Mary Oliver says in her poem 'Wild Geese'. Mary Oliver recognised the importance of nature to *'announce our place in the family of things'*.

The lake was quiet for the whole of the winter. The moorhens and coots scuttled away and the mallards flew off noisily whenever I approached. March remained cold and the fields dull. Then late in March the geese returned. First a pair and then, a few days later, there were seven geese on the lake. Might we be more patient with our practice, just being with what is here, listening to the longing in our hearts, without turning away with disappointment? At last the geese return, they bring some of their grown goslings with them and again I enjoy their antics. Spring always comes and longing is part of the journey.

Planting seeds is an excellent patience practice. First, they take a long time to germinate; you watch and wait, just bare earth. They take ages to grow big enough to make an impact. You can't hurry them; they come in their own time. In the end your patience is rewarded with a harvest or a display of colour. It is usually worth the wait.

We cultivate patience as a matter of faith each time we do a practice and this extends to our daily life. If we can remember to be present with the breath, with the body, as we wait for that phone call or stand in a supermarket queue then we are developing a habit of practice. It takes a lot of practice to be mindful when we are challenged by a child or loved one but this, too, can be an achievable aspiration.

Many times we are just too restless to stay with the moment. Pat found she couldn't sit still for more than five minutes in her meditation practice. She would jump up without thinking in the middle of a meditation. She decided to be very conscious of this urge and to stay with this intense restlessness for an allocated time. She started with one minute and gradually and intentionally increased this into longer time periods. She learnt a lot about the nature of restlessness. She recognised that she was also very impatient in her daily life. The opportunity to spend a little time studying this changed her approach to life.

> *Do you have the patience to wait*
> *Till your mud settles and the water is clear?*
> *Can you remain unmoving*
> *Till the right action arises by itself?*

– Lao Tzu

Trust

> *Watch the dust grains moving, in the light near the window.*
> *Their dance is our dance.*
> *We rarely hear the inward music,*
> *but we're all dancing to it nevertheless.*

– Rumi

'Developing a basic trust in yourself and your feelings is an integral part of meditation training' says Jon Kabat-Zinn (1990). Trust also includes trusting the process, trusting that the practice is worthwhile, trusting in awareness. Trust in yourself and your own basic wisdom and goodness. Trust is an antidote to the doubt we touched on in Chapter 2.

So how do we cultivate this trust? As we practise coming back to the breath or other focus of attention we are developing this trust. However, being open to the present moment can be challenging at times and trusting in this process even more so. For example, might we be able to trust that we can manage a future event without excessive planning or worrying? A few years ago I realised that I sometimes used my meditation time to go over my busy schedule of the day or the week ahead. When I paid attention to this I noticed a slight leaning forwards in my posture and a clenching feeling in parts of my body, particularly my jaw and abdomen. I saw that this planning was my way of ensuring that I didn't 'screw up'. I also saw that I could trust myself to work it out at the time. In the same way I noticed a tendency to go over incidents in the past and realised that ruminating about these things didn't change or fix what had happened. Gradually I was learning to come back to the present instead of time travelling.

When we closely pay attention to what happens in our mind we may notice that this tendency to plan and worry happens a lot. It can make our practice quite unpleasant as we notice how certain thoughts dominate our meditations and we can be sure that these thoughts are also prominent within our lives. We notice the thought patterns, let go and refocus on being mindful of the present moment. Being anxious about the future doesn't change the outcome.

Beginners new to meditation will often feel they are not doing the practice right and it's not just beginners, many of us can feel that. There is a subtle or strong feeling of wanting things to be different, not liking this moment and thinking the experience should be something else. We are closed to the moment rather than open. Might we trust enough in awareness to become intimate with this feeling rather than fighting or running away from it? How would it be to turn towards, to open, to fully trust whatever arises in this moment without the desire to attain a special state? The subtle expectations we bring to the practice create an extra layer to our experience. Being willing to open to our experience, staying with feelings may be an opening into compassion, both to ourselves and to others.

Sometimes, self-doubt or the feeling 'I'm not good enough, I am not doing this right' arises during the practice or in life itself. They are often core beliefs that we may have carried since early childhood and created by fear, which is caught up in our perception of our identity.

This sense of separation and disconnection is a place worth investigating. Can we trust ourselves to stay with the feelings and sensations rather than push them away? Might acknowledgement of these feelings and trusting ourselves to become intimate with them lead to a greater openness?

A friend, SHANTI, told me how one night she was overwhelmed by loneliness. She said at other times when she felt this she would try to distract herself; maybe watch telly with a few glasses of wine. This night she decided to sit with the loneliness, with awareness and curiosity, in spite of feeling very afraid. It brought tears and great pain but eventually something shifted and she felt a sense of spaciousness and a sense of being connected at the heart to others.

This has been my own experience at the times when I have had the courage to open up to strong feelings. There has been a sense of connection, a sense of reaching out with compassion to others who suffer.

Sometimes, we don't know who we are. This is a frightening place to be. Might we be able to trust this 'don't know' space as a place of possibility? One person said that this open space felt like being on the edge of a cliff. Can we trust this space and the possibility that we may have wings? As the Japanese poet Issa said:

> *Simply trust*
> *Don't the petals flutter down*
> *Just like this?*

Non-striving

For after all, the best thing one can do when it is raining is let it rain.

– Henry Wadsworth Longfellow

There is a subtle difference between effort, which involves discipline and striving which implies straining. Trying hard in meditation defeats the purpose. It will create tension and tightening. We are often goal-orientated in our lives, our whole conditioning from school onwards is to strive to achieve goals. However, our intention here in the practice is to notice how we bring this tendency to meditation. We practise with an open mind and intend to be with our experience without striving for it to be different.

Choiceless awareness as a meditation focus helps us practise non-striving. Our awareness is receptive to whatever is arising in the present moment and this means a giving up of control. Our effort, like a guitar string, is fine-tuned; too tight and it will break, too loose and it will be flat and energy-less. We need to be constantly fine-tuning our effort in our practice so that we are not too tight and tense at breaking point, nor are we flat and dull and slack. Balance is the practice.

KRISH said he couldn't 'do' the choiceless awareness practice. He preferred focusing on the breath as a task he could 'achieve'. When we talked about attitudinal foundations he recognised that 'non-striving' was a significant attitude for him. He identified that striving caused him stress and indeed anxiety in his life. He was invited to stay with choiceless awareness. As he struggled to stay focused he first experienced a wandering mind and then switched to sleepiness. He became frustrated with himself. Yet this time he was able to notice the critical voice, the frustration. He identified that the frustration in the practice was linked to a perfectionist tendency that directed him in many parts of his life.

The need to be perfect causes anxiety. Of course, it is important to do a good job, but the emotions generated by perfectionism can be hard to live with. Sometimes, the critical voice pushing us to be perfect is a voice from the past.

Interestingly, we all have a picture of what a good meditator would be like and most of us fall short of our expectation. But what if it is not what we think it is? What if being with this uncertainty is part of a meditation practice? We are learning to live with uncertainty that is life itself.

ANWEN decided to set an intention of non-striving during an all-day retreat. She was very surprised how this intention, which she kept coming back to throughout the day, gave her practice some vigour. She said, 'I am aware that all my life I have been striving in one way or another and I really felt it on Saturday during the practice. When I felt my body expressing this striving I let go a little and softened. At the end of the day I felt so much more ease.

'In the last practice, which was not guided, I was aware of a lot of negative thoughts. Each thought like: 'How long is this going on? When will it be finished?' With these thoughts I noticed my jaw tightening up and a wanting that the thoughts go away. I remembered the poem The Guesthouse by Rumi. So I treated each thought as a new visitor. I said, "Welcome, come in and sit down quietly while I carry on with this". Soon there was a crowd of them quietly sitting around me. It made me laugh (silently, of course) and some of the tension evaporated.

'Mindfulness was helpful in seeing a pattern of striving. It hasn't rubbed that pattern out. It's still there, but now I am able to do something like go to the gym for 20 minutes (instead of it stopping me by saying "What's the point"). I now go, OK, fine, it's 20 minutes (instead of the goal of an hour) and by the time I've done that I will feel better anyway.'

JIM commented, 'I always have to get everything right; I'm a perfectionist. So having permission to try my best and if I didn't hear the end of the tape because I fell asleep, it was OK. I wasn't failing. It was fantastic. A real shift in my attitude. Just developing kindness to myself was the key thing.'

Letting Go or Letting Be

A little letting go brings us a little peace, a greater letting go brings us a greater peace.

– Jack Kornfield

'Letting go' is part of the zeitgeist of our culture. We often hear people say, 'just let it go' and it sounds a bit like the order to 'chill' or 'just relax, can't you?' It's not a particularly effective directive, is it?

Letting go is more open-handed than pushing things away. And yet, if my hand was always open or my hand was always tightly closed, I would be paralysed. We need the flexibility to both receive and to let go. Maybe sometimes this involves an easing out, as we gently unpick our experience rather than dropping it suddenly. 'Unhooking' from a train of reactions may be more effective.

In meditation we are constantly practising letting go when we let go of a thought and come back to the breath, the body or sounds. Sometimes, we may acknowledge sticky thoughts or persistent thoughts or patterns and this helps us to let go, and other times we may choose to explore the body sensations under the thoughts, expanding our experience to both body and mind. It is more like letting be, which leads to letting go.

We may find certain thoughts tend to preoccupy us. In particular, anxious or angry thoughts can have a strong hold on our thinking patterns and cause us much stress. Bringing frequent awareness to negative repetitive thoughts and their impact on the body may well help us let go of them.

When I notice tension in my shoulders or around my eyes I naturally let go a little. Sometimes, as we sit in meditation, we try too hard – parts of our body may tell us this. Thus, as we let go of the tension of trying too hard, we are able to bring a kinder, less striving attitude to meditation practice.

I wonder if we ever really 'let go' of anything! Perhaps, particularly in meditation practice, what we do is to redirect our attention into cultivating something else. So, we don't let go of something but simply refocus our attentional capacity on something that is more wholesome and fruitful – while we are cultivating what is useful and skilful, we are not cultivating our destructive patterns and habits. So, we are not really letting go of something and this I think is far more useful than telling ourselves to 'let go' because no matter how many times we do this it generally doesn't happen. This is somewhat akin to someone telling us to 'relax!'. It usually has the opposite effect.

– John Peacock

'Letting be' is an essential requirement for an easeful life.

Many years ago ELSA and TANIA shared a work assignment. Elsa thought it went well. She enjoyed working with Tania and was pleased with her own contribution. Tania had done the task several times previously but it was Elsa's first time. At the end of the job, Tania gave her some feedback about areas she could improve. At the time it affected her like criticism usually did and she felt herself curl into herself and withdraw. The numbness she felt meant that she finished the work assignment with a false smile and a heavy heart. However, the next day she attended the funeral of an old friend and immediately afterwards found herself visiting her new grandchild who had just been born that day, surprisingly early. Her sensitivity around being criticised seemed to be of no real significance in the light of this new baby and in the sadness surrounding the death of her friend. It seemed so small in light of birth and death. So she let it go.

KATHERINE was an artist. Her challenge was that she had too many ideas for one project and had to narrow these down. Sometimes, she was working with something interesting but it didn't fit properly into the concept she was working towards. She had to let go of ideas and work that didn't quite fit and this meant giving up on some of the work she had spent time and energy doing.

However, the following example illustrates that if we let go of everything we will also be hampered.

EVELYN was an author; she had the plots for several novels but no matter how much she wrote she felt the necessity of completely re-writing the first chapter. Some of her stories had 10 or more first chapters. She kept letting them go and rewriting. Sometimes letting go means letting go of perfectionism. 'A poem is never finished, only abandoned' is a famous quote, attributed to Paul Valery. Thus, in the knowledge that 'perfect' is impossible we can let go of the idea of the perfect piece of work, the perfect meditation practice.

There is an old teaching story about letting go. In India, coconut shells are used as monkey traps. A banana is pushed into a small hole in a coconut husk. The monkey can squeeze his hand into the hole by extending his fingers. He grabs hold on the banana but because his fist is clenched his hand has become bigger and now he can't get his clenched hand with the banana out through the hole. He needs to let go of the banana in order to free himself. He just can't let go of that valuable banana and therefore is trapped.

How many bananas are you holding onto in your life?

Acceptance

Radical acceptance can keep us from becoming progressively constricted and diminished in the face of painful experiences. It invites us to fully experience the richness of life even when things seem to be at their worst.

– Williams, Teasdale, Segal and Kabat-Zinn, 2007

The purpose of this acceptance is not to develop passivity but to get as close to our experience as we can... being aware of it is the path to wisdom.

– Susan Salzberg, *A Heart as Wide as the World*, p.82

Accept it or change it, the Serenity Prayer declares. Sometimes, we need to fully realise the pain of a situation and experience some deep emotional reactions of fear, denial, anger or grief before we can fully accept the things we cannot change and the things we can.

Acceptance is not passive. It does not mean that you accept bad practice in the workplace, or injustice in the world. It does not mean that you tolerate cruelty or corruption or avoid making changes in your personal life or for the good of society or the planet. Nor does it mean resignation, putting up with things. Acceptance is understanding and taking responsibility for your own feelings and situation.

Acceptance is a willingness to see things as they are. It is a key component of a mindfulness practice because its opposite, avoidance of experience, 'is too risky' (Segal *et al*, 2002). You are more likely to know how to act if you have clear vision rather than seeing the world through a filter of your own emotional judgements, prejudices and fears or from a self-serving attitude. How does anger feel? Sadness? Resentment? It may be hard to own up to some of these emotions. To accept that 'I'm feeling resentful' can be disappointing to say the least. Yet knowing in the body the twists and turns of resentment may help us to understand both within ourselves and in the world the possible motivation for negative behaviours. It may help us to understand universal suffering.

Acceptance is intrinsically linked with kindness. The practice is essentially a practice of the heart. In turning towards our difficulty, we are turning towards ourselves with acceptance. We are practising acceptance over and over again as we practise coming back to the present moment, to this breath, to the body. In this moment we may be aware of what's pulling us away from the moment, of our attachment to a thought or memory or an aversion to our experience, a pulling away from or placing a wall between ourselves and a strong feeling, emotion and bodily sensation.

There may be times when we encounter the big stuff. These moments of awareness are an opportunity for acceptance. As we practise acceptance towards our emotions and corresponding body sensations time and time again, we might notice that the impact of them lessens. The waves that came up to our heads, knocked us off our feet and totally overwhelmed us, gradually become smaller.

Sometimes, when we look back at those difficult times we may be able to see that they were part of the story of our life, and our acceptance has deepened our understanding of what it is to be a human being. William Blake said this in the 17 century say:

> Man was made for Joy & Woe
>
> And when this we rightly know
>
> Thro the World we safely go
>
> Joy & Woe are woven fine
>
> A Clothing for the soul divine
>
> Under every grief & pine
>
> Runs a joy with silken twine.

For JANE 'It's about tolerance. Yes, it's OK to be feeling like this now. I can't figure out why I am feeling like this [when experiencing a negative emotion such as sadness or anger] but there doesn't necessarily have to be a reason for it. The acceptance feeling takes the resistance out of it, frees it up and makes it softer and therefore the negative feeling is ultimately dispersed'.

Here is a poem by Jody Mardula, who had a brain haemorrhage in 2011 while she was the director of the Centre for Mindfulness, Research and Practice. This poem describes how she is now in 2019. She has written a book called *Mindfulness and Stroke*. Jody's poem is an example of how a mindfulness practice can augment acceptance.

I abandoned growing up a long time ago

> But I have gone off,
>
> As I do
>
> Constantly straying from the point.
>
> The thoughts in my head
>
> The words from my mouth
>
> Passing as water

From one bucket
Into the night.

An ever flowing
Stream of thoughts
And information
Drowned
Strangled
Discarded
Poured out and thrown away.

This is Dementia.
And this is only the beginning.

I must learn. Again,
To let go
Sink into the water
Let it take me where it will

I become a reflection
Of myself.

Sometimes
Someone
Will catch a glimpse of me
Here, in the water.
Some recoil with fear.

Only children
See what's hidden here.
And it was always so.
Dementia just lets go
The Adult world of woe.

I dance again with children

And remember now

That I abandoned the abandoning adults

Long, long ago.

– Jody Mardula

Non-judging

I always think it is useful to clarify that this is not the renouncing of all judgement but only of self-critical judgement. Judgement is a necessary criteria for life and hugely important in developing an ethical sensibility. So, it is only a particular type of judgement that is being dropped not all judgement, which if in fact we could do this would be hugely dangerous.

– John Peacock

When I write I feel like an armless, legless man with a crayon in his mouth.

– Kurt Vonnegut

Vonnegut wrote fantastic novels, despite his inner critic. When we practise mindfulness on purpose in a particular way, we are practising accepting our experience as it arises. We may be making judgements such as we don't like this sensation, this thought, this memory; however, we just notice it non-reactively, notice how it can change and leave of its own accord. We don't need to add an extra layer of judgemental thought. Yet when we meditate these judgemental thoughts seem to be amplified. We start to notice how judgemental we are and when we notice this we become judgemental about judging too! Layer upon layer of judgement.

We can practise working with non-judging when we notice critical thoughts that come up because the mind is wandering or because we feel sleepy or when there is a sense of 'I can't do this'. Then we may begin to notice a whole barrage of critical thoughts, which comment and judge ourselves and others. We then realise that these are frequent visitors that are sometimes barely detectable. However, they may have a strong impact as they can cause low mood and even have the power to change our behaviour.

We may be responsible for wrong-doing or mistakes and feel that our self-criticism is justified. However, it is possible to be responsible without constantly punishing ourselves with negative statements that undermine our sense of wellbeing. A skilful way of doing this may be to acknowledge any mistake, feel it and then bring some kindness in. This is a way of turning towards ourselves with compassion, then letting it go. We can do this by either cleanly dropping it or by noticing how we are ruminating over and over the same old self-critical thoughts and deliberately saying: *'There I go again'*, and then letting go.

Taking responsibility for mistakes or deliberate wrong acts enables us to contemplate what we can learn from them, and how we might consider ways to make amends or repair the situation, if possible. We can decide what to do and then act. It is not helpful to feel guilt or shame. We may even need to say silently to ourselves: 'I forgive myself and take responsibility. I have done everything I could to make it better. Now I can let go. Regrets and guilt are useless'.

We also need to be aware of the difference between deliberately acting with malice and being caught up in other people's blaming attitude towards us. Sometimes, we may need to acknowledge that the interpretations of others are not our responsibility.

We can believe self-criticism is useful to us because it could lead to self-improvement but mostly it inhibits or sabotages our response to situations. Some psychologists (Gilbert, 2005) have suggested that it is helpful to name self-criticism as 'the inner critic' or, my own personal favourite, 'the judge'. We can identify the voices by finding names for them.

> CERI named his criticising voices after his grandparents. Both his parents had one fierce bullying parent (his father's mother and his mother's father). Whenever he noticed a nasty note creeping into his thinking, especially after making a mistake, he would thank Richard or Molly and say he was fine without their help. This helped to take the sting out of the judgement. Also, by skipping a generation it took the blame away from his parents. He was able to break an age-old cycle of the unskilful conditioning and behaviour of generation after generation.

OLWEN said she was more aware of her self-critical voice when she did movement practice than when she did the body scan. The 'should try harder' and 'you're not good enough' narratives seemed to accompany her practice throughout. She noted that this 'try harder' instruction had been useful in the past and, although it was trying to help now, it was not relevant. In fact, it was redundant at this time in her life.

GRACE added that the movement practice had been so useful for her because she had learnt to accept that her over- achieving had led to injury and that now she was more able to accept her limitations and practise cultivating a sense of friendliness to herself and her body.

'I used to be super fit and run in marathons, but since hurting my back a year ago in a car accident I have been unable to move it very much. This steady, gentle movement with awareness of how my body is in the moment is perfect for me. I can stretch and feel the sensitivity and ease into and out of the movement. It has really helped my body get stronger and made me more mindful. I am so thankful to this practice and the attitude of gentleness that it encourages.'

Ways of working with the self-critic or judge

When we hear ourselves thinking or saying 'should, ought and must' it could act as an alarm bell to warn us that we are possibly being self-critical. The self-critic often has the benefit of hindsight: 'You should have said...' 'You should have done the other thing rather than the thing that didn't work out so well.'

We can notice the following words:

- I ought to...
- I should have....
- I shouldn't have done that
- If only I had done that

and change them to:

- Next time I will...
- I am choosing to/have chosen to do this, maybe it will prove to be the interesting choice!
- I could
- I would like to
- I want to do that

Other words to watch out for are absolutist words such as everything, nothing, completely, always and never:

- My mind wanders all the time
- I will never be free of this sadness
- I have nothing to say when the family is together.
- I always get the blame.

These absolutist words are very common in depression and anxiety online forums and even more so on suicidal ideation forums. These words can make us feel stuck, and it is useful to be able to spot them in our practice and in our life.

Sometimes we may notice self-critical thoughts that undermine and overwhelm us. The work here is to notice and bring kindness to that moment. One way to do this is to imagine yourself as a small child and bring kindness to that image. Another is to put out the welcome mat. 'Hello, I know you are trying to help, thank you but I don't need this comment now'. Humour is a good tactic, to smile or laugh at the critical voice. Or to say, 'Oh, here you are again, would you like to sit down and have tea?'

Another way might be to count how many critical thoughts you can have in a meditation sitting. Keep a record and be amazed not judgemental.

AMARA worked with judgemental thoughts by being aware of their sheer volume and how destructive they were. 'I felt unable to lay off myself and got myself in a tighter and tighter knot, like unpicking a great tangle of wool. When I realised how horrible I'd been to myself and noticed the stuff I was saying to myself regularly I was shocked. And I found out other people do it to themselves… eroding their self-confidence. Then I tried to stop it so I was working at another level.'

It is also very useful to check in to the body. Notice the effect of that criticism physically; where in the body do you register the thought? You may tighten in the belly or in the chest area (heart ache). You may twinge, tighten, burn or go cold. Your shoulders might rise like the hackles rising on a defensive cat or your face express itself with a frown or grimace.

Another consideration is to treat yourself as you would a good friend. What would you say to a friend who criticised her/himself in a severe manner? Would you be more tolerant of their mistakes and weaknesses than you are of your own?

Exercise: working with the self-critic

What are your most frequent critical thoughts? Write down at least five of them. Then go over them one by one, taking a moment to pause and investigate any sensations in the body that arise as you recall them. Then ask yourself the following questions:

- Is this critical thought or judgement true?
- How do you know if it's really true? Or just a self-belief that has become fixed in your mind?
- How does holding on to this belief or judgement serve you? What do you gain from it? Who would you be without it?

Ask yourself:

- Is this true?
- Is it necessary?
- Is it kind?

Exercise: who is or was the voice/voices of the self-critic or judge?

Can you identify the voice or voices of the self-critic as a voice from childhood? Could it be a parent, caregiver, grandparent, teacher or an influential figure when you were quite young?

Can you identify the voice? It may be a sibling or a peer? In fact, a sibling could sound like a parent or other adult with influence.

The voice may have been activated by concern. Telling you not to be lazy, to work harder, to look a certain way so that you could be successful in life. Or it may be repeating their old conditioning from their childhood, repeating the sayings of their caregivers or seeking to control or have some power over you because they had little power in their own lives.

Would understanding where the judge or critical voice is coming from make it easier to live with and become independent from?

Moving towards the positive

'You never can have too much joy', exclaimed SYLVIE, aged eight. She had made a cake and iced it with her own design sketched beforehand on paper. Half of the cake was winter, white with a penguin and Father Christmas sitting on lumps of meringue icebergs. The other half was summer, with a sun and fruit made out of tiny sugared lemons and oranges. Flowers were represented by sprinkled colourful hundreds and thousands. She said, 'Shall I have more flowers and cover this half with sprinkles? I think I will. You never can have too much joy.' I agreed with her whole heartedly.

In his book, *Hardwiring Happiness*, Rick Hanson writes that it is important to register positive experience, which in time will re-orientate the brain towards a more positive outlook. It was necessary way back in our evolutionary history to be primed to be alert to threats, in order to fight, flee or freeze. The brain naturally leans towards a negative threatened bias. But this can be counter-productive in our life today. He advocates intentionally cultivating joy and other happy states of mind, so that we consciously register our pleasant experience.

Often, we can miss happiness, let it glide away. We can change the neural circuits in our brains and strengthen our propensity towards happiness. We can develop and strengthen these neural circuits of warm feeling, joy, happiness and love just like we can strengthen our muscles by a regular practice at the gym lifting weights or regular exercise. So, notice a child's smile and register a feeling of warmth. Notice the bird singing at the window and see if sometimes there is a corresponding surge of joy. Don't miss it.

In my own garden when I have no preference and let all the plants grow, the burly weeds will overwhelm my efforts at planting a seedling or a tender plant and it will not thrive or even survive. We are the same. Our negative thinking and the self-critical voice are like weeds. They are habits with long roots into our conditioning and, like weeds, will soon overwhelm the tender growth of kindness. As a result we also will not flourish. Cultivation of the tender plants of acceptance, non-striving, non-judgement, trust and friendliness to ourselves is essential and as this friendly inclination to ourselves becomes stronger it, like the flowers, will give strong bursts of colour and beauty.

If we don't cultivate these positive attitudes, we may well get overwhelmed by negativity.

As a gardener I choose to have a regular presence in my garden in order to nurture the areas I want to develop and strengthen. We are growing fruit and vegetables and it's not just weeds that get in the way of a good crop – blackbirds were stealing the strawberries we planted last year before they were barely red. Did we want strawberries or lots of fat blackbirds singing in the garden?

I am happy to feed birds, in fact we give peanuts and seeds to the tits, goldfinches and chaffinches all winter and throughout the summer too while they are feeding their young. Even the young come to the feeders and look like little punks with their feathers ruffled. I am happy for the blackbirds to feed on the windfall apples but the strawberries are for us. My husband John and I decided we would stop play. John is a wonderful improviser so out of spare bits of wood and not quite enough netting we made a makeshift fruit cage. We had to improvise the last part with some chicken wire and odd cut-offs from another job. It was satisfying and fun as we worked together in the sunshine, hammering in nails to hold the sides of the cage and then stretching nets over poles. Now the blackbirds will have to seek out other nutritious berries instead.

The metaphor? Sometimes the cultivation of kindness and other attitudes is not enough to live a wholesome life. We may have to work out ways with our mind to go forward. Problem-solving and analysing in a situation is often useful.

However, this comes with a caveat that sometimes emotional problem-solving does not work. We cannot think our way out of an emotional situation or be mindful and hey presto all is well. Problem-solving is just one strategy. Another is to be aware of what hinders us and, rather than pretending it is not there, turn towards it. Chapter 4 will signpost ways to do this.

Nevertheless, the physical or emotional pain may be too much and we need to build a protective structure around our tenderness. Mindfulness can be a guardian that holds us in safety against the dangers that beset us. Although we need courage and kindness we also need the wisdom to look after ourselves.

Practices to promote positivity

Think not lightly of good, saying, 'It will not come to me.'

Drop by drop is the water pot filled.

Likewise, the wise one, gathering it little by little,

Is filled with good.

– Dhammapada 9.122

The following meditations are concerned with promoting a positive attitude to your life. This more directional kind of meditation is expanded upon in later chapters.

'Focusing on the positive' meditation

Grounding: Feel into whatever is supporting you. This could be your feet on the floor, your bottom on the seat. If you are lying down, you can feel the back of your body making contact with the floor. Feel into this contact with the ground, allowing the earth to hold you.

Breathing: Feel the breath in the body.

Recognise something positive in your life by bringing to mind one or more of the following:

- Something pleasant about your experience in the present moment
- A pleasant moment from your day or yesterday
- Something you like or love in your life. It could be the warm sunshine, a pet, a child

Find something good in your situation, something you are glad about.

Think about things that make you feel one or more of these: grateful, calm and peaceful, loving, loved, happy.

Acknowledging and absorbing: Choose one thing and stay with it awhile.

Once a positive feeling comes to the front of your awareness staying with and re-imagine the story around it. Picturing it. Hearing it. Using your senses.

Investigating: Where are you feeling it? Where in the body? Acknowledge the pleasure or the delight you feel by staying with it, lingering with it. Are you feeling a sense of warmth or maybe coolness? Lightness or heaviness?

Nurturing: Staying with this feeling and nurturing it. It's OK to be here, enjoying it. If any judgemental thoughts come up, accepting them too in the moment and soothe with kindness. There is this judgement and also this positive feeling. I'm OK and it's OK to feel the way I do.

Smile meditation

Grounding: Feeling the connection with the floor. Your feet contacting the earth, your bottom on the seat. Being aware of your whole body sitting or lying here. Noticing any parts of the body that feel tight or tense.

Breathing: Focusing on your in-breath and your out-breath for at least three breaths.

Expanding your awareness to hearing sounds and, as you do so, become aware of the space around you.

Then: allowing an image of a smile to come into your mind. It could be a friend's smile, a child's smile. Notice how the body feels with this imagined smile. Maybe there is a sense of warmth or ease connected with this image.

Now go to your eyes. This is often an area we hold tight, creating tiny wrinkles. Letting go of any tension or holding of tightness in the area of the eyes. Softening around the eyes. Maybe feeling a sense of brightness here under the eyelids. Soothing your brow.

Imagine a smile at the corner of both eyes and allowing this area to soften further.

Now **inviting** a small smile to move your lips ever so slightly. Softening and relaxing the muscles in your face, noticing how your jaw feels and softening here as best you can. Let the tip of your tongue touch the roof of your mouth. Notice if your eyes are still smiling. Allowing the smile at your lips to grow if that feels right.

Now bringing the image of a smile to your throat. What happens here? Maybe a sense of opening. If you are noticing tightness allowing it to be held by the smile.

Moving down the body now to imagine a smile in your chest. Feeling the smile in the region of your heart.

Acknowledging all the feelings in this area. Maybe you are feeling heavy-hearted or light-hearted... whatever emotional tone is in your heart, letting the smile sit alongside these other feelings, a sense of openness and allowing all your experience with kindness.

Allowing the smile in your heart to ease the tension in the body. Visualise sending ripples of ease through the shoulders and along the arms, down into the belly and buttocks and through the legs all the way down to the feet.

Allowing the aliveness, energy of a smile to brighten up the body. Holding your experience with kindness and warmth. When your mind wanders reminding yourself to be kind, to befriend your experience of the moment.

(Adapted from Tara Brach's *Radical Acceptance*)

A simple practice from Thich Nhat Hanh

Breathing in, I calm body and mind.

Breathing out, I smile.

Dwelling in the present moment, I know this is the only moment.

Thich Nhat Hanh, from *Being Peace*

Movement practices cultivating attitudinal foundations

The following two movement practices are from a Zen retreat with Melissa Blacker and David Rynick.

Walking meditation

Step with the right foot and say 'This moment'

Step with the left foot and say 'Calm'

Step with the right foot and say 'Present moment'

Step with the left foot and say 'Only moment'

Continue for 5, 10 or 15 minutes

Clearing the space or letting go of stress

This goes very well with a movement practice or can be done before a sitting practice, even as an intentional practice. It is wonderful when done outside. This practice focuses on the attitudinal foundation of letting go.

Standing with your feet hip-width apart, or if needed this can be done sitting. Feeling the ground beneath your feet. Feeling the contact with the floor and the earth itself.

Breathing, feeling the movement of the breath deep in the belly.

1. Now raising your hands above your head with your palms parallel to the ceiling or the sky and breathing in. On the out-breath pushing your stress away from your head so your arms lift up in a pushing motion. Clearing the space above you.

2. On an in-breath bringing your arms down to shoulder height. Having the palms of the hands straight and flat and on the out-breath push the stress or distress away from the sides of your body. Clearing the space to the sides of you.

3. On an in-breath bring your arms together in the front of your body at your chest; touching your palms together. Now turning the palms of your hands to face outwards, on the out-breath, pushing the stress or distress away from the front of your body. Clearing the space in front of you.

4. On an in-breath bringing your arms back and on the out-breath, turning the palms to face downwards, pushing the stress or distress down to the ground. Clearing the space below you.

Coming back on the in-breath and repeating the sequence twice more.

A reflection on attitudes

From Hedwig's Personal Journal (2013)

'I am letting go of the "striving", of wanting to do it right. I "saw" myself sitting enveloped in a blanket as "a whole", like I was witnessing myself from the outside. I felt connected with all the other living creatures sitting in this way, in this moment, all over the world.

*'It was warm inside the blanket, cosy. I remembered this is not permanent, this is not mine, this is not me. **I felt grateful**. For the first time in a long time my neck and shoulders were not disturbing the sitting, they were not too tight.*

*I reflected on "**trust**", feeling trust in this moment of calm awareness, this trustful moment of presence. I wonder if perhaps, by relaxing the shoulders I had **let go** of some fear and anxiety. And surely, the fact of being able to care for myself around the tension in neck and shoulders gave me confidence in myself, trust.'*

The Drawbridge

For Sarah

The bulwarks are bolstered for invasion
Are they strong enough?
'I am feeling wobbly'
You say with a catch in your voice.

The boundaries
You have erected against delusion
And cruelty –
'not strong enough' –
You worry.

Your dad died.
No one protected you
Yet you came through.
'I did not want to give up on love'
You give me faith

That the practice of love
Can surmount serial neglect.

Others fall from the parapets
Pedestals of pride.
Surviving your own history,
You are resilient, you spring back
From destruction to deep adaptation.
'I had to trust or die'
You allow me to trust
The wayfarer's way –
Awareness.

When conditions are right
The strong fortress lets down
The drawbridge.
The gateway of the heart.

– Annee Griffiths

The Seven Attitudinal Foundations

(with two extra inherent qualities)

patience

non-striving

acceptance

letting be

beginner's mind

trust

non judging

generosity

kindness and compassion

To help us remember to cultivate these qualities continuously in our practice and in our daily life, pin this up where you will see it often or cut each one out and pin them around your living space. Bringing creativity into our practice may help us reinforce positivity by engaging physically not just mentally …get out the felt tips!

by Staying Mindful student Emma Gibson (illustrator)

Chapter 4:
Working With Difficulty

'No mud, no lotus'

Attributed to The Buddha

PHYLLIS was in the middle of a family crisis. Her relationship with her husband of 20 years had shifted and they were negotiating new living arrangements. She found it very hard to cope with the sense of blame, the ups and downs of deciding what to do and felt that she was unable to stay calm and mindful during the turmoil.

She said, *'It's like being in a corner with darkness raining down on me. I feel a failure not just in my marriage but also as a mindfulness practitioner and a mindfulness teacher. How can I guide others when I have failed in my own life and my practice hasn't made it all right?'*

This is a pitfall that so many of us fall into, thinking that having a mindfulness practice will save us from future suffering and that if we just focus on our breath we can stay calm and avoid stormy weather. Living in a maritime climate like Wales we know that we will always get weather and that it will change constantly. In fact, although the climate may not be so changeable, there is nowhere in the world without weather.

While Phyllis was speaking, I had a picture in my head of a woman on a storm-tossed boat. The waves were high, the wind and rain were lashing at the boat. What do we do in a storm? When it is impossible to mend the broken nets, we must just hold on to the mast in order to save ourselves from being washed overboard. We can fully experience the storm because we know that in this moment there is no escape. This is what Phyllis experienced when she described the darkness raining down.

However, in the very next moment she rained more arrows of darkness onto herself by judging her experience. *'I shouldn't be feeling this'. 'How can I be a mindfulness teacher when I can feel so hopeless and lost?', 'I am not good enough', 'I will never be good enough'*. This is how our self-critic or judge often speaks. We resort so readily to use the judgemental and final words 'always' or 'never'. It is either 100% or nothing! So why is it that we want to believe the exaggeration? This is the second dart mentioned in Chapter 2.

The first step is just to be with the storm. As we turn towards all those emotions, including the emotion of shame that we are not coping, then we are experiencing storm. Acknowledging what is going on, we notice that our threat system is fully activated. At some point in the storm, in the emotional difficulty, we notice the emotions that are present and fully turn towards the wind in our face, the feeling in our body. This is the approach mode.

Three types of emotional affect systems that influence our behaviour

Adapted from Paul Gilbert's Compassion-based Therapy

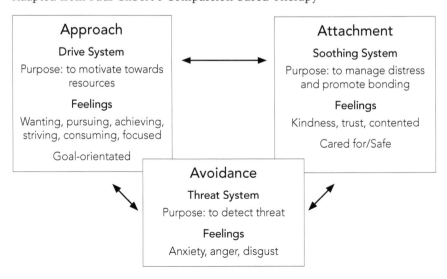

Phyllis fully experienced both avoidance and approach mode. That is experiencing the storm, hating it and herself, then approaching it with curiosity, noting the full disruption and after some time realising that she was being hard on herself. She was in a difficult situation and needed to 'soothe' herself, to be kind and self-compassionate.

It can be so hard to remember this. Sometimes our emotional behaviour can be linked even further than our own childhood to that of our parents and grandparents. This family cycle of shame is activated from generation to generation. An awareness of this may well alleviate some of the sense of blame and failure. The three emotional affect systems devised by Paul Gilbert explains this.

Avoidance (threat-orientated)

Avoidance is a behaviour we may use in life to escape from feeling the full effect of the present moment. It is a coping strategy that may be useful sometimes but is not a long-term solution. We can notice this in spontaneous reactions to life situations and sometimes during meditation we have a heightened awareness of this avoidance behaviour. It can show up as restlessness or sleepiness and, when this is very strong, we need the other emotional affect systems to help us be with it.

Threat-focused behaviour was an essential function in man's early history but now it often plays out against us. We react to criticism or negative experiences with the same amount of adrenaline as we did for sabre tooth tigers or other predators. This is a survival mechanism. Often, we perceive a potential threat and react by either flight (anxiety) or fight (stress, anger and impatience) or we freeze (numb out, withdraw, hope we will not be noticed).

This behaviour has been located by MRI scan in the part of the brain called the brain stem. This is the most primitive part of the brain (reptilian) where we perceive threats and potential threats. This urges us toward fight, flight or freeze behaviour. The hormones that fuel this behaviour are adrenaline, noradrenalin and cortisol.

Approach (goal-orientated)

Approach mode is goal-orientated behaviour that helps get things done. It leads us to seek out pleasurable behaviours and motivates us to work, seek mates and make our lives comfortable. It is a wanting and achieving state, however, it can lead to over-striving and driven behaviour. It has energy and vitality. It can also lead to stress. In meditation and in life, approach mode encourages us to make an effort, to be curious about our experience, to turn towards difficulty. However, it also may lead to tension as we often try too hard.

The mid-brain area called the cortex (mammalian) is responsible for this behaviour and the hormone released when this is activated is dopamine.

Attachment (bonding-orientated)

Attachment mode describes our need for connection and safety. It is often a non-wanting state, a more un-selfish system based on nurturing, kindness and soothing with a social motivation. We often need to encourage this nurturing state in order to regulate the other two systems. All three are necessary for our survival; however, we may need to consciously work at cultivating this nurturing state towards ourselves. We develop this in meditation by being gentle with ourselves, deliberately evoking kindness when we notice harshness and self-judgement and also by self-compassion, befriending and loving-kindness meditations.

The pre-cortex, a higher region in the brain both in position and in evolutionary history (primate), is responsible for this behaviour. The hormones that fuel it are serotonin and oxytocin.

How to apply this to our own experience

1. Noticing the threat

The activated **Avoidance** system is acknowledged. We notice and acknowledge that anxiety or anger or adrenaline is here. The impulse towards a fight, flight or freeze reaction is noted within a mindful pause and a choice made about whether to go with the habitual reaction or not.

2. Turning towards this with mindfulness

We deliberately activate **Approach** mode with a 'goal' of seeing this for what it is. This could be to notice what's here in this moment and experience how it feels in the body, take in what is going on in our whole experience (body, emotions, thoughts) and step back and observe our experience mindfully. This being curious about our experience will lessen our anxiety; the brain cannot register curiosity and anxiety at the same time very well. The curiosity of the approach mode often overrides the anxiety and fearfulness.

3. Bringing kindness to ourselves

We tune into **Attachment** mode by nurturing and soothing ourselves. We can use the breath for calming and soothing ourselves. We can use words to bring kindness to ourselves. We can see ourselves as a vulnerable child and imagine sending kindness and warmth to this child. We can gently stroke or squeeze ourselves either physically or in our mind's eye. The practices later in this chapter – the breathing space working with difficulty and RAIN meditation both work with being with emotions. The practices in Chapter 6 emphasise self-compassion.

Being more inclined to an Approach mentality can enhance wellbeing. Welcoming new experience and being curious about people as well as our own reactions opens up the world. We find more courage when we approach the world with a friendly curiosity. Mindfulness with its attitude of Beginner's Mind and fresh eyes can give us a new perspective and a new interest in our lives, which may have been previously inhibited by fear. We don't know what the future holds but we can be curious and open and trusting that we will not only cope but will actively find something positive in our experience.

Examples of working with the three emotional affect systems

Avoidance affect system

SEREN came home from shopping completely shattered. She had 'shopped til she dropped' with no break for lunch or even a cup of tea. She knew she was not looking after herself very wisely but considered it a necessity for preparing for Christmas. She was already feeling grumpy because she had not been very successful in finding any presents except a funny pair of socks. Seren was self-critical as she judged her present buying ability to be very poor. This proved she was a failure as a friend and even as a partner and mother. Once the trigger had been touched it opened a whole can of worms!

When she got home her husband was sitting on the sofa enjoying the last episode of a TV series. She made them a cup of tea and ate some biscuits and watched too. He said he wasn't hungry so didn't feel like cooking tea. She felt uncared for. She had been out all day – why couldn't he cook something? She began to sulk, feeling uncared for, thus triggering another core belief – she was 'unloved'. When he realised she was 'in a funny mood' he started offering to cook but what did she want? 'Nothing,' she answered. She was hungry but she didn't want any of the things he offered. They all made her feel sick. She stayed in a bad mood all night. She had become frozen. She cried when she went to bed and felt unloved and useless.

She recognised these as old patterns from when she was a little girl. Yet she couldn't shift out of the negative thoughts. '*He* should *have made a meal, he didn't care*'. She felt worthless. Her mouth turned down in a pout, her tummy tight. She was frozen. Eventually she was able to escape the treadmill of negative thoughts, check into her body and just notice and stay with the uncomfortable feelings. When she woke in the morning she rehearsed the ancient litany again. How interesting that she felt so drawn to these negative thoughts, she really wanted to get stuck in them again.

Luckily, her husband wanted to talk about what was going on. She presented her argument from the stance of the little girl who wasn't loved and he told her it wasn't true. He had been happy to cook but she had rejected everything he had offered. She meditated after this and saw how she had been stuck in an old story. She touched into the feelings in the body, felt the frozen heaviness. She was shocked about how strong the belief in the old story was and how, if conditions were right, it could still have so much power. She was shocked at how strong the desire was to avoid being fully present with the whole experience and to stay with the negative thoughts.

The meditation opened her to really feeling the dissatisfaction and to see that this was not the whole story. This led her to feeling self-compassion; to see that the child's experience had been so strong, that the threat system of shame, anger and hurt had overridden everything for an extended period of time. Her drive for survival, towards resources of food and comfort, even to explore mindfully had been overridden. Her self-compassion and even her compassion for another had been overridden too. The threat-focused, avoidance affect system had taken over. She was interested to notice this and hoped that maybe next time she might be quicker to realise what was happening.

Approach affect system

Ten years ago, FLORA had difficulties at work. She had been very unhappy and wanted to leave her job to escape her unsympathetic line manager, Donald and colleague, Ceri, who had criticised her work. She regained the confidence she had lost by working with her mindfulness practice and moving to another department. She now was receiving positive feedback for her work.

Then, with the development of a new project, the two departments were set to work together. Flora was very anxious about this. Could she work with them again? Should she go off sick or refuse to work with them? She felt that they would criticise her again and she would lose ground and become incompetent while trying to work with them. She felt that she would have to prove herself. She also felt that she should have got over it after this time.

Flora explored her feelings in meditation and could feel the fear as a tightening in the gut and a feeling of nausea. She recognised that the deep sinking feeling she felt in the body felt like despair and hopelessness. As she explored this deeper she felt a vortex opening up in her abdomen area; it was black and apparently bottomless. She just wanted to cry. The feeling felt like abandonment, a feeling of deep rejection. She recognised a core belief of not being good enough. She felt fear and shame.

This was Approach mode. She had turned towards the feelings but it had rendered her even more fearful, because of the strong inclination to believe this long-held primary belief. She needed to have enough self-compassion to let this go. She asked herself, *'Is it true? Is it useful? Is it the right time'?*

Flora also needed to engage the attachment soothing system. She asked herself what her strengths were? What qualities had she brought to the work? How did she value these qualities? She reflected on her successes, the praise of her new manager and the gratitude of her clients. She discovered that, although her style was very different from her colleagues', her warmth and friendliness gained the confidence of her clients, and that too had an important part to play in the success of their work. She had to let go of her pride and the image of herself as not being competent or up to the job; the job that she had done thousands of times since the original setback.

She decided to use her practice when working with these colleagues. To keep coming back to the moment, to feel her feet on the floor, to be with her breath and even stroking her arm as a comforting gesture. Flora set an intention to remember her positive qualities, which reflected her values of cooperation, kindliness and love.

The collaboration day involved a joint presentation. Flora decided that the courageous thing to do would be to insist that she managed the day and did the presentation in order not to feel cowed by them and to confront her inner judge. However, after reflecting some more she asked herself what she needed in this situation. She needed to feel safe and not activate the threat system. She decided that this was not a situation where she had to prove herself. Flora told Ceri she would be happy if Ceri took the lead in this. Ceri did the presentation but respectfully included her at intervals. It was a win-win situation. Flora had kept her self-respect and enjoyed the day. She felt less hostile to her colleague who had apologised for her earlier behaviour. Flora recognised her colleague's strengths and was able to learn from her.

Soothing affect system

Mindfulness was a useful tool to help HANIYA cope with the sudden death of her husband, Zavi.

'My life is very different at the moment. I'm working out how to deal with it after feeling a lot of loss after Zavi dying and the children leaving home at the same time. I can feel a bit all over the place. I could feel disorientated but mindfulness practice has the opposite effect. It focuses me and anchors me so that I can feel stronger to deal with anything that comes my way. I can sometimes feel immediate benefit.'

She acknowledged that, initially, mindfulness was a useful anchor that gave her solace by calming and soothing. Then, later on, she was able to turn towards grief and anguish to experience the full ferocity of emotion with both mind and body. She allowed herself to feel the fullness of it and found this very powerful. Haniya was engaged in her life and yet she was not avoiding the many depths and shades of her grief. She said:

'It's difficult for us to quantify sometimes how it helps us. It's a mystery. It's more than a tool to make me feel better and I am still exploring and thinking about it. The more I practise the more I might understand it. I am in touch with my sadness and anger but I also feel comforted, soothed by my practice. It's as if the grief is not the only thing in my life. I can appreciate that I am alive.'

Being overwhelmed

Rough winds do shake the darling buds of May,
And summer's lease hath all too short a date.
Sometime too hot the eye of heaven shines,
And often is his gold complexion dimm'd

– William Shakespeare, Sonnet 18

There are occasions when it is neither possible nor appropriate to work with difficulty by turning towards it. Sometimes physical pain is alleviated and made bearable by painkillers. In a situation of abuse, flight or removal from the situation is usually the right response. Where a person has suffered trauma it is often not wise to invite them to turn towards these feelings while experiencing the numbing affect, which is a survival strategy in itself.

This is the reason we ask people to delay coming to a mindfulness course if they have had a bereavement of a loved one or a traumatic event. This certainly isn't avoidance in a negative sense. In turning towards unbearable difficulty we can become overwhelmed. In these cases, we make a wise choice to withdraw skilfully. We are not running away but taking compassionate action, looking after ourselves. This may well involve a conscious intention to wait for an appropriate time to turn towards the difficulty. Mindfulness work is always about choice.

Jackie came to the Staying Mindful course several years after she had done the eight-week course. When we started with the body scan for home practice she said she had always slept through the practice. I asked her to see if there was any particular pattern to this and to note where in the body she was when she fell asleep. She noticed that she always fell asleep at the thighs and missed out the lower trunk all together.

Molly said she just couldn't lie still for the body scan. Just the thought of lying still made her so horribly restless that she would jump up after a few moments and run out of the room. I emphasised that there was no necessity to lie still and that she was free to go or to move whenever she wanted to. However, I invited her to be curious about this extreme restlessness which seemed to contradict her sincere intention to do the practice. I suggested that she could give herself permission to get up after a certain short time, maybe one minute or two. If possible, to stay with the uncomfortable feeling for that short time and notice where it was in the body, what kind of sensation was arising and how she was breathing in those moments. She did this and found she was able to stay with the scan longer.

Both women discovered that scanning through the body in this mindful way had felt extremely threatening to them. Their reaction had been to run away either by sleeping or by moving and therefore avoiding the unpleasantness. Eventually, when they were ready to stay with the body scan, both women retrieved early memories of abuse. They then felt ready to have support in therapy to help them come to terms with this traumatic memory.

Sometimes we take quite a time to heal. Mindfulness is not about forcing ourselves or becoming hardened to our sensitive areas. Often it is about giving space for things to unfold in their own time. Jon Kabat-Zinn compared our work in doing meditation practice to the slow unfolding of a chrysalis into a butterfly. It must happen in its own time, no forcing and no holding back. If we try to force the butterfly to emerge we damage it. A gentle patience is required. Sometimes the wise choice is to wait until we are strong enough to engage with the difficulty, with the suffering. To let it be.

SUANNE was distressed because she felt a lump in her throat throughout meditation. She just wanted it to go away. She explained that she knew it was because she wasn't allowed to speak out as a child. She told herself: 'It's OK now.' She expected that she could relax in meditation and then it would soothe her throat and make it go away. 'I am trying so hard to make it go away' she said. We explored the sensation in class, but Suanne found it hard to stay with it. She kept asking herself: 'Why is this here now?' I asked her to forget the why for now and to focus on the how of it. 'How does it feel? How big? Is it hot or cold? What's the texture of it?' She was able to do this a little but became overwhelmed.

AKIRA brought in her own experience. She said that at the beginning of the meditation she could feel a big stone boulder weighing her down deep in the abdomen. 'It didn't move, I stayed with it a while and breathed into it, holding it closely with my attention. I breathed into it gently. Eventually it became smaller and lighter still, until it dissolved and was no longer there'

Suanne said, 'I want to understand it and make it go away.' Her whole body tensed up as she expressed this, visibly gritting her teeth and clenching her fists. It seemed alien to her to simply allow it to be there for a while. I reminded her that noticing it and allowing it to be there, as in the coping breathing space, was part of the practice, but being gentle with herself and kind through this difficulty was also important. She had a choice to stay with it or to mindfully move, back to the breath or another focus. In the end we decided that at that point in time her movement practice was more helpful than her sitting practice and that trying to make tension or pain go away does not work.

After the death of her daughter, Catrin had carried on stoically at her workplace. For a whole year she had held out and not shed a tear. At the end of a retreat she broke down and cried all night. Like a storm breaking her grief was tumultuous. She said, 'Nothing can take way the pain, there is no cure for this and yet there is some relief for me in being able to cry in this way'.

Things fall apart; tread the path with care.

– The attributed last words of the Buddha

Guided meditations for working with difficulty

Three-step breathing space – when facing difficulty

1. **Acknowledging** your experience in the body, heart and mind. Becoming aware. Checking in with yourself. Asking yourself, 'How am I right now? What's going on with me'? Noticing the thoughts you are having, the emotional tone of the moment and any corresponding sensations in the body. Often there are strong sensations in the body when emotions are present.

2. **Gathering** your attention to focus on the breath and/or grounding your attention with feet on the floor. Noticing how the breath is. Is it tight, shallow, caught, held? Where are you feeling the breath in the body? Not trying to control it, merely being aware of in-breath and out-breath. In a difficult situation this maybe more challenging than usual; your mind and body will feel disturbed so notice thoughts and simply being with the breath as best you can.

3. **Expanding** your attention to be aware of sensations in the body, these may well be the emotional feelings you felt in Step 1 but also including the feel of your feet making contact with the floor and if you are sitting, feeling your bottom on the seat. Noticing how your hands are – held tightly or clenched? Checking in with your shoulders, your belly, your chest, your throat, or any areas where you may hold tension. You may say to yourself that it's OK to feel it. Now expanding the attention still further to be aware of sounds, near and far. Being aware of your whole body and the space around you. In this expanded awareness we realise that strong feeling is a part of experience, albeit a powerful part, but it is not the whole of our experience. We are held in ABC: A Big Container of Awareness.

A useful guided meditation for this practice can be found in *Mindfulness: A Practical Guide to Finding Peace in a Frantic World* (2011) by Mark Williams and Danny Penman.

The Oxford MBCT app also has useful guided meditations: http://mbctapp.oxfordmindfulness.org/

IONA said that although the invitation had been to think of something small, the big stuff came crowding in and she didn't want to go there. Instead she felt numb, not feeling anything. I asked her if she was able to stay with that feeling and was that OK? She said: 'Yes, it's like I am in a warm cocoon and I can't feel anything; people want me to behave in a certain way, but I am fine doing this my own way'.

Numbness is there for a reason; after a shock, a trauma or a grief we are especially tender, and like the chrysalis of the butterfly, we need to unfold in our own time.

It is important not to force ourselves to stay present with something that feels too painful in the moment – to acknowledge it and our wish for it to go away may well be enough for this moment. We are not trying to fix ourselves but just to notice with kindness and gentleness what is here. If we have suffered trauma it is not helpful to force ourselves to confront it, to go right into it – instead we need to find a way of nurturing ourselves. We focus on self-compassion later in Chapter 6.

No and yes meditation

This is an invitation to come up close to resistance.

Take up your meditation posture. Feeling your body on the seat and your feet on the floor. Focus on the breath for a few breaths.

When you are ready, bring to mind a situation; something you recently experienced, when you felt angry, sad, frightened or a strong sense of resistance. Something manageable or current. Maybe it is physical or emotional or both.

Think about the story of this and allow it to come alive. You may see the person or hear them in your mind's eye. What emotions are present? How is your body feeling and where are you feeling the emotion – maybe in the chest, guts, belly heart area or shoulders? What is your facial expression as you re-live the situation in your mind?

Experiment with saying 'No, not this, I don't want it.' Embody 'No'. Feel it in the body. No – to the emotions, push them away. No – to the situation, this should not be. No – to physical sensations, to grief, anger, despair, fear. If the exercise seems difficult and you can't get into it, say 'No' to that. Experiment with allowing a stroppy teenager to appear in your life. It could seem like a parody. You can ham it up with a very dramatic 'No' or two. Or, if you are feeling fragile, just listening to the vulnerability as you say 'No'. You can say 'No, I don't want it'. ➜

Check in to the body – what is the effect of this 'No'? How do the belly, the guts, the heart area, the jaw, the area around the mouth or eyes feel? What are your feelings about the situation when you are saying 'No'? What happens to your painful feelings?

Take a few deep breaths and let go of 'No', opening to the breath and to sounds in the moment. As best you can allowing yourself to move to a neutral place. Again, feeling your bottom on the seat and your feet on the floor, feel the support of the seat and the ground.

Then, recalling the painful situation again, imagine it, the story, the people the feelings. But now saying 'Yes, welcome' or 'It's okay.' Embody 'Yes'. 'Yes': to the situation, to the memories, to the feelings both emotionally and physically. Yes – to the tightness in the body. Yes – to sounds you can hear in the moment. Yes – to this breath.

Exploring 'Yes', the effect of it on your body. What do you notice in your chest, tummy, abdomen, your face? What do you feel in your heart? Does your body and mind relax a little, soften? Let your feelings float, held in the energy of 'Yes'. How does it feel to accept yourself just as you are in this moment?

Then coming back to a neutral place, noticing the breath, feelings in the body, sounds in the moment, feeling your feet on the floor and your bottom on the seat.

There is no right way to feel here, it is an experiment with being with our feelings and working with resistance and acceptance. There is no desired outcome, just open-mindedness as we play with 'No' and 'Yes' and see if it allows us to take a different perspective. An investigation into our different stances. A mindful enquiry into 'Yes' or 'No' which may guide us to be more compassionate to ourselves.

(Adapted from Tara Brach's *Radical Acceptance*.)

JOSIE was working with resistance to practice, feeling that the practice was dull. She said: 'What's the point of being in the moment anyway? I could hear the wind in the trees, feel my breath but it wasn't enough. I have been plagued by this "it isn't enough" before. I am feeling dissatisfied in a grumbly sort of way. Maybe I want more lively entertainment, something juicy. More likely, I am avoiding what has shifted me into this low mood in the first place.'

When we began to deconstruct this she told me that she was ruminating over the story of not being included in a dining table conversation as she was sitting on the far side of the table. She couldn't hear and therefore was unable to join in. 'Ahh the return of the Invisible Woman complex!' she added.

She realised that her passivity was initially instigated by a work issue. Josie had been asked to do something she didn't want to do and had taken a passive stance that led to her to complain about it to herself rather than making an active choice to either do it or decline the work gracefully.

When we did the 'No'/'Yes' meditation' she was very intrigued by her reaction, especially the call to invite her inner rebellious teenager to arise. This involved staying with the hurt, accessing the anger and feeling it in her body and then bringing a sense of kindness to this horrible feeling.

Josie's next practice was very dynamic as she allowed the stroppy teenager to say **No**. 'No, it wasn't fair. No, I didn't want this burden. No, I don't want to feel like this'. She said that the energy generated felt good. 'I felt the tightening of my body, the defiant tilt of my jaw, the clenching of my innards and my teeth. It was interesting. I found a lot of things to say "No" to, including the very strong feeling that I shouldn't be behaving in this way!'

When she moved to the next stage of the practice, she relaxed, took a few breaths and just experienced being in a neutral place. Then she revisited the situation again and invited herself to play with saying 'Yes' with enthusiasm.

Curiously, the tension and tightness that had arisen from the negative feeling did soften, did lessen, did ease. Jon Kabat-Zinn says that 'mindfulness is a radical act of sanity and love'.

Allowing yourself to say Yes to the life that's here. When we say Yes our hearts awaken to love.

The RAIN meditation

This practice is a useful one when working with difficulty or when any strong emotion is present.

Bring to mind a particular situation that has been difficult for you, a minor mishap where you have felt judgemental or aversive. A situation you have not liked. On the scale of 0–10 when 10 is major, let it be a 1 or 2 and at most a 3.

Begin by **Grounding**.

Feeling the contact of the floor, the seat. Allowing this contact to really support you. Focusing now on your breathing. Feeling the breath in the body wherever it is the most vivid. Staying with the breath to calm and steady yourself. Then bringing to mind a difficulty, a hurt, a disconnect that is disturbing you at this time. This could be at home, in a relationship, at work. It could be your own or someone else's aversive behaviour or obsessive behaviour. Make it something relatively easy to be with, not a big difficulty or trauma. A place where you feel some awareness would help.

Move into RAIN:

R is Recognise your story as a story. Go to the situation. Relive it in your mind. What emotions are present? What is the most uppermost feeling here? What is your facial expression while thinking about it?

Ask yourself 'What is happening inside me now?' What emotion, judgement or negative thought is here in your head at this moment? As you go over the story what bites, what grabs you, where do you get stuck? Freeze the frame here. →

A is Allow, Accept. Pause. Allowing yourself to accept and be with these feelings.

Saying to yourself:

'It's OK to feel this, to stay with these feelings. Just letting it be here. Yes, to this feeling in this moment.'

Allowing yourself to feel into the resentment or anger or hurt or despair or fear, whatever is here, however it is in this moment. Accepting that this is suffering and allowing these negative emotions. The feelings maybe unpleasant but letting them be there. Saying 'Yes' to the experience you are having at the moment, not to make it go away, but in order to spend more time with it, in a more objective way.

I – Investigate Investigate where you are feeling the most vulnerable. Where are you feeling this in the body? What wants attention? What am I believing here?

This is a difficult place to stay with as it can be really painful. It is important to investigate with kindness and a strong motivation of curiosity. Remember you are not analysing or problem-solving, but moving from the story, the fixed ideas of your thinking to the feelings in the body i.e. staying with sensation and bringing curiosity to it. After feeling into these body sensations asking yourself what am I believing here about myself? This may lead to determining core beliefs about yourself which may be very old, perhaps gained when you were very young.

The four foundations of mindfulness may be helpful here.

1. The Body: Where are you feeling sensation and how? What is your facial expression, your posture? Is the place you feel this in the body: constricted, contracted, tense, tight, hard and solid, or trembling, or numb, or squeezed, hot or cold, heavy or light? Let your posture express the feeling. Maybe your body tenses or sags, your chest caves in or pushes out? Your hands tighten into fists, your forehead frowns, your mouth pouts, the jaw clenches?

2. Feelings or Perception: Is it pleasant, unpleasant or neutral? There may be a mixture of feelings.

3. Mind: What are the thoughts here, the core beliefs? What am I believing about myself? What emotions does this bring up? (Anger, sadness, hurt, fear, despair, shame, unworthiness or other?)

We can question whether this is a fixed belief i.e. one that has been with us for so long we assume it is true. Core beliefs such as: 'I am unlovable', 'I'm not good enough', 'I am a failure', 'I am useless', 'I am hopeless', 'I am worthless', 'I am bad', 'I am stupid', 'I am inferior', 'I am not attractive'. Questioning whether these fixed beliefs are true leads us to ask yourself what is needed in this moment? What do you need right now?

4. Nothing is solid or fixed, things change: When you see that your story is impermanent (a fleeting story, like a scene in a film), when you see the story is not who you are, and as you weaken your identification with the story, it becomes weaker and loosens its hold.

N: Non-identification or Nurture

Meeting your experience with a compassionate heart and letting go of taking it personally. →

Things are not fixed; you are not the same in every situation. You change throughout your life. Can you see that you are making it a solid, unchanging thing? Can you see you may have a fixed idea of yourself and not take it so personally?

What do you need? Can you bring some loving attention to yourself? You can keep company with yourself as a kind witness. You are bigger than just this hurt or angry part of you. You can relate to rather than from that place that needs help. Maybe you can give yourself a loving touch, placing a hand on your heart or maybe feeling your arm or stroking your hand with your other hand. Maybe finding some words for yourself: 'I see you', 'I love you', 'I accept you the way you are,' 'It's OK to be like this', 'You belong', 'You are allowed to be like this'.

It may help to bring to mind someone who loves you – this can be your pet, or it can be an archetypal figure like the Buddha or Jesus Christ or Mary or Kuan Yin, the Chinese female Buddha of compassion, or the Dalai Lama. Someone who can love you, unconditionally, without questioning.

If aspects of this nourishing guidance don't ring true to you or you feel yourself resisting, go back to the R, A and I – recognising, allowing and investigating how you are feeling in this moment. There is no need to force yourself to feel a particular way.

Each time you open to the vulnerability and practise bringing kindness to this, you are practising to become free of these negative thoughts. They may not go away, but their power will weaken. You are learning to hold with compassion the wounded place. You are opening to your own vulnerability. Breathing in and connecting with your own kindness to your own vulnerability.

Saying to yourself when you are immersed in the difficulty, in the suffering, 'Is this who I really am? This is not who I am completely, maybe it is just in this moment.' Can you identify with the whole of your experience? Maybe hearing a bird's song or feeling the contact of your feet on the floor, maybe noticing a pleasant sensation, like the sun on your face or even the refreshing drops of rain.

We need both sun and rain to nourish us. And as we continue to do this practice regularly we will experience the freedom we crave.

> *Keep looking*
> *At the bandaged place. That's where*
> *The light enters you.*

– Rumi

Working with RAIN meditation

LOK was feeling down. He had done a movement practice and decided to sit for a while. After a few moments steadying himself, grounding and breathing, he began the R of RAIN. This is what he told me.

'Recognising: What's here? I was feeling a bit down; I felt doubtful about the practice in general. There was no joy in the movement practice. I felt heavy and just like I was going through the motions. The thought was "What's the point?" The feeling was doubt and apathy, the body felt heavy. →

Allowing: I said to myself, "It's OK to feel this. It's unpleasant but it's here. I am saying Yes to this". Just feeling myself settling into the feeling of heaviness.

Investigating: What was happening inside of me? Heaviness! I asked myself: "What do I believe about myself?" I answered "I believe that I just don't get this practice. It's a waste of time because I can't get it. I am a failure".

My body felt heavy, my shoulders down, I felt slumped, my lips had a sneer. Then I remembered I could investigate with kindness. I said to myself: "I am feeling heavy; I don't like it. I don't think I am getting anywhere so the body is reacting. This is an old belief. I don't think I'm good enough".

I said to myself: "It is not like this always, what else is here?" I could hear the birds singing and the sound of the wind and the rain.

Non-identifying: This heavy feeling is not how I feel all the time. It is not all of my experience in this moment. The birds were singing sweetly, I felt myself smile. I realised that my experience is not fixed. It changes. I am not always a failure! I can nurture myself in this moment, taking in the sounds.

Then I put my hand on my heart and soothed myself. I said to myself: "You don't have to be any different in this moment, it is enough just to hear the birds and sit quietly, expecting nothing, just being here".'

The Guest House

This being human is a guest house.
Every morning a new arrival.

A joy, a depression, a meanness,
some momentary awareness comes
as an unexpected visitor.

Welcome and entertain them all!
Even if they're a crowd of sorrows,
who violently sweep your house
empty of its furniture,
still, treat each guest honourably.
He may be clearing you out
for some new delight.

The dark thought, the shame, the malice,

meet them at the door laughing,

and invite them in.

Be grateful for whoever comes,

because each has been sent

as a guide from beyond.

– Rumi, translated by Coleman Barks

JANE talked about her difficulty in a one-to-one session. She was being very critical of her friend who was always busy. She did the RAIN exercise. In the recognise part she said she was uncomfortable about being so critical of her friend. She asked, 'Why does she rush around like a fly with a blue bottom?' She remembered hearing her friend boast about how busy she was.

When she did the Allowing, pausing part she said that she felt irritated and angry and maybe felt fear. When she investigated she said, 'I feel that I am not worth her attention, that she is just like my mother, too busy to pay me any attention'. Where was she feeling this in the body? Jane said 'I am feeling tightly squeezed in my abdomen area, I can't breathe properly. It's a hollow feeling. I am thinking I am unlovable; no one loves me, I am tiny and insignificant.'

She realised that this was a very young part of her, left over from childhood. When she explored what she needed, Jane said, 'Hand on my heart, I am thinking about my husband and how he has time for me and how we can spend easy time together without an agenda. I am feeling good, better than I was. Also, I am thinking about her – her restlessness, her fear of missing out and I'm feeling sorry for her and not envious anymore. But I am worried I will get into this again.'

Of course, we often worry that we will fall back into the hole time and time again. It is like a muscle that you need to keep exercising. Each time we open to the vulnerability and practise kindness, we practise becoming free of negative thoughts. They may not go away, but their power will weaken. We are learning to hold the wounded place with compassion; opening to our own vulnerability and connecting with kindness.

Here is a Zen story from ancient China. Don't try to understand it. Just enjoy it and see that being too busy and stressing about it is an age-old predicament.

Yunyan is sweeping the ground. Daowu his brother monk says, 'Too busy!'

Yunyan answers back, 'You should know there's one who's not busy.'

Daowu laughs, 'Oh, you mean there are two moons?'

Yunyan then holds up the brush and says, 'Which moon is this?'

Jane realised that she didn't have to compete in a world that was too busy. She had time for the moon.

EMMA was a keen mountain athlete. After an injury with her back she found herself limited in her usual athletic activities. She wrote this poem after a Staying Mindful course in 2017.

Where has superwoman gone? I thought, where has superwoman gone?

I look down

I see a body that cannot run,

a body that cannot climb mountains.

Where has superwoman gone?

I used to bounce when I hit the floor!

Not think twice about leaping, jumping, climbing and cavorting like a lunatic!

Where has superwoman gone?

Where is unbreakable, unbeaten, unchallenged?

I look deeper...

Where is defiant and strong willed?

Where is brave and strong minded?

Where am I?

Where were these things when I needed them?

Then I remembered...

They were chipped away once,

superwoman dwindled, slowly, slowly, over time

Away...

Then there came a time when I became more mindful of where I am now and I realised that the super is

still in the woman,

because how would anything less than super have remained
standing tall and strong and defiant after all this.

– Emma L. Lloyd

No Compass

Where do we go from here?
What is beyond?
Not knowing I am fearful
And ask for certainty or at least a compass
To solid ground.

There is a station existing between two tunnels
You must travel through darkness to arrive there.
Keep along the tracks when the sun goes down
Carrying all you can. No straight line to awareness
The only currency is kindness.

What is beyond imagining?
Summer in midwinter
Snow on a hot June day.
God in heaven.
No solid ground.

What is beyond bearing?
A world without you.
The death of a child.
Leaving home...

The sun is weak in January but you will be safe in the woods.
Some call them the dark woods. The moss is a carpet of stars
Clothing the trunks of trees, alongside ivy and lichen.
There are no wolves only foxes.

When you stumble on the stream follow it by sound
To the river and all the way to the sea.

I am determined to stay on the path.
Alone in a strange country
Beyond sun and shadow

With no compass.

– Annee Griffiths

Chapter 5:
Working With Anxiety

All shall be well and all shall be well, and all manner of things shall be well.

Julian of Norwich (13th Century Anchorite)

You can't stop the waves, but you can learn to surf.

Jon Kabat-Zinn (1994)

There is a Scandinavian folk story called The Lindworm:

Once upon a time there was a childless queen who lived near the Arctic circle. Desperate for a child, she consults a wise witch who tells her to eat from a magic bush that has a white and a red flower. She must eat only the white flower otherwise something terrible will happen. So delicious is the white flower that she can't stop herself from trying just a mouthful of the red flower. Surely one tiny bite won't make any difference? She can't resist another tiny bite. Then seeing as it has almost gone, she finishes it. She has eaten both the white and the red flower. At the consequent birth the queen gives birth to a black serpent, a Lindworm. It is flung away out of the window and into the forest. She then gives birth to a beautiful boy. →

Of course, the fearful thing hasn't gone away – what you push away usually returns with a vengeance. When the prince wants to marry, the Lindworm returns to the castle and insists he, the elder brother, must marry first. Princess after princess is given as a bride to the Lindworm and he eats every one of them.

Eventually, there are no more princesses left to eat and the king orders a shepherd's daughter to marry the monster. Terrified and unable to escape, she consults with the witch about what she should do. The witch tells her to wear many dresses, one on top of the other. She is to ask the serpent to shed a skin before she takes off her dress. Surprisingly, he does just this. He takes off a skin; she takes off a dress. She is wearing 12 dresses and he has only 11 skins. Believe it or not, under all the skins he is indeed a handsome human being who she embraces and loves happily ever after.

The snake which cannot cast its skin has to die.

– Friedrich Nietzsche

We have to be prepared to be brave, to take a risk to turn towards and shed layer by layer our fear.

Perhaps everything terrifying is deep down a helpless thing that needs our help.

– Rainer Maria Rilke

Even in the Lindworm story the castaway needed love.

Can we tell ourselves that all will be well? Does that work or do we need other strategies? The emphasis in this chapter is on turning towards anxiety. In 2013 there were 8.2 million cases of anxiety in the UK. A briefing paper from the House of Commons in 2018, asserted that 5.9 % of the population suffered from Generalised Anxiety Disorder, with considerably more cases in the north of England (Baker, 2018).

Many people come to mindfulness training because of anxiety. 'Be Mindful Online' is an online mindfulness course offered by the Mental Health Foundation. Research on the online course in 2013 found that for the 273 people that completed the course there was, on average, a 58% reduction in anxiety levels.

Children from quite an early age are experiencing stress and anxiety. The specialist Child and Adolescent Mental Health Service in Wales (CAMHS) is under more pressure than ever before. The last four years have seen a 100% increase in child anxiety referrals according to a paper published by the Mental Health Foundation in 2016. Schools in Britain and North America are beginning to teach mindfulness to children to help them cope with the demands of our culture. My friend and colleague, Sarah Silverton, has been involved in the Mindfulness in Schools Programme from its early days and has now developed, with primary school teachers, a programme for young children called 'The Present'. This is being rolled out by the Welsh Government.

The part of the brain called the amygdala in the frontal lobe is particularly active when we experience fear. The more we experience anxiety the more active this part of the brain becomes. It grows more sensitised like an alarm bell wiring us up to emotional reactions throughout the brain stem. We can overload the system with these threat alerts, which can become habitual. It's back to the story of the second dart. A man is hit with one arrow and instead of attempting to seal the wound by attending to the pain he spends his energy worrying about who sent the arrow. The stimulus of the first arrow or dart that hits us may well be a problem that we need to sort out. The second dart is a self-inflicted injury. We need to unhook from this extra layer of fear that accumulates around the first dart.

The emotion of fear, like anger, often totally overwhelms us and we are caught in its reactive clutches. Thoughts, feelings and even actions become out of our control. The mindfulness practice of turning towards and exploring the physical aspects of the emotion help to loosen its power. When we pay attention to the physical effects of that emotion and use our thinking power, perhaps to verbalise what is going on in the body, the frontal lobe is better able to regulate the limbic system.

The awareness of fear is not fear. The thought that tells us we are anxious and the awareness of this in the body is a step removed from fear. Caught up in our fear is the sense that we cannot cope with what is happening. We feel unworthy, we feel shame. Anxiety makes us contract and withdraw. By becoming more aware of how we respond to fear and the stories we tell ourselves, the judgements around it, the mind and body states surrounding anxiety, we can become more present to all aspects of our life.

Can we relate to fear rather than from fear? If we can get to know its territory rather than be dominated by it we can begin to identify with a greater sense of self rather than a narrow one based on our fear. We can notice how things don't stay the same, that our world is changing constantly. By connecting to the present moment we can see that the thing making us fearful is only one part of what is happening.

However, in the case of traumatic experience or extreme fear we may need to create safety. Rather than mindfully working with fear, we need to take time to strengthen ourselves, to feel safe and to feel connected. This inward strength allows us to stay present and curious so that we can be both careful with ourselves and interested in the experience.

We cultivate mindfulness and compassion and learn to work with the challenge of fear and, through doing this, fear lessens. Meditation practice re-forms the neural pathways, helps us to unhook from our habits, our obsessive behaviour. We pay attention with care and friendliness and create a sense of space.

In recent months we have all been affected by fear. The modern plague of Covid-19 has united the whole world with similar fears. Will I or my loved ones get the virus? Will I get into debt or not be able to afford food or rent? Will the changes it makes to our world be insufferable, insurmountable? Things will never be the same. For me, when I realised how my mind was proliferating by projecting a terrible future, one of my ways of coping was simply to sit in our garden and bring my attention to sounds. The sounds of the blackbirds with their spring song stopped my mind in its tracks. When the nearby song stopped, I opened my eyes and there she was perched right by me. I wrote this poem:

> Sitting still
>
> Blackbird's not singing right now
>
> She's eating the ivy berries
>
>
> Right now
>
> No fear.

At other times during the Coronavirus crisis I used specific meditations, in particular, the RAIN meditation found in Chapter 4 and Tonglen found in Chapter 6. The following meditation was very useful.

Working With Fear meditation

Grounding. Scanning your body for any tension. Are there any areas where you are clenching, tightening? What's here in this moment? Feeling your feet on the floor, your bottom of the seat, a sense of being rooted, secure, held by the seat and by the floor, by the earth itself.

Noticing your breath. In and out. Paying particular attention to the out-breath. A sense of exhaling into spaciousness. Your out-breath mingling with the air, flowing into the space around you. Resting in a sense of openness and space.

Bringing your attention now to sounds, simply listening. Noticing spaces between sounds. Focusing on near sounds, far off sounds, hearing the most distant. Widening your awareness. Sounds arising and leaving in the space. Sensing the infinite, boundless nature of space.

Now bringing to mind a situation which evokes fear. Something you are worried about perhaps. As best you can, making this something not too serious, but enough to cause some sense in the body. A 3 or 5 in the 1- 10 scale of anxiety. This could be a difficult situation, maybe around health, perhaps around a loved one. Or something that's present for you at this moment. 'Maybe I won't sleep tonight, or the journey home will be long and stressful.' Asking yourself: What am I really afraid of here? →

Noticing the story but not getting pulled into it. Keep checking the body for any physical sensations. The story is the fuel in the fire of your feelings, which show up as physical sensations in the body. Going over the story in your mind, seeing it, hearing any conversation around it, sensing it, feeling it.

How does your mouth feel? The muscles in your face, any holding here? What is your facial expression? Pay attention to your throat, and any sensations in the chest and tummy.

Inviting the fear in, allow it to be here.

Maybe you are aware of other emotions: sadness, helplessness, confusion, anger, self-doubt, despair, shame.

What are the sensations in the body? Keep checking in. No matter how subtle these sensations are or even if your attention glances quickly away from it.

It's OK if you draw a blank, nothing here.

Simply just coming back to your anchor of the breath, of the feet on the floor, whenever the feelings get too strong. Allowing it to be here. It's OK to feel like this.

Letting the in-breath touch the area of your body that feels vulnerability. On the out-breath letting go, sensing the breath touch the space around you.

How does it feel? Where in the body do you feel it? Does the sensation change or move around? How big is it? What kind of texture does it have? Is it solid or moving? Hard and tense or fluttering and vibratory? Maybe an image comes to mind or a colour?

Just allowing whatever arises to be here.

How is your mind? Is it constricted? Noticing any judgement that arises: 'I shouldn't be thinking this'. What is the tone of voice of any thoughts here?

Focusing now on your breathing. Realise each in-breath as a willingness to be alive. And each out-breath: a letting go into the space around you and the earth that holds you. Feeling the whole body supporting you.

Breathing-in – bringing kindness to the feeling. Breathing-out – sensing the vastness of experience that contains your fear. Trusting here in A Big Container (ABC) of awareness. Coming back to connecting with your feet on the floor.

You might like to reflect that many people are experiencing fear in this moment and bring compassion to yourself and others.

Knowing that fear is only part of your experience. You are not your fear. Don't identify with this as you or yours. Realising that this is just a tiny part of your experience.

Now bringing a sense of kindness to yourself in this moment. Saying to yourself: 'I'm OK, no matter how I feel. It's OK to have emotions, it's part of being human.' If you don't feel anything or don't feel you can do this exercise, that's OK too. →

How would it feel to bring kindness to yourself in this moment? Maybe a sense of touch, touching your arm or hand and gently stroking it. Or maybe feeling the warmth in your chest area as a sense of well-wishing towards yourself. If it's OK with you, you may like to reinforce this feeling or bring about this feeling by placing your hand on your heart or belly as a kindly action.

Now bringing your awareness back to your anchor. To the breath, the feet on the floor, the sounds in the present moment.

Inspired by and Adapted from Tara Brach's Radical Acceptance

Personal stories of the Working With Fear meditation

MARGARET was a manager and a member of the teaching staff involved in an inspection of quality at a college. Although she did the eight-week course some time ago, this inspection was the first time that she remembered to be mindful in a tricky situation. She experienced the encounter with the inspector and was able to function well. Yet, at the same time, she was aware of feeling waves of anxiety. She noticed herself being swept away with these for moments before coming back to coping with the inspector and his challenging questions. At the same time she noticed the physical sensations of anxiety.

She commented to me that the Staying Mindful course had helped her through the difficult moments of the inspection process. The Fear Meditation, where we practised turning towards and staying with anxiety, prepared her for the real event. After the encounter with the inspector she was able to slip away to the bathroom and take a few mindful moments with herself. She felt mindfulness actualised in the real world.

SIWAN considered herself to be of a nervous disposition and often suffered from anxiety. Nevertheless, she managed to work in a professional capacity at a very high level. She was able to manage her anxiety in the workplace with few knock-on effects in her life. However, her teenage daughter had a serious health problem that Siwan had to monitor and manage. This had a detrimental effect on Siwan, and she began to suffer from her own health problems. Consequently, she had to take leave from her job for a stress-related illness. She came to the Staying Mindful course to reinforce the benefits from practice that she had gained from the eight-week course.

She had a Eureka! moment after we had done the 'Fear Meditation' in class. She was awake in the middle of the night worrying about her daughter and trying to work out what she could do to help her. She could feel her heart race and flutters of anxiety in her chest area, which felt constricted. Although this feeling was quite familiar her attitude towards it changed that night. Instead of panicking about the sensations and trying to get rid of them, she found she was able to become curious about them. She stayed with them a while and found that both the sensations and the thoughts driving them receded. She began to focus on her breath and eventually became aware of a feeling of deep peacefulness. She fell asleep with the awareness that she could 'bear' her anxiety, that these were sensations in the body and that she was able to manage. She realised that she was always trying to problem-solve her way out of her anxiety, but the thoughts fuelled the situation rather than fixing it.

She was able to let go of the thoughts in this situation and consequently at other times when the anxiety was taking over. She is grateful to her mindfulness practice but admits she is more likely to practise seriously when things are tricky.

The 'STOP' meditation

We can use this instead of the three-step breathing space if it feels appropriate:

Stop and slow down

Take a few deep breaths

Observe thoughts

Proceed with awareness and curiosity

Marooned in the Morning

Awake
Adrift on the black ocean.
Ship's bells chime three.
Morning, dark morning.

Black night presses down.
Siren voices
Threaten to ship-wreck
A fragile craft.
The voices, ghosts from distant shores.

Waves crash over the waterline:
Ambushed by thoughts:
'Could do better
'Not good enough.'
Waterlogged

Down, down, down
To the depths.
Plunging from head to belly
Where the whirlpool eddies.

Riding the whirl,
Round and round and round
She goes.
Nauseous and trembling,
Bodyful

Reaching for the raft
She floats on the waves,
Up and down; in and out.
Breathing.
Rhythmic
Rocked on the raft
By ebb and flow.

The blackness bursts
Into tiny petals of light.
The dislocated thoughts
Disappear with the dawn.

This boat of breath carries her.
A gentle wind that blows
In and out of safe waters.

– Annee Griffiths

There is a famous meditation story about MILAREPA who lived in a cave in Tibet in the 11th century. He reputedly lived on nettles and therefore turned green. One day he came back from collecting firewood and found some fearsome demons had taken over his cave. He asked them politely to leave but they settled down in the cave and created mayhem. He tried everything but couldn't get them to go.

He got very angry. He fought them and pushed them away. He tried to ignore them. Finally, he turned towards them. 'OK,' he said, 'I surrender. Let's live together. Let's have a cup of tea'. At this all but one demon left the cave. But one was left.

He was the fiercest, most ugly and terrifying demon of them all. He didn't know what to do with this one – how could he surrender even more? Then he ran up to him and put his head right there in the demon's mouth. 'Eat me!' he said. At this the demon disappeared and he was left alone. He realised that these fears and ugly demons were merely projections in his mind, all the fear and violence and anger that was unacknowledged and unresolved. He only had to face it or go right into the heart of it. He had stopped resisting or avoiding the unpleasant and trusted in his practice completely.

ELINOR told the class she was having difficulty with focusing on the breath. I noticed she was touching her throat and asked her what she was experiencing here. She said that she felt tightness was in this area and around her chest.

'It's a horrible feeling. It is a difficult time for me. A number of friends and family have died in the last six months and I have changed jobs. I am all right in the day – I don't feel very much and I can function – but when I wake up I feel abject terror and I can't breathe. I don't know what it is. Then when I focus on my breath in the meditation I feel it again, the tightness, and the inability to breathe properly. You talked about turning towards difficulty, but I don't know if I want to stay with this.'

I said to her: 'You don't have to do anything that you don't want to, you are aware of it and you also need to be kind, to do only what feels right for you. No forcing. What's happening now as we are talking? Can you feel it?'

'I feel empty inside. There is a big hole here (points to her middle). It's all empty, it's frightening.'

I asked her if she was OK to explore this a little. She said she was. So I asked her what happens if she placed her attention on the edge of the hole. She said:

'It's jagged and rough. The edge is red'.

'And inside the hole?'

'Black.'

'How deep is it?'

'It's very deep. I don't want to go there.'

'It's OK just to touch on this. To acknowledge it and to be curious and then to bring some kindness to yourself. This is not easy to be with.'

She said it was a weird feeling and I agreed saying that I too had experienced something like this and I have known others who have too and it is usually OK.

We then did a breathing space meditation where Elinor focused on sounds rather than her breath. She said the feeling had gone and she felt a little better. The next week she said that that feeling was no longer there. She felt something had shifted. We reflected on how being curious had allowed her to be more detached, to step back and reframe her experience, which led to a change.

The Rock and the Hard Place

Rough, grey rock.

Wedged in the mountain,

Your shoulders are squeezed

Stuck in a crevice.

Frozen like a rabbit

Fixed by the fox's eye.

He is able to trick you

Into believing he is real.

Red for you.

You believe you are crushed,

He takes you limp and powerless

Into the deep dark hole of his lair.

You are stuck

Deep in the darkness.

Afraid.

You dreamt you held a little girl in her arms.

Her mother has left her.

The child clings, frozen and stiff.

Waking from the dream

You know your mother loved you

And then she forgot you as she struggled

To fight for love for herself.

That's when the fox used to find you

And carry you limp to his hole.

In dreams you ran from foxes, pirates, dragons.

Now you move in close, ask:

"Who are you and what is it?"

Facing the fox, softening,

You stop being stuck.

You are out of the hard place.

The route through the rock

Is carved by a swift stream.

You know the way

It opens out to a vast blue sky.

– Annee Griffiths

I was on a walk by the sea with my walking group. I had the misfortune to wander off the path. I lingered behind the others and failed to see them take a path of the middle of the beach. I went to the end of the beach and around a rocky corner. As the path on the beach got rougher and rougher and the boulders became ever bigger I suspected that this wasn't the path. And yet... wet and slippery as it was, another part of me was deluded into thinking that it was the path and if I just persisted I would catch them up. When I came to a dead-end, a dangerous climb down the wet rocks to a very rough sea, I finally realised that I was wrong. I was lost and fearful. I felt like a child, a lost child, helpless and lonely. I was caught up with the story of being lost and afraid and I was tearful.

Then I remembered the STOP Meditation.

I Stopped.

I became aware of Taking a few deep breaths (tight, restricted, held in my throat).

I Observed thoughts ('I'm lost', 'They don't care').

I Proceeded with awareness. That is, I became aware of my environment – the wild sea swirling on the rocks beneath me; the cold wind blowing my hair; the sea birds crying. I became aware of my inner experience. I checked into my body and noticed the sensations that were swirling around. Naming the emotions fear and anger, judgement and blame, took my mind off the drama and calmed me. As I noticed each of these emotions, including the incipient tears, I also felt connection with others who had ever been lost and fearful and upset. I said to myself, 'This is what it feels like' and imagined those in war zones, scattered refugees from Syria or parts of Africa who have nowhere to go and only the shelter of the bare bushes against the cold harsh night. I felt a sense of connection with others who were suffering. Yet, in truth, there was very little danger for me. I had my phone and there was a signal!

At that moment John phoned me and asked with alarm: 'Where are you?' I couldn't go back as I was cut off by the tide and could only go upwards. We arranged to meet at the top of the cliff. I beat my way through brambles and bracken to the top, I climbed over sheep fencing and barbed wire and saw John waving with arms opened wide. I was rescued.

What was interesting about this experience was how I was convinced the path was one way (it wasn't) and how the emotions whipped up the thoughts into old stories of fear, loss, abandonment and judgement. How hard it was to just experience the emotion in the body when the thoughts were so dominant. I also took time to calm myself by watching the waves breaking, strangely comforting. What was really sweet was the concern of the rest of the group – when I finally caught up with them I received a very warm welcome and although I was feeling sheepish, their kindness connected me again into the fold!

Sometimes, we can be really happy and carefree and then something happens. When I lost my purse after a birthday outing I experienced a range of emotions. Uppermost was anxiety, but also sadness and blame were equally present. My body reacted in shock, I could feel my lips tighten and whiten and strange fizzing in my abdomen. Then a blank numbness came over my body. I retraced my journey back to the restaurant's car park but searching about with the light on my phone in the dark proved fruitless. I went to bed and the adrenaline kept me awake nearly all night. A body scan, with deep breathing and some soothing kindness phrases helped to ease the anxiety and the self-judgement. The next day after cancelling my cards and beating myself up some more I found my purse at home.

I was reminded of this incident recently at the end of a long walk when a good friend of mine patted her pocket and realised she had lost her mobile phone. Panic ensued. She began to lament and beat herself up for carelessness, even for stupidity. She was anxious and very self-critical. A good friend offered to do the entire walk with her again to look for it. This coastal walk had taken us six hours of meandering. I waited in the car park to give her a lift home. The friends raced across sand dunes and wet sea flats only just missing the incoming tide and the gathering dusk.

They didn't find the phone but knowing that people cared and were not judgemental calmed her anxiety and her foremost emotion was one of gratitude. Naomi Shihab Nye wrote a poem called Kindness. It is one of my favourites. She said: 'Before you know what kindness really is/You must lose things'.

Friends can often reassure us and soothe our anxiety. Befriending ourselves with an awareness of the moment and a refusal to escalate self-deprecating thoughts can be helpful. The internal friend may be as helpful as the external one. The next chapter focuses on this.

Cold Shock

I drowned in the lake tonight

And was reborn

Naked in the womb

Abandoning my beliefs

I take them off on the bank

Alone, I dive into my deepest fear

"Wake up,

Wake up to the truth"

For once I see clearly

Delusions fall away

Sinking in the darkness

There is only the rain

Rejoicing on finding its source

Dancing on the water's surface

I am reunited with that old friend who is myself

In the hands of God

I feel his warmth

He is holding me

He is watching, after all

I am alive

I am healed

I am complete

– Meilyr Wyn Jones

Chapter 6:
Basic Friendliness and Self-Compassion –
'Accepting myself as I am'

Your task is not to seek for love, but merely to seek and find all the barriers within yourself that you have built against it.

– Rumi

Wake up and love more.

– Kate Tempest

ANGHARAD lay awake in the middle of the night worrying about her teenage son. He was smoking a lot of skunk marijuana. He dropped out of school and was acting in a dysfunctional way. Smoking from morning until night, his eyes were often glazed over. He seemed unable to communicate with his parents and hung out with his friends until the early hours of the morning.

Angharad catastrophised about the future, thinking that he would continue to be like this and get progressively worse. He would gravitate to hard drugs and addiction and she would lose the boy she loved. He would become a burden to the family, would become homeless, a social outcast. He already seemed lost to them apart from the occasional re-emergence of the boy they had known.

Lying awake one night unable to sleep because of anxiety, Angharad remembered the befriending meditation we did in class. She wished him well and said:

'May he be happy. May he be safe. May he be well. May he have ease in his life'.

She repeated the phrases over and over. She also said the words for herself and her husband. As she repeated them over and over she became more peaceful and she was able to sleep. Now her son has grown up and, luckily, none of her fears were realised. It was a fleeting episode in their lives. In this they were fortunate. She saw her meditations as a way of coping with the moment, not fixing the problem. She realised that for others in this situation no amount of wishing or prayer can prevent addiction.

This meditation can have quite a number of different reactions. But, for Angharad, her anxious problem-solving mind was reassured that she had 'done' something and she felt more peaceful. She learnt a lot about meditation in those sleepless nights.

In Japanese and Chinese writing the character for 'mind' means heart as well as mind. Heart–mind is the character. How would it be to describe mindfulness as heartfulness? Mindfulness meditations focus on being aware in the present moment with kindness. Compassion and befriending meditations focus on generating feelings of warmth, friendliness or compassion. This might include visualising or invoking a feeling or silently saying words that point us to a more positive place.

Words can be used as a focus that can be similar to a concentration practice, such as placing the attention just on the breath. Compassion practice has two wings like a bird. One wing is being aware in the present moment; the other wing is actively asserting an intention, a wish for self and others (maybe for some a deep prayer). With these two wings we learn to fly.

Befriending or loving kindness meditation emphasises the wish to be happy and safe. Compassion meditation focuses on the suffering we meet as human beings, both in ourselves and in others. It is founded upon an inherent intention, a wish for self and others to be free from suffering.

Live in joy and freedom, even amongst those who are sick or troubled.
Live in joy and a peaceful heart, even among those in conflict. Quiet
the mind and heart and find the sweet joy of living.

– The Dhammapada

Befriending meditation for yourself

This meditation combines a contemplation focus with mindfulness of body awareness.

Bringing your attention to your body, in particular your feet on the floor. If you are lying down, feeling the contact with the body and the surface you are lying on. This is grounding. This helps us connect to our body and stabilises us here in this place, to establish an intention to be here in the body, rooted in the moment.

Bringing your attention to your breath. A deep and gentle in-breath and a slow out-breath. Slowing the breath, feeling the breath in the body where you can feel it the most vividly. Take three of these deliberate slow breaths.

Then, breathing normally, feeling the sensation of breath. Stay with the breath for a few cycles, allowing the calming quality of the breath. Letting the breath or the feet on the floor be an anchor. A place that you can come back to at any time during this practice. Accepting this breath in this moment. Befriending yourself. Caring for yourself.

Checking through the body, noticing how it is in this moment. What sensations are here? Softening the tummy area. Is it possible to feel the aliveness of the body, the energy in the body? You may be aware of the warmth of the hands, the secure feel of the ground beneath you.

Focusing your attention now on your heart area. Whether you can feel your heart beating, a sense of aliveness here or just a sense of the heart, its kindness, its warmth. Maybe just placing your hand here in the area of your heart and feeling the warmth under the hand. Directing the in-breath to the heart area and breathe out from the heart area.

Bringing to mind a person or an animal that you feel friendly towards. Someone with whom you have no issues, someone who you can feel an unconditional regard towards. Maybe a small child or baby, a favourite pet or, if no one comes to mind, you can imagine accepting someone as they are. Making the choice easy for yourself, not hesitating too much over your choice, just choosing the first one who come to mind without making anything of it.

Allowing yourself to feel into the experience, the warmth. Placing your attention in the heart area you may feel a sense of warmth here or expansion in the chest or maybe you can imagine a smile here as you think of the loved one. Trusting your love for them and their love for you.   →

Can you now bring this sense of friendship and acceptance to yourself? If this feels uncomfortable or difficult, you may like to imagine or remember yourself as a baby or young child, back to the time when you had no expectations of yourself, a time when there was no need for perfectionism. Perhaps saying to yourself: 'It's OK, just to be as you are, there's no need to improve yourself. It's OK to be as you are right now.' Be a friend to yourself. If this seems unreasonable or unacceptable then be curious about the thoughts, feelings and body sensations that arise in resistance to this. This too is rich material.

Explore how you can bring a sense of kindness and friendship to yourself at this time, no matter what your thoughts are about yourself.

If it feels right, you can send yourself some good wishes. Wishing yourself well with words such as:

'May I be kind to myself, as kind to myself as I would wish others to be kind to me.'

'May I be at ease.'

'May I be safe.'

'May I be happy – feel the possibility, visualise or imagine what this would feel like.'

'May I accept myself as I am.'

'May I love myself.'

'May I forgive myself'.

Or saying:

'Appreciating myself, I wish for my happiness.'

'I wish for my safety.'

'I accept myself as I am.'

'I can love myself just as I am.'

'I can forgive myself.'

'I am wishing for ease.'

These phrases may not suit you. If so, adapt them and find your own friendship phrases if you choose.

Say these phrases to yourself, maybe once or maybe up to three times in whatever order seems right. Notice how saying the phrases makes you feel. What is your intimate feeling with yourself?

Is it possible to feel friendly to your life as it is right now?

Is it possible to feel friendly to your body even if you feel it is letting you down at this moment?

Can you befriend your mind now in this moment, letting go of any shortcomings you may be feeling?

Now, returning to the breath as an anchor, stay focused on the breath in the body until you wish to finish the meditation.

You can also say these phrases for someone else.

Befriending or loving kindness in a nutshell

We invite ourselves to bring to mind an object of love, a person (maybe a child), an animal or a favourite place. In this way we are consciously generating a feeling of warmth. Then we focus on the following phrases:

'May I be happy and enjoy the roots of happiness.'

'May I be safe.'

'May I be as healthy as it is possible for me to be in this moment.'

'May I care for myself with joy and ease.'

Or you can make up your own words to express your heartfelt wish to yourself or another. Maybe by bringing happiness or safety to mind we may feel a sense of happiness or wellbeing or love or kindness. We have generated this feeling.

Traditional 'metta' meditation

The traditional 'metta' or befriending can be seen as a list. This is practised in many meditation centres.

Oneself – this is often the most challenging person to direct kindness to, the most important and often the most difficult. Nevertheless, we need to look after ourselves and bring kindness to ourselves first before we can really do this for others. Similar to the advice on an aeroplane where you are told to put on your own face mask before helping others; you need to be there in order to help others.

- Someone you respect, a teacher, close friend or loved one.
- A neutral person, an acquaintance you see regularly, such as a delivery person or shop assistant.
- A person with whom you are experiencing difficulty.
- All living beings.

The following list can also be used. Add variations of your own choosing. We start with ourselves and expand further and further into the world around us:

- Self
- People in the room or house
- Family or close circle
- People in the town or county
- Country
- Continent
- World or planet
- Universe

Practise kindness all day long to everybody and you will realise you are in heaven right now.

– Jack Kerouac

Self-compassion

Soko Morinaga Roshi was my first Zen teacher in Kyoto, Japan in 1976. These words of his resonate for me:

> *If you desire to gaze out over wide vistas, you do well to climb up to a high spot. But if you wish to gaze into the human heart, you must climb down and look from a low place.*

Compassion means 'to suffer with'. The root of the word compassion is 'com' meaning 'with' and 'pati' meaning 'to bear, to suffer'. Compati is to suffer with. It is sometimes defined as the heart that trembles in response to pain, the heart that listens to the cries of the world. How can we manage our wish to alleviate the suffering of others without feeling overwhelmed, helpless or burnt out? Compassionate training is a way of cultivating altruistic love, allowing it to grow so that we have 'courage' (*cor* means heart in Latin, which is the root of the word courage) to act with integrity and kindness.

The first step in feeling compassion for others is to feel it for yourself. Self-compassion is being open in a non-judgemental way to your own pain. It is opening your heart to your own humanity. You are kind to yourself as well as to others. When you notice personal failings you can gently work with this mindfully by bringing awareness into the present moment and cultivating kindness to yourself whenever you notice negative judgement.

Compassion practice shapes the mind away from negative thinking about ourselves and others. Sometimes, when we feel resentment or dislike of others it is tempting to go along with this strong feeling and indulge in it. It is a form of hatred. We practise overcoming these inclinations – to understand ourselves first and then understand the roots of the suffering of others. Compassion is not to be confused with pity; self-pity or pity for others is disrespectful and disempowering.

Cultivating compassion can free you from being utterly overwhelmed by the suffering in the world. The troubles of your friends and acquaintances, the appalling distress of the people and children in war zones, in famine areas, people suffering from disease and difficulties are hard for us to witness, never mind experience ourselves. As we reflect on the pain of others we realise that our own suffering is not unique. We are not alone; our vulnerability is in common with most of humanity. Some people have tremendous difficulties and hardships to face. It is not a competition. Each one of us may be heartbroken or bereft at some point in our lives. Sometimes, people who appear to have a good life from the outside are filled with despair, depression and suicidal wishes. Comparison is not useful.

We can despair or become 'compassion-fatigued' if we merely stand by amid the horrors that occur. It may seem that it is not enough just to do these meditations. We may consider it self-indulgent or that we are indulging in magical thinking. Acknowledging the suffering of yourself and others, rather than simply ignoring it, may be an act of witness. We may not be able to change it but we can keep our hearts open and be ready to respond with action when needed. We can have an intention, a deep commitment to act whenever we can. It can be preparation for action in the world. A warrior training. We become more courageous by first understanding our own pain and then connecting with the suffering of others. It is a practice of discernment and understanding, resilience and strength. Nonetheless, it is important to realise that we can only reach out to others and help in a limited way. To feel the need to make vast changes is an impossible task and will lead to despair. So we ask ourselves 'What can I do?' We do what we can.

> *Life is mostly froth and bubble,*
> *Two things stand like stone.*
> *Kindness in another's trouble,*
> *Courage in your own.*

– Adam Lindsay Gordon

Compassion meditations

May I be free in the middle of difficulty

One way to practise compassion meditation is to focus on suffering and our heartfelt wish to be free.

First, we focus on grounding, by feeling our feet on the ground and our bottom on the seat. Then we shift our primary focus to the breath wherever we feel it most vividly. Then we focus our awareness in our chest area, the region of the heart. We may focus on sounds if that is a gateway into the present moment.

When we feel quite settled, maybe after about 10 minutes, we can say the following phrases for ourselves and then for others:

May I be free in the midst of enmity and danger.

May I be free in the midst of mental danger.

May I be free in the midst of physical danger.

May I care for myself with joy and ease.

We can say these phrases over and over again as we stay connected to how we are feeling in the body.

Adapted from Melissa Blacker and David Rynick's CMRP workshop, *Kindness, Compassion, Joy and Balance* (May 2015)

Compassion for yourself

This meditation is about cultivating compassion for yourself, focusing on body, mind and heart.

Bring your attention to your body, in particular your bottom on the seat and feet on the floor. If you are lying down, feel the contact with the body and the surface you are lying on. This is grounding. This helps us connect to our body and stabilises us here in this place. We establish an intention to be here in the body, rooted in the moment.

Bringing your attention to your breath. A deep in-breath and a slow out-breath. Slowing the breath, feeling the breath in the body where you can feel it the most vividly. Take three of these deliberate slow breaths. Three in-breaths and three out-breaths. Then breathing normally, feeling the sensation of breath and letting go of any thoughts as best you can.

Reflecting now on the life of your body, how it is now. Consider how it was in the past. Considering how it may be in the future. Becoming aware of the cycles of your life.

You were born, were a child, a young person, you are ageing, and you will die.

Reflecting now on the joys of the body. Remembering an occasion when your body delighted you. A physical activity – maybe running or dancing, maybe eating a delicious food, hearing or seeing something wonderful. Remembering the warmth of a loving touch, perhaps remembering what your body was like as a child or a delightful experience from yesterday.

Reflecting too on the frailty of your body. Remembering that it is subject to illness and pain. Reflecting on your life's seasons. Noticing any resistance to the changes you experience in your body. The sadness, the fear and blame we can experience in these changes. Feeling the connection with other bodies who also experience this.

If there is any part of your body feeling pain or intensity or difficulty at the moment then bring your attention to this part.

Is it possible to hold pain and illness and frailty in attention without blame?

Softening around the stories we tell ourselves about the body, about illness, about ageing. The way we despair and imagine the worst that can happen and believe that the difficulties will never alter or change. Sensing the impermanence of our experience.

Holding it all in your attention, rejecting nothing. Allowing it to be there. Saying to yourself:

May I accept myself as I am.

May I be free in the middle of change.

May I find peace.

Expanding now to your mind. Acknowledging that you are at times confused or obsessed, and that you can also experience calmness and peace. Acknowledging that you can experience anxiety, judgement, resentment – and moments of ease, clarity, wisdom. →

Sometimes, your mind can get lost in judgement and resentment. Sometimes, you feel righteous or rebellious. Sometimes, you are at ease in your mind and your thoughts are friendly to yourself and others. Recognising and reflecting on the suffering – the pain and sorrow when you are not at ease.

Saying to yourself:

May I be safe.

May I be free in the midst of anxiety and confusion.

May I be peaceful.

Acknowledging now your emotional life, your heart.

Reflecting on sadness, loss and grief, loneliness. Reflecting on your anger or jealousy, mistrust, blame or resentment.

Sensing too the moments of happiness and love. Tenderness and generosity.

Bringing compassion to moments of heartache, turmoil and darkness.

Offer to yourself compassion:

May I have ease in loving.

May I accept and bring compassion to pain I can't avoid.

May I find peace.

Resting in the present moment. Taking a breath and opening up to sounds. Sensing the openness of space, for a moment holding this vastness in your consciousness. The immensity of the blue sky, the earth, the universe. Softening into accepting what's here at the moment. Holding yourself in compassion. Coming back to feeling your body sitting or lying on whatever is supporting you. Feeling the floor beneath you and the earth beneath.

Bringing your attention to the in-breath and the out-breath. Anchoring in the present moment with the breath.

(With acknowledgement to Christina Feldman for inspiration)

Self-compassion break

A useful short practice to come to when you are feeling distressed.

1. Say to yourself: This is a moment of suffering. (Mindfulness)

Bringing mindfulness to this: What are the thoughts? The feelings and emotions? The body sensations?

2. Say to yourself: This is part of life. (Connection) This links you with others/common humanity.

Imagine all the other beings in the world who are feeling like this at this time. →

3. Put your hands on your heart or both hands on opposite arms, or just one hand on the opposite arm, give yourself a self-hug or just rub your arm gently. (Soothing yourself or Self-compassion).

Feel the warmth of your hands, or feeling under the hands the breath moving in the chest.

You could say words of your own choosing to bring some kindness to yourself, or:

May I be kind to myself.

May I accept myself just as I am.

Created by Kristen Neff

Tonglen practice

This is a compassion practice from Tibetan Buddhism.

Feeling the contact of the ground beneath your body. If you are lying down, feel the whole-body making contact with the floor or bed. If you are sitting, feel the contact of the support of the floor with your feet and the contact with your bottom on the seat.

Stage 1

Resting in the present moment. Taking a breath and opening up to sounds. Sensing the openness of space, for a moment holding this vastness in your consciousness. The immensity of the blue sky, the earth, the universe.

Stage 2

Imagine breathing into the heart and out from the heart. As we breathe in, imagine a hot, dark, heavy, sticky breath. As we breathe out, imagine a cool, light, bright breath, a freshness.

Practise this for a few breaths.

Stage 3

Now bringing to mind a painful situation. Breathing in the emotional feeling, your pain, your sadness, the difficult emotion we wish to escape from. Breathing it in as heavy, painful, dark.

Now breathing-out light, spaciousness, coolness. Practise this for a few breaths.

Thus, the practice is inhaling acceptance and exhaling compassion and kindness.

Inhaling suffering and the uncomfortable, and exhaling love and care. Relaxing, taking your ease. As best you can, softening and relaxing into the inhale as well as the exhale.

Staying with this just as long as you feel you are able.

Stage 4

Remembering that others in the world feel a similar pain to yours. Widening your attention to connect with other people who are also suffering and wishing them well.   →

Now returning to being aware of the breath as it comes in and goes out without visualising. Just breathing. Taking in the feeling in the body and aware of sounds coming and going.

Just sitting quietly with the breath.

In the middle of the Covid-19 virus in April 2020, I began to do Tonglen meditation regularly. It was a shortcut to RAIN meditation for me. It was a time of high anxiety. It was also a time full of valiant stories about NHS health workers and carers and the other essential workers risking their lives every day. There are so many stories of courageous efforts that deserve their own book. And there are small gestures also of people helping each other, like shopping for those who have the virus, maybe driving many miles and leaving the parcels on the doorstep; the little acts of kindness.

When I sit down for my daily practice, I find that the mind is looking out for danger. I do Tonglen. Tonglen helps me work with an intention to both acknowledge my anxiety and to be present with what is actually happening now in the present moment. The envisaging of darkness and light in the exercise is practising an intention to be with the difficulties (darkness) and to counterbalance them (lightness) by the realisation that my experience is more than just difficulty. An intention to balance both.

The following is a glimpse into my Tonglen practice in the midst of the Covid-19 virus.

I acknowledge the dark thoughts. I imagine the proliferation of anxious thoughts like black smoke. Thin at first and thickening out as more and more thoughts swirl into my mind. I do this on the in-breath.

On the outbreath I let this go. I sense the present moment. What is here in my immediate experience? I hear birdsong. A sense of lightness.

I take another in-breath: I allow the anxiety, the 'what ifs' spin for a long in-breath before I let go. I imagine them as dark sticky black smoke.

Out-breath: 'I ask what's here? What's now?' Bird song and light behind my closed eyes. I imagine light around my heart area, spaciousness.

In-breath: Anxiety and 'what ifs' still here in my mind. I focus on my body. Anxious sensations in my heart area; sensations of tightening, fluttering, squeezing.

Out-breath: A letting go. An expansion in the chest area. A sense of lightness and warmth. (This can be imagined and may well appear on its own with practice.)

In-breath: Anxiety – the specific story: 'What if the people I know with the illness die?' 'What if I die or anyone in my family?'

Out-breath: Letting these thoughts go. Allowing for a sense of spaciousness. Acknowledging that my mind's activity is only part of my experience at the moment. Inviting in other sensations, in the senses, in the body. Feeling a sense of compassion for myself. *'Yes, you are worried about X but this is an anxious time. We are all feeling anxious to some degree'.* (Connection)

In-breath: A sense of other people in the world struggling with this fear of being ill, losing a loved one, losing their livelihood, the darkness of the time.

Out-breath: Wishing them all well. May we heal from this disruption and heartache. Forming an intention to connect with others. To generate positive, caring, and supportive thoughts for others.

I need to take long, deep breaths for all this to happen. It takes practise, like all meditations, but I have time. I am not going anywhere. I am staying home and staying safe. For me, mindfulness practice has been essential during this time.

I sit with the breath in the present moment, allowing the in-breath and the out-breath to come and go without direction. To finish I sense the ground beneath my feet and my bottom on the seat.

The Four Immeasurables or Heavenly Abodes

Metta or loving kindness or friendliness is the first of the Four Immeasurables or Heavenly Abodes described by the Buddha. Compassion is second. Appreciative Joy is the third, and Equanimity the fourth.

Appreciative Joy

The third Immeasurable or Heavenly Abode to cultivate with practice is appreciative joy. This can be to cultivate happiness when others are successful, especially when you feel envious or inadequate. A practice that counterbalances envy when your sibling wins the race, when your friend has bought a house or car or some possession you covet. The envy you may experience when someone is more popular, more successful, more attractive than you think you are.

Appreciative Joy

May I know appreciative joy for happiness and achievements of others in my world. Maybe when I compare myself to others, I feel small or slighted. Maybe I feel their glory diminishes my own, I feel resentment, envy. Noticing how this is in my mind. Noticing any corresponding feeling in the body, where is it located? Acknowledging this or having an intention to change. When experiencing the pang of envy acknowledging it and practising saying: 'I am glad for them'.

Repeating to myself:

May I feel joy for the success or happiness of… (name) or others.

May I feel appreciative joy towards… (name a key person).

Or if you don't like using the term 'May I', just say:

Appreciating your efforts.

Rejoicing in your achievements.

Delighting in your success.

Like a flower in a garden I too have my place and am not diminished by the beauty or power of the other plants.

Equanimity

The fourth practice from the Four Immeasurables is equanimity. This is to hold your own peace in the face of whatever life throws at you.

Aware of how I feel this moment, asking myself or feeling: Is there ease here in the body in the mind? Maybe some parts feel tense – being aware of this, aware of ease and dis-ease, cultivating a sense of ease.

May I be easeful, live my life with ease, have ease of being.

Now bringing to mind someone in your life and saying to yourself:

May he or she know ease of being.

Knowing I cannot change the other, may I feel peace. May any negative action towards my Self not affect me, knowing that it is their reality not mine.

Just like me

This exercise cultivates an intention to expand our compassion and understanding to the whole of humanity. The benefits are often a surprisingly feel-good factor for yourself.

On a busy crowded street, or any place where there are people, choose a person unobtrusively.

1. Say to yourself: Just like me he/she wants happiness in his/her life.

2. Say to yourself: Just like me he/she wants to avoid suffering in his/her life.

3. Say to yourself: Just like me he/she has known sadness and loneliness.

4. Say to yourself: Just like me he/she wants to fulfil his/her potential.

5. Say to yourself: Just like me he/she... find words to express something you hold in common.

'As a solid mass of rock

Is not stirred by the wind,

So a sage is not moved

By praise and blame.

As a deep lake

Is clear and undisturbed,

So a sage becomes clear'

– Dhammapada 81–83

Advantages of cultivating friendliness or loving kindness

According to the Buddha. Taken from the Sutta Anguttara Nikaya XI.16

'You sleep better.

You wake up happy.

You don't have bad dreams.

You are liked and loved by human beings and non-human beings.

You are guarded and protected by angels.

You cannot be harmed by fire, poison and weapons.

You easily become concentrated when meditating.

Your appearance is serene.

You will die without feeling confused or panic.

You will be happy even after death.'

Although some of these benefits may seem strange to us now, remember that this is an ancient practice that originated from a completely different culture – 2,500 years ago.

From the Christian tradition, another religion that puts love and suffering at its heart:

> *'Though I speak in the tongues of men or of angels, but do not have love, I am only a resounding gong or a clanging cymbal.'*

– The Bible, Corinthians 13:1

> *'Your task is not to seek for love, but merely to seek and find all the barriers within yourself that you have built against it.'*

– Rumi, from the Sufi Islamic tradition

The Metta Sutta

From the Buddha

This is what is to be done:

1. To reach the peaceful state

One skilled in the good should be

Capable and upright,

Easy to speak to and straightforward,

Of gentle nature and not proud,

2. Contented and easily supported,

Living lightly and having few duties,

Wise and with senses calmed,

Not arrogant and without greed (for supporters).

3. And should not do the slightest thing that the wise

Would reproach them for.

[One should reflect in this way:]

"May all beings be happy and secure.
May all beings be happy-minded.

4. Whatever living beings there may,
whether weak or strong,
Tall, large, medium, or short, small or big,

5. Seen or unseen, near or distant,
Born or to be born,
May they, without exception, all be happy-minded.

6. Let no one despise another
Or deceive anyone anywhere.
Let no one through anger or hatred
Wish for another's suffering"

7. As a mother would risk her own life
To protect her child, her only child,
So for all beings one should
Guard one's boundless heart.

8. With boundless friendliness for the whole world should one
Cultivate a boundless heart,
In all directions,
Without obstruction, without hate and without ill will.

9. Standing or walking, sitting or lying down,
Whenever one is awake,
May one stay with this recollection.
This is called the best and most sublime way of dwelling in this world.

10. One who is virtuous, endowed with insight,
Not clinging to wrong view,

And having overcome all passion for sensual pleasure,

Will not come to lie in a womb again.

– Karaṇīya mettasutta, Sutta Nipāta 143–152, translation by John Peacock

Research on compassion and befriending practices

Neuroscience research has shown that generating compassion towards the sufferer makes the experience of being with or witnessing someone else's suffering more bearable. Richard Davidson and Antoine Lutz carried out research with 16 long-term practitioners of compassion training, Tibetan monks. The control group had two weeks of compassionate training.

The 32 subjects were placed in the fMRI (functional magnetic resonance imaging) scanner. They were all asked to practise compassion meditation or refrain from it. At different intervals they were subjected to negative and positive human vocalisations designed to evoke empathic responses. Examples of this were the sound of a woman in distress, a baby laughing and background restaurant noise.

The research found that the monks could induce loving feelings and that there was increased brain activity in the insula (the region identified with empathy and body awareness) and the temporal parietal juncture in the right hemisphere (a region of the brain where emotions of others are perceived). The control group of less experienced meditators did not experience the same effects (Lutz *et al*, 2004; 2008a).

The findings support Davidson and Lutz's working assumption that through training, people can develop skills that promote happiness and compassion. This could be a way to work with burnout or 'compassion fatigue'. Generating compassion and altruistic love could be a skilful way to work with our own difficulties around the suffering of others and may give us more energy when in a caring role, and this includes our own self-care when we are suffering.

Davidson, Lutz and Tania Singer have developed a secular compassion training for professional helpers and carers. When the meditators visualised and empathised with the intense suffering of others, they experienced burnout and helplessness. When they meditated on compassion and unconditional love, they did not experience negative results but felt resolved to do what they could to alleviate the suffering.

Davidson has also shown that people were more compassionate towards themselves after two weeks of compassion-based meditation. A practical result was that the meditators gave more generously to a charity when asked to donate their honorarium to a cause of their own choosing (Lutz, 2007).

Research at the University of North Carolina found that befriending practice increased positive emotions, a sense of purpose in life and social support. It reduced depressive symptoms and decreased illness symptoms including improved cardiovascular health (Fredrickson, 2013).

Anna Dóra Frostadóttir's research in 2015 showed that metta (loving kindness) meditation has demonstrable positive effects on the brain and that there is a shift towards positive emotions and life satisfaction. This unpublished study was conducted in Iceland for an MSc thesis at Bangor University.

Challenges of metta and compassion practice

In Chapters 4 and 5 we looked at turning towards difficulty and anxiety. For many people these befriending and compassion practices also bring up difficulty. Often, the very mention of befriending ourselves or self-compassion can create difficulties, negative thoughts and aversion.

These meditation invites us to be aware of our whole experience, including negative and aversive thoughts towards the meditation, ourselves or others. This meditation may bring up resistance or difficulty. We are not able to feel happy or warmth to order. The words seem mechanical and false. However, if we approach the meditation with curiosity then we can learn something about ourselves. We have an opportunity to explore strong reactions to this practice in a mindful way and experience how this feels in the body, heart and mind rather than struggling with what we think we are expected to feel. Like mindfulness meditation, this meditation is not outcome related, we do not have to feel happy or safe, just notice and be curious about our own experience, without adding more layers of judgement.

The practice can bring up intense feelings of anger or hurt and sadness as we bring to mind relationships and our own disconnect with ourselves or others in our world. Bringing to mind a loved one may be difficult either because that person is now no longer with us or because there is some conflict with him or her. We can feel inadequate if we are not able to feel friendly or compassion towards certain people in our lives. If the meditation is extended to all beings we may well disagree with the inclusion of some people. We may feel angry when we think of an individual or politicians who we believe have destructive policies. We may feel sad about the misfortunes of others. We may well feel despair and a sense of hopelessness and impotence in a world steeped in suffering.

I remember seeing the Dalai Lama in the Albert Hall, a huge venue that was filled to the brim. He told us that it was no good merely wishing for peace in the world, we had to find peaceful solutions. In other words, to merely wish for peace on its own is magical thinking, we have to find peace in our own lives first and then we can move in the world to do what we can. We can start with this intention and repeat it over and over as a preparation for action.

As a child GINA was both physically and emotionally abused by her stepfather. As an adult she'd experienced a number of similar relationships and although she felt mindfulness meditation could heal her and help her live her life differently, she found it very difficult to engage with it. She found she could not close her eyes, and focusing on her body caused her distress. When she placed her attention on the breath her throat began to tighten, which felt life-threatening.

She tried to do the befriending meditation and found that it was impossible to consider a warm feeling of kindness to herself. So she decided to bring to mind her dog. She found that if she visualised her dog and noticed the love in his eyes she was able to stay with the meditation. She was able to feel love for the dog and feel warmth in her heart. Gradually, she was able to direct this feeling towards herself and realise that she might be equally deserving of love as her dog. Eventually she was able to gently stay with sensations in the body and develop her mindfulness practice.

This practice can be an uncomfortable one for many people. To generate a feeling for oneself or another may seem false and not authentic. Some people find the word 'happy' challenging. One person changed this to: *'May I be content'.* When I asked her how that felt, she came to a conclusion that she didn't deserve happiness. It is sad that we can have such deep-rooted ideas about ourselves. We all deserve happiness.

For some people another barrier to this practice is the form of the words in the traditional well wishing. Saying 'May I be…' or 'May he be…' (happy, well, at ease, safe, etc) sounds religious, like a prayer to God, to some people.

GEORGE was outraged when he first tried the befriending or metta meditation. 'This is cloying and sickening', he said, 'It's too much like prayers. I've had enough of empty prayers in my upbringing, I need to be self-sufficient.' I asked George to note what emotions were present. He said he felt angry and resentful. I asked him what feeling was there in his body. He described a churned-up feeling around his heart and his guts. He closed his eyes for a moment and stayed with his sensations. 'Hmm… interesting,' he said. 'I am feeling quite emotional about this.'

I suggested that he had choices to make around this practice. He could practise 'RAIN' (Recognise, Allow, Investigate, and Non-identify and nurture) and explore these powerful feelings or just as validly he could choose to stay with the breath as an anchor and as a way of befriending himself in this moment. He reported later that something had shifted and he felt OK to do this practice in an exploratory way.

Another challenge can be wishing that all beings be happy, that all beings be free from suffering. Our minds acknowledge the impossibility of this, but as one person said there is no harm in wishing it. In fact, the act of wishing it, the act of imagining a world where there is no conflict, can make us feel happier.

Many people don't like loving kindness meditation because it feels too soft, 'it's flaky, fluffy, bunny land'. However, it is anything but soft. It can often feel quite tricky for people and brings up strong feelings of resistance and aversion.

'Back-draft' is a term sometimes used for the effect that happens to a person who has long been deprived of compassion towards themselves. The metaphor comes from firefighting – when a fire has been deprived of oxygen and someone opens a door, a massive explosion occurs. When we decide to explore more loving and accepting feelings towards ourselves it can cause an explosion of difficult feelings and even more self-critical or judgemental negative thoughts may arise.

Some positive responses

Even though it is challenging, many people find self-compassion a helpful practice. My friend and colleague, Judith Soulsby, found it so transforming that she went to train in America and has since become a leading teacher in self-compassion. It has transformed her life.

LEWIS liked the idea of befriending himself and whenever he noticed self-criticism, asked himself: *'Would I judge a friend like this?'* To sit with himself as a friend became the centre piece of his meditation practice.

MISA wrote this:

'I chose a friend from my youth and observing the feelings I have towards her, besides the tender and warm feelings which made me smile, I suddenly discovered a feeling of pity and of contempt. I was so shocked and ashamed of that feeling. I remembered that my father also disrespected people who were not very intelligent. I realised I am just like him in this vice. I also realised how terrible such a feeling can be. I lost courage and had to cry a little.

'Most of the time I like to be alone rather than with others. Relating to others often brings a lot of stress, often being unsure if things are all right between us. Perhaps this is due to the difficult relationship I had with my father, even up to his death. I was always trying to please him, to make him feel proud of me, to make him love me for my realisations and successes. Nothing worked: he never could allow me to be different from himself.

'In the meditation I was crying about our human condition, about our incapacity to love and be loved, to be imperfect and accepting of each other. Always judging one another and oneself. I also judged myself for having difficulties with choosing a neutral person. I realised that even with a neutral person I don't know, there is for me immediately a feeling of like or dislike. There is already a pre-judgement. ➔

> 'At this very moment, writing this down, I realise I skipped the next step: self-compassion! I was judging myself and realising it, then broadening my suffering about being imperfect to all living beings, and I got stuck in my sadness about our human condition and forgot to add compassion and self-compassion!
>
> 'I got stuck again in self-criticism: thinking I had to improve myself, that it was not OK to be as I am. I'm glad this insight struck me at last, I hope and intend to remember it during the next days, each time I hear the critical voice again and maybe I can feel grateful as well for being aware of this. I must remember what the Dalai Lama says: "Kindness is my simple religion. There is no need for temples".'

Here is a story from my own life:

It was the middle of winter and I had been ill for several weeks. From my bedroom window I am lucky enough to see mountains and they were covered in snow throughout my illness. I longed to go there. When I felt a bit better on a bright and sunny day, I set out for the hills to a high lake in the Snowdonia valley, Llyn Idwal. I imagined it would be sparkling in the sun just like it was in the summer but even more beautiful by being surrounded by snow on this January day.

The highlight of the trip was the journey there. I stopped on the roadside at Lake Ogwen, stepped out of the car and marvelled at the shining lake with clear reflections of the snowy mountains. I then set off to walk up the mountain pass to the higher valley.

I hadn't considered that Llyn Idwal is a north-facing valley and the sun does not rise over the surrounding mountains at this time of the year. The path was icy, the sky grey. The sun was not even touching the tops of the mountains. No shining lake here, all was dull and wintry cold.

I started to get fearful that I could fall on the icy path and freeze to death. All alone. This imagined scenario led me to dramatise even further, to feel resentment. Why hadn't my husband offered to come with me? Didn't he care?

On one hand I felt resentment and anger, on the other I reasoned that I had insisted on coming on my own. My husband was going with the walking group the next day and didn't want to go to the same valley twice and he had fencing to do. I had felt good setting off, independent, making my own way. A kind of pilgrimage, a mini retreat where I could be in solitude, in the moment.

My experience was initially thinking resentful thoughts; then waking up to noticing them as thoughts; then acknowledging the emotions present; then feeling this in the body (tightening and clenching); then noticing shorter breath and letting go into the huge mountain landscape I was standing in. At some point I noticed that I was being unkind to myself because of the judgement. It was very interesting to be processing this experience amid such a vast space around me. A space of harsh rugged beauty and wilderness. I alternated between an appreciation of this environment and imagining that I could freeze to death all alone with no phone signal. Kindness was indeed required.

Here is an outline of my experience:

1. Noticing negative thoughts

2. Labelling feelings

3. Bodily sensations

4. Focusing on the breath

5. Experiencing a sense of space

6. Kindness

7. Back to thoughts.

I felt disappointment on two counts. I experienced dark, bleak scenery rather than the walk I anticipated, a bright, sparkling, snowy mountain landscape. I was also disappointed by my aversion and reactivity. However, the experience was actually richer because I learned so much about mindfulness and also self-compassion practice. I was able to work with these emotions and hold them literally in a vast space. Through this process I softened into a kinder approach.

We imagine that as a mindfulness practitioner, teacher even, we will be free of such pettiness. But it is useful to 'know' how resentment feels, how fear feels and what a privilege to be able to work with this in such an environment. And then to bring kindness to feeling resentment, to feeling abandoned and unloved. I acknowledged that these feelings came from a place deep inside me that was pre-rational, a very young place, a leftover from my childhood. How to hold and take care of the petulant young child inside that feels such a raw emotion. To acknowledge that the child had felt unloved at some point and that this was stored deep in my consciousness.

When I got home, I still felt some of the aversion, even though I knew I was being reactive. The final piece was to communicate this to my husband, who articulated the rational side. He said that there were people about so I wouldn't have frozen to death, and pointed out that I had wanted to do it on my own. He hadn't wanted this – I could have asked him to come. We both had made our choices and that was a healthy way to relate to each other – with trust that the other can manage, with love to give the other freedom, with acceptance of the different needs of the other.

It is interesting to me that, although I had worked through it on my own, on this occasion it still needed to be communicated in a mindful and loving way. Although that could have gone horribly wrong!

The next day, the walking group walked out of the gloom into a top-of-the-world experience. They went into the same shaded cold and grey valley and rose through the cloud to the sunny peaks. All around they had views of mountain peaks covered with snow shining in the sun. They even saw a Brocken spectre, a natural phenomenon that I have long wished to see.

Since then I have had to work with feeling 'appreciative joy' that my husband and friends had a 'peak experience'. A unique and never-to-be-repeated wonderland of a walk. When they talk about it (and they do), and when I feel envy, I have to remind myself that I wasn't well or fit enough to do that walk. I looked after myself and had my own valuable experience too. And it gives me a wonderful opportunity to practise appreciative joy, a delight in another or others' delight!

Sometimes I go about pitying myself, while I am carried by the wind across the sky.

– Chippewa song

Night Quawk

Heron stands still by the bridge
The tiny circles around her legs
Embrace, expand, engulf the lake.

She waits, watches beneath reflections
Surveys the undercurrent.
Preying.
Come mid-morning
Heron lifts her legs
Takes off on her airplane wings
Prayers answered.

Touch the sky.
Reveal the boggy under belly.
Don't get sucked into the swamp.
Don't get sucked into the swamp.
Fight for freedom.
Care with your sky heart Heron.

Yet how far the sky?

Can we count the wing beats?

It is beyond reckoning.

'Quawk! Quawk' she cries

Vibrations ricochet.

The lady of the waters. Night Quawk

She shrieks into the net of heaven.

Let there be love.

– Annee Griffiths

Chapter 7:
Interconnection

'No man is an island,
Entire of itself,
Every man is a piece of the continent,
A part of the main.
If a clod be washed away by the sea,
Europe is the less.'

– John Donne

> *'On the eight-week Mindfulness course I began to notice nature more. It came into focus and I noticed trees and birds and the light. The Staying Mindful course has made a difference with the people that I was previously finding difficult to communicate with. Mindful communication has really made a difference at work. I am more present with people. I listen to them now instead thinking about what I am going to say. I am more likely to work out a better solution.'*

– Davy

As we feel more at ease with ourselves, we become more at ease in our relationships, more connected to the world. This, in turn, may motivate us to practise. We may be more creative, more attentive to people with whom we work, happier to give, able to be more altruistic, to contribute to society.

> *'A hundred times a day I remind myself that my inner and outer life depend on the labours of other men, living and dead, and that I must exert myself in order to give in the measure as I have received and am still receiving.'*

– Albert Einstein

Realising our interconnectedness allows us to shift away from the delusion that we are separate from the whole, from the world. We are dependent on many levels with other beings, plants and the planet itself. Global communications, activism and the media, particularly as it focuses on aspects of climate change, mean more of us are becoming conscious of this reality.

Early conditioning

Stress patterns in relationship are often so deeply ingrained that we become stuck in habitual reaction. These conditioned reactions may have been learned in childhood from our significant relationships. They are usually created as a coping strategy for difficult situations. These reactions, which we developed to protect ourselves, might well be inappropriate for our life today. In order to function fully as a loving human being, it is helpful to understand our personal barriers or hang-ups that may stand in the way.

Early patterns of relating are repeated over and over again in our lives. In his poem *My Heart Leaps Up*, Wordsworth describes the child as *'the father of the Man'* (1802):

> My heart leaps up when I behold
>
> A rainbow in the sky:
>
> So was it when my life began;
>
> So is it now I am a man;

So be it when I shall grow old,

Or let me die!

The Child is father of the Man;

And I could wish my days to be

Bound each to each by natural piety.

The attachment theory of John Bowlby (1969) described a child's predisposition to form a strong attachment to a primary caregiver or givers in order to survive. Children who are neglected or abandoned may not have experienced early attachment as an infant and consequently they may have difficulties with relationships later in childhood and adulthood. Adults who experienced insecure attachments generally find it difficult to manage their emotions. A study by Schore (2003) shows that caregivers' behaviours and how they attach to their infants in the first two years of life affects the structure of the brain. However, many recent studies and the developments in neuroscience show, through brain scans, that the brain has neuroplasticity and patterns can change. So, although 'the Child' may be 'Father to the Man' in one sense, as Wordsworth put it, he or she can change and transform in spite of deep conditioning.

We are sensitive beings, particularly as children. Parents are not perfect, and children are not either. The tricky behaviour of either parent or child can set off chains of reactions. Those of us who were lucky to have formed loving attachments in infancy have still got deeply ingrained habits that we developed to protect ourselves from perceived danger. This is what we can work with in meditation and or therapy.

ELSIE told me this story. Friends had gathered for a dinner party after a general election. While they were eating their meal a disagreement arose. Views differed and voices were raised. She found herself becoming withdrawn, almost frozen. Her strategy was to freeze and become numb. She spent the rest of the evening feeling unreal, insubstantial, invisible. It was as if she was skating on ice.

The next day during meditation she associated the upset feeling to her childhood experience of loud, emotional, violent rows between her parents at the dinner table. During meditation she was able to feel constriction in her guts and tears came. She did the RAIN meditation (recognising, allowing, investigating and nurturing) and felt a little better. She was able to give herself the love and care that she had missed out on during her parents' power struggle. She said she didn't blame them, they were having difficulties. Nor could she blame her friends whose passion also made her feel disconnected for a while.

Mindfulness courses for parents can help parents to understand and communicate more effectively with the family. My colleague Eluned Gold has developed a 'nurturing parents' course. She says:

'Young children learn their emotion regulation from their carers; when we attend to our own emotion regulation by acknowledging, observing and letting go we are better prepared to deal with the situation. When we are able to forgive ourselves for being less than perfect we are much more ready to apologise and show our kids that mistakes happen – people mess up and relationships can be repaired. Mindfulness and self-nurture are important qualities to cultivate in order to be more at ease with ourselves during the turbulence of life especially family life.'

We are interconnected but it takes courage to acknowledge our dependency on another. It takes courage to trust another, to trust someone enough to let them in. We need reassurance, we crave and fear intimacy. We don't wish to appear needy or clingy. In the western hemisphere we have developed a culture of individuality and independence that is at times unhealthy. We can feel isolated and lonely, threatened and self-protective.

If we give to others our full attention, our presence, we lessen our isolation. We need to be both receptive to others and prepared to communicate what we need. Effective communication is essential for good relationships. A relationship is like a dance.

'A human being is part of a whole, called by us the "Universe" — a part limited in time and space. He experiences himself, his thoughts, and feelings, as something separated from the rest – a kind of optical delusion of his consciousness. This delusion is a kind of prison for us, restricting us to our personal desires and to affection for a few persons nearest us. Our task must be to free ourselves from this prison by widening our circles of compassion to embrace all living creatures and the whole of nature in its beauty.'

– Albert Einstein

Seven steps for mindful communication

1. Notice, pause and breathe

Bringing mindfulness into communication especially when it is a difficult one is a real challenge. The first step in this as a practice is to remember your intention. Then, as in the three-step breathing space, bringing awareness to how you are in the moment. This might be feeling the contact of your feet on the floor and to bring awareness to your breath. The intention here is to become grounded in the moment. The practice of: **Two feet. One breath**.

When you are in strong disagreement with a partner, child or colleague the thought 'I am right' and the feeling of heat and agitation is foremost. The need to push out in an aggressive manner or to retreat into a passive-aggressive sulk may be very strong.

This is the time for the mindful pause. A pause may enable you to see any negative habitual patterns that are acting out in this communication. A mindful breath allows a pause in ruminative or blaming thoughts and gives rise to the possibility of less judgement and some kindness toward yourself. Finding middle ground is not always easy, but sometimes it is important to decide whether you need to prove yourself right or whether you want to be happy. The need to be right can sometimes be stronger than the need to be loving and understanding. So sometimes it is wise to ask ourselves what we are trying to prove. What is our motive? Is it ego or pride? Is it point-scoring in an attempt to be the dominant person? We may need to compromise in order to be peaceful in our relationships.

GLENDA brought a very painful communication to the class. As she sat with RAIN, the working with a difficulty meditation, she felt her anger and despair. Her mind was talking all the time and as she took her attention to the body she became aware of the intense sensations around her chest. She experienced palpitations around her heart and felt very hot. This was a powerful physical feeling and rather frightening. As she turned towards these feelings in the body the constant nagging of the thoughts stopped and when she turned to the class to explain her situation she said she felt some relief from her relentless thoughts.

Her previous partner had been a bully and very abusive. Her parents had also been threatened by this man and were very negative about her new boyfriend whom they had not met yet. She told us that she was endlessly ruminating about her situation. The act of feeling into her body and then finding some words to soothe herself like: *'I respect you, you have had a hard time, you deserve a loving partner'*, gave her a pause from the suffering and some relief.

2. Mindful listening

To listen deeply to what the other has to say is often a challenging experience. This means giving your full attention without being defensive or fighting back, without freezing, withdrawing, numbing out or running away.

Check that you are not judging or criticising while you are listening. The self-critic or judge could sabotage interactions and spontaneity could be lost. Check that you have heard and understood what they are saying by repeating what they have said and summing up what you think they are saying, for example 'Are you saying…?'

Attend and befriend is the principle. Be open-minded as best you can. When you listen to another you need to take care that you are:

■ not thinking about how to fix it for the other

- not problem-solving

- not giving advice

- not mind reading, that is, not assuming you know what the other is thinking

- not adding to the discussion by bringing in your own examples when you are thinking about what you want to say rather than listening to the other.

In a paired mindful communication exercise, which required one person to speak and the other to just listen, YAZMINE noticed an inclination to give advice and to compare and share her own experience when she was listening. On the other hand, when she was talking, she was so grateful to be able to just talk without interruption or interpretation. She realised that if her partner in the exercise had made a judgement on the person in her story and said, 'What a mean person', it would have reinforced her own negativity rather than allowing a shift to a more impartial view. She ended up feeling that the difficulty she had been talking about wasn't such a big deal after all. The story that had been bugging her all week was really 'quite trivial'. She also noticed that she often gave advice to others and that her mother did too. Although it irritated her when her mother gave advice, she delighted in doing so herself. After the exercise she realised it was a habit that she would like to change.

3. Speak assertively

People have different views and it can cause hostility. This is often all too obvious in a close family relationship or friendship. How do we cope with this or with the person with strong opposing views who we encounter on the street or on social media? Sometimes, we increase hostility by directly confronting or belittling them. How can we weave a dance so that we bring them in closer, so that they are not alienated and feel the need to return the hostility?

Often we become angry about an injustice, either perceived or real, in our world. There are many examples where disrespect causes murder and mayhem. How can we temper our anger so that we can be effective but not invoke more hostility? How might we bridge the gap between the way things are and the way we want them to be?

The following list is a guide to further assertiveness:

- Use active 'I' statements like 'I feel…', not passive like 'You make me feel…'

- State clearly what we want. 'I want you to…'

- Avoid generalisations like never, or always e.g. 'I never get my way; you always get yours'. 'No one listens to me.' 'You always do that.'

- Be aware of mind reading, i.e. thinking you know what the other is saying, and avoid making assumptions.

- Be wary of 'should', 'ought' and 'must'. For example: 'You should have done that.' 'You ought to do as I say'. 'You must know what I mean.'

- Find some common ground. Use questions and statements like:

'How do you see this working out?'

'How do you feel about this and what is your expectation of my feelings here?'

'This is very difficult for me, I am not feeling heard.'

'You make a good point.'

'I hear you and I hadn't seen it in that way.'

JOANNA found it very difficult to be in a relationship where the ex-wife of her partner kept interfering in their plans. His ex-wife used the children as tools to hurt the relationship with their father. Joanna was finding it very difficult to keep her peace. To speak out would be damaging, to be silent felt too much like being a doormat.

She used the mindful pause a lot. She felt her anger and her frustration in her body and was surprised at the intensity of the physical feeling. After a discussion on assertiveness skills she decided she would try speaking assertively at home. She gave a lot of thought to of how best to express her needs in a way that would be fair to all concerned. She stated to her husband that she needed to talk to him about how he was feeling about the situation with his ex-wife. She let him speak first and then repeated what he said back to him (mindful listening). She then told him she was feeling upset around the lack of boundaries. Could they work out a strategy that better met all their needs? The discussion between them cleared the air and she felt empowered, although the situation continued to be an ongoing negotiation.

4. Mirroring

Our interconnection and interdependence on others have been obvious from our early history, and it is still relevant. This age-old propensity for empathy was physically demonstrated when mirror neurons in the brain were discovered by neurological research in the 1990s.

Facial expressions, body language and emotions are often mirrored in communication. This can be subtle but is picked up by the brain and reflected back to the other. Brains 'hook up'. Seventy per cent of communication is non-verbal.

Bringing awareness to our body language, our facial expression and posture makes a difference to how we are received. It is skilful to be aware of your own expression and not merely to reflect the emotion on the face of the other, which could escalate the emotional response.

In an area of conflict or difficulty it is important not to be defensive. Repeating back what someone says accurately and mirroring them can be helpful. We could say, 'Let me see if I understood what I thought you said'. Then 'Tell me if I have missed anything'. Then 'Have I got it?' or 'I heard you say... is there any more about that?'

Mirroring the other can be obvious to us when we are looked on with love and kindness. We can feel it. On the other hand, when we pick up negative signals, we may not be aware that we are reflecting the same signals back, possibly magnified. How important it is therefore to be aware of how we are feeling and how we may be projecting that out in a hostile manner. Using 'the pause' to be aware of an emotion internally can break neural circuits not only in your own brain, but also in the 'hook up' between brains.

The following story is taken from a chapter, 'Mindfulness and Carers' by Vanessa Hope in *The Mindfulness Breakthrough* by Sarah Silverton.

LAURA cares for her 20-year-old son Dan, who had a motorcycle accident two years ago. He is now not only in a wheelchair but also suffered injury to his brain, which means that her previously easy-going boy is now prone to dramatic mood swings, made worse by the fact that he does not always understand what is being said to him. Sometimes communicating with him in a way that means he can understand and help with the simplest tasks seems impossible. Laura can sometimes feel at her wits' end.

One day, Laura had to get Dan in from the garden early to go for a hospital appointment. He often got angry at having to stop what he was doing and did not understand why the appointment was important. As she steeled herself for an argument, Laura paused and took a breathing space. She came in touch with how she was bracing herself for a battle. As she stayed with this tightness, she became aware of a heavy feeling around her heart and found that underneath her frustration was immense sadness for herself and for the strongly individual little boy her son had once been. She felt the tightness dissolve and she gently put her arm around him, saying: *'Time to go in now, Dan, and get ready for your hospital appointment.'* To her surprise, he hugged her back. Laura then realised how often just expecting confrontation made the situation worse. She also realised that it was the first time for a while that she had simply given her son a hug, and how good that simple, wordless communication felt.

5. Taking a kindly attitude and not taking it personally

Friendliness is an essential prerequisite for mindful communication, especially friendliness towards ourselves. This means an awareness of judgement. It means vigilance around the use of 'should' or 'ought'. It means a willingness to forgive when we have slipped into being judgemental and the continuing intention to be kind to ourselves in that moment, in spite of the judgement; to recognise that it is a difficult or painful moment that needs self-compassion and that kindness is enough. Remember the self-compassion break. Sometimes we may need to step back, and not take it personally, even when it appears personal.

JULES loves football. If his team loses, he takes it personally. He thinks he is a failure and so is the whole team. He is on minimum wage and feels his team have to be successful and win or else they and he are nothing. He is upset about his own status in the world. He needs his team to win in order to gain some personal status. When they lose, he is depressed – the team are rubbish and so is he.

This global thinking has led him to be both aggressive (wanting to fall out and fight with people) and passive (taking to his bed for several days). Part of his mindfulness training was to become aware that he was more than his team's successes and failures. If people were rude about his team it didn't mean he was nothing. He learnt to be more aware of the moment, to take a mindful breath and to see that there was more in his life than this need for status.

6. Sometimes you can be flexible rather than trying to make the other change

The need to change someone else to suit ourselves may expend a lot of energy getting nowhere. It can be a power struggle for who is right or who is in control. Perhaps it is possible to compromise sometimes and soften a little? We all tend to be selfish and think about ourselves first. How to truly accept the otherness of someone we love, to appreciate their difference, is the work of relationship, as we discover over and over again: otherness and togetherness. We might change ourselves, adapt to the situation or decide to allow the behaviour that we want to change.

My husband is very quick to make decisions and will stick with them no matter what. I, on the other hand, am slow. I like to deliberate, to ponder over all the options and sometimes I just can't make up my mind. We have had to come to some understanding. He makes the unimportant decisions like what car is the most efficient for our purposes and I make the important decisions like whether God exists! Joking aside, the adjustments we have had to make around the decision-making process include his recognition to give me ample time to make a decision and the necessity for me to let things go once a decision has been made or find some way of altering the decision.

7. Smile!

'Smile and the whole world smiles with you' are words from a popular song from the 1920s. The muscles in the face are directly connected to the brain's nervous system and a smile will affect our mood for the better. Even a false smile can make us feel happier. In a famous experiment from the 1980s undertaken by Strack and his colleagues (Strack *et al*, 1988) some subjects were asked to hold a pencil horizontally in their mouth (resembling a false smile) and other subjects held the pencil in their hand. They all looked at the same cartoon. The subjects with the pencils in their mouths reported the cartoons funnier than the control group. Try your own experiment: *'Smile though your heart is aching...You'll find that life is still worthwhile, if you just smile'* (accredited to Charlie Chaplin). Most people will smile back. Experiment.

Thich Nhat Hanh gives us this:

Breathing in, I calm body and mind.

Breathing out, I smile.

Keep a communications record

It can be helpful to keep a daily communications record. This can be a daily record of the situation plus thoughts, feelings and body sensations.

Do you notice any patterns that are repeated in the difficult communication? What is your usual reaction? Do you tend to fight, flee or freeze (withdraw, go numb) when the communication becomes challenging? When did you first notice the communication being problematic? How long after the communication did you feel the effects?

The five-column technique

Aaron Beck developed this technique for the Beck Centre for Cognitive Therapy. Use five columns on a sheet of paper to divide your experience into useful areas.

1. The first column is 'The situation', i.e. the story in your life that is troubling you at the moment.

2. The second column is headed 'Negative emotions' that you identify which are provoked by the story.

3. The third column is headed 'Thoughts', i.e. the thoughts you are having linked to these emotions.

4. The fourth column is headed 'Body sensations' and records the sensations in the body that are caused by thoughts and emotions around the story.

5. The fifth column is an opportunity to re-evaluate the initial experience and is headed: 'What do you feel now?'

The situation	Negative emotions	Thoughts	Body sensations	What do you feel now?

Anger and Forgiveness

'Anger is like drinking poison' said Nelson Mandela. Anger is one of the Buddha's three poisons, alongside greed and delusion. Sometimes the hot fires of anger, like the larva of a volcano, erupt and then turn into resentment and bitterness. They harden into a protective armour.

It is useful to investigate what is underneath anger. It could be emotions such as frustration, powerlessness or helplessness, anxiety, vulnerability, hurt, sadness, loneliness or a sense of not being understood or respected. To acknowledge these underlying emotions within the anger may help to soften and transform anger.

A Poison Tree

I was angry with my friend:
I told my wrath, my wrath did end.
I was angry with my foe:
I told it not, my wrath did grow.

And I watered it in fears,
Night and morning with my tears;
And I sunned it with smiles,
And with soft deceitful wiles.

And it grew both day and night,
Till it bore an apple bright.
And my foe beheld it shine.
And he knew that it was mine,

And into my garden stole
When the night had veiled the pole;
In the morning glad I see
My foe outstretched beneath the tree.

– William Blake

RAIN meditation – working with anger

Begin by Grounding. Feeling your feet on the floor and bottom on the seat. Placing your attention on this connection with the earth for some moments. Held here by gravity.

Bringing your attention to focus on your breath. Stay with the breath for about five minutes. When you are ready, bring to mind a situation that makes you angry.

RECOGNISE that anger is here. Go over the story. Hear the words that you might say to yourself or another. *'This shouldn't be like this, it's not fair, this is not right.'* Feel it in the body. Go over the story in your mind. Relive the drama.

ALLOW yourself to feel it. Perhaps saying, *'It's all right, let me feel it'*, allowing the emotion to be there. Freeze frame the part of the story that ignites your anger the strongest.

INVESTIGATE the feelings in the body and any other emotions that are present. Asking yourself, 'What emotions are underneath this anger?', identifying the emotions and the sensations in the body. If you are not feeling sensations in the trunk of the body allow your posture, your face to express the emotion. Noticing this is anger. This is what it feels like. Is it also hurt or shame or sadness? Notice whatever emotion is present.

Asking yourself, *'What is my unmet need here?'*

NURTURE What would you say to a good friend who is feeling like this? Or to a young child? Placing your hand on your heart or simply rubbing your arm or even your finger as you sit here. Perhaps saying, *'I love you'*, *'I see you'* to yourself. Perhaps there is a phrase from the befriending meditation that you can use.

'May I accept myself how I am.'

'May I be safe.'

'May I forgive myself or another.'

'May I be strong.'

'Accepting myself as I am at the moment.'

Or another phrase that suits you in this moment.

NON-IDENTIFYING Don't take it personally. The anger shown towards you or the annoying reaction of the other may be more about the other person than about you. This is passing weather, like a thunderstorm in the mountains.

Forgiveness Practice

Nelson Mandela said:

> *'Forgiveness liberates the soul, it removes fear. That's why it's such a powerful weapon.'*

He forgave his jailers after his liberation. In 1995 he had lunch with the state prosecutor who, in 1963, had favoured giving him the death penalty rather than imprisonment. Forgiveness is not easy but often the rancour and bitterness that not forgiving creates hurts the victim rather than the perpetrator. This is why it is an important practice.

'The weak can never forgive. Forgiveness is the attribute of the strong.'
– Mahatma Gandhi

We can't forgive without opening to and validating our own pain. Forgiveness is not about condoning hurt but about letting go of the anger and resentment that is not serving us.

Sometimes we can hold a grudge for the longest time, sometimes a lifetime. Sometimes the hurt is so immense that it seems unpardonable, impossible to forgive. But to not forgive continues to hurt the victim.

EVA KOR was a member of a group of children who were alive for one reason only – to be used as human guinea pigs.

'During our time in Auschwitz we talked very little. Starved for food and human kindness, it took every ounce of strength just to stay alive,' she said. 'The moment I forgave the Nazis, I was freed… The day I forgave the Nazis, privately I forgave my parents whom I hated all my life for not having saved me from Auschwitz. Children expect their parents to protect them; mine couldn't. And then I forgave myself for hating my parents.' 'Some survivors do not want to let go of the pain. They call me a traitor and accuse me of talking in their name. I have never done this. Forgiveness is as personal as chemotherapy – I do it for myself. I do it not because they deserve it, but because I deserve it.'

To read more about this astonishing woman go to:
www.theforgivenessproject.com/eva-kor.

We may not have such a horrific story around forgiveness but the message 'I do it for myself' is an important one. We forgive to have ease in our lives. We all make mistakes. These can be caused by our conditioning, our culture our upbringing (carers, parents and grandparents). Maybe it is not my fault, not their fault. It is useful to understand the causes and conditions of our own and others' actions. The example I give below is so minor compared to the above examples. When I was about 10 (about 60 years ago!) I was thoughtlessly cruel. We were a group of three girls. For some reason two of us decided to exclude another girl and run away at playtime. Our friend went home hurt.

I can't remember if we made it up, if she forgave me; maybe she didn't, but a group of girls ran away from me about four years later at a new school, and I have witnessed my siblings, children and grandchildren all being hurt by similar situations. I can still feel her pain on that cold January day when we ran away to deliberately exclude her. At that moment she was 'the other' and was isolated and rejected. I use this memory to practise both asking forgiveness of another and forgiving myself.

> *'There is a simple practice we can do to cultivate forgiveness. First, we acknowledge what we feel – shame, revenge, embarrassment, remorse. Then we forgive ourselves for being human. Then, in the spirit of not wallowing in the pain, we let go and make a fresh start. We don't have to carry the burden with us anymore. We can acknowledge, forgive, and start anew.'*

– Pema Chodrun from Comfortable with Uncertainty P. 193

Forgiveness meditation

The forgiveness practice is in three parts:

1. Asking forgiveness of others. 'Forgive me for the hurt I have caused.'

2. Forgiving myself for hurting myself or others.

3. Forgiving others who have hurt me.

First settling into a meditation posture. Feeling the support of the ground beneath your feet and the support of your seat. (If lying, feeling your body making contact with its support). Breathing in and breathing out. Staying focused on your breath for several minutes.

1. Asking for forgiveness

Bringing to mind a situation where you have hurt another. Make this a small misdemeanour when you first do this meditation. It may be your angry words or your cold withdrawal. Maybe you were unkind or selfish or just careless, not being aware of the hurt you were causing.

As you think about your own situation, notice what emotions are present. Judgement against yourself, guilt, shame, sadness or justification. Then as you picture the person or the people you have hurt, ask for forgiveness. Consider how you impacted upon another. In your mind you can say their name or names and saying to yourself:

'I am aware of the hurt you have felt, the hurt I have caused you.

'I ask your forgiveness, please forgive me.'

Then just sitting for a few moments feeling into the possibility of being forgiven.

2. Forgiving yourself

Bringing to mind the same situation where you have hurt another, or a recent situation where you have been unforgiving to yourself. This could be a time when you have been hard on yourself, when you have sat in judgement on yourself. You may have made a mistake or deliberately chosen to be mean or negative towards another or yourself. →

There may be understandable reasons leading to mistakes or you could be under stress or maybe an old button has been pressed and you have reacted from habit. Notice what emotions are also present, the feeling of discomfort, the pain of shame. Allowing yourself to feel this in the body. Fully acknowledging what's here in the thoughts, emotions and physical sensations.

Offer forgiveness to yourself by saying the following words that are appropriate to your situation:

'May I begin to forgive myself for causing this person harm.'

'May I forgive myself for my shortcomings.'

You may offer yourself compassion as well as forgiveness:

'May I be free from shame.'

'May I accept myself as I am.'

If you feel unable to forgive yourself at present, setting an intention that you will work towards forgiveness.

'It is my intention to forgive myself as best I can when I feel I am able'.

You can also say this aspiration towards forgiveness to yourself if it feels like you are just going through the motions, and you don't feel sincere. Although it may feel inauthentic, it is important to be aware of all the aspects of your emotional response and note that in attempting to do this practice there is a need to be forgiving.

It may be that you fall into the same habitual reaction of hurting another or yourself time and time again. To be aware of this reaction and the suffering it causes and holding onto the intention to forgive yourself is more constructive than endless guilt and whipping yourself.

3. Forgiving others

Bringing to mind a situation where you were hurt by another. Again, it is best to choose to start with a minor hurt rather than a major traumatic event. As you think about it visualising the scenario, allow yourself to feel the pain. At first only staying for a moment rather than trying to feel the full impact.

Noticing the different emotions and body sensations present. Fully acknowledging the pain you feel around this situation. It may be possible for you to sense the pain that they may have felt when they hurt you, even if this pain is the numbness of insensitivity.

Then saying to yourself:

'May I forgive you for the suffering you have caused.'

'May I begin to forgive you.'

Or: *'It is my intention to work towards forgiving you for the pain you have caused.'*

Repeat several times holding the person in your mind's eye. Be patient – forgiveness practice is an advanced practice. It may take a while before you are able to forgive. It is a work in progress.

Adapted from Jack Kornfield.

To believe, what is it? Guarding a town

Until acceptance comes.

Forgiveness, what's that? A way through thorns

To an old enemy's side.

Beth yw credu? Gwarchod tref

Nes dyfod derbyn.

Beth yw maddau? Cael ffordd trwy'r drain

At ochr hen elyn.

From Pa Beth Yn Dyn?

– Waldo Williams a Welsh poet, translated by Tony Conran

Giving and receiving compassion with equanimity meditation

The meditation practice of equanimity is useful for those times when you are unable to help someone or change a situation.

Bringing to mind a person who can exhaust or frustrate you. Someone who is suffering. A person you feel close to or who is bound up in your life.

Take a few minutes to settle, by grounding, feeling contact with the ground and the seat. Then repeat these words to yourself:

Everyone is on his or her life journey.

I am not the cause of this person's suffering,

Nor is it in my power to make it go way

Even if I wish I could.

Moments like this are difficult to bear

Yet I may still try to help if I can.   →

Aware of the stress in your body, inhale drawing in compassion for yourself.

Exhale sending out compassion for the other or for all beings.

Breathing-in for me.

Breathing-out for the other.

Peace and reconciliation work

'An individual has not started living until he can rise above the narrow confines of his individualistic concerns to the broader concerns of all humanity.'

– Martin Luther King Jr.

Many people are working towards a peaceful world. The fascinating work of peace and reconciliation uses the same principles as mindfulness communications. I first became aware of this work after the Truth and Reconciliation Commission was established in 1996, after the abolition of Apartheid in South Africa in 1994.

A few years ago I visited Corrymeela, a centre for peace in Northern Ireland. Although the 1998 Good Friday Agreement meant far fewer violent attacks on both sides, the region was still extremely divided into Protestant and Catholic factions. I was impressed by the work Corrymeela was doing with groups and, in particular, schools on both sides of the conflict.

I was teaching an eight-week course to Northern Irish teachers and health professionals who believed that mindfulness training would be useful in alleviating some of the difficulties of the area. We had interesting dialogues over mealtimes and breaks. Although 'The Troubles' have lessened over the last few years, the participants on the course, both Catholic and Protestant, told me that to have these discussions anywhere else in their country was almost impossible. Here, they felt more free to have a dialogue around the 'struggles' in Corrymeela than anywhere else in their lives. One woman who married into the 'other' religion lamented that their mutual in-laws were hostile to each other.

David Rynick, my Zen teacher, wrote in his blog (http://davidrynick.com) about the division of the United States after the election of Donald Trump as the President of the United States. In the blog he quotes Paula Green, a peace activist, founder of the Karuna Center for Peacebuilding and recipient of the 2009 'Unsung Hero of Compassion' awarded by the Dalai Lama:

'The felt sense of being respected, or its opposite of being ignored or humiliated, has a much more powerful influence on people's opinions than rational arguments...The pain of being humiliated and excluded is

147

unsustainable. Sooner or later, shame seeks a scapegoat, someone to blame in a misguided attempt to reduce the pain. The excluded demand their place at the table.'

David Rynick asks how we can amend this division:

'How do we, as Paula Green says, "enlarge our boundaries of inclusion?" How do we join with those who have felt so disrespected and left behind by our country? A friend who voted for Trump is also appalled by the racism and violence he incites and suggested we might form a "coalition of the reasonable" to protect those who are vulnerable.

'How do we go beyond being shocked and outraged and begin forming new coalitions and taking strategic action? This is not the time for playing nice and pretending everything will take care of itself. All of us who pay lip service to compassion, democratic principles and economic justice need to be behaving in new ways.'

After a recent election here in Britain, as after the Brexit referendum, the population of Britain are also polarised in their views. Social media plays a role in emphasising this division as we can become easily enraged by comments from people who oppose us. Again, we come back to investigating what is a mindful way forward, a way that does not include spreading acrimony and hate.

Anger is war, forgiveness is a seed for peace.

– Eva Kor

Letter to the future

Imagine a time in the future, perhaps in a hundred years' time, a time when a descendant, a grandchild or relative of yours or a descendant of a friend has grown old. He or she is living in an entirely different world from the world we live in now. Write to this person telling them about the good things in your life. Tell them about what you hold precious in your life. The love, the beauty and the friendships.

Now tell them of your fears for the future. Perhaps acknowledge in this letter trends that threaten our peace and survival. Be succinct or choose one aspect of your apprehension. Maybe include a recognition of the pollution already present and the animals and insects endangered with extinction. You might like to finish the letter by a description of one of these creatures as a eulogy, a praise poem in hope of their survival.

While I was finishing this book I took a trip to London. I was going to the Tate Modern to see an exhibition when I found out there was an exhibition on Buddhism at the British Library. So, I went there instead and thus missed a terrorist attack on London Bridge. This made it more personal: 'There but for fortune go I.' It was brought home to me by this tribute by Dave Merritt for his son, Jack Merritt, who was killed in the attack:

'Jack believed in the inherent goodness of humanity and felt a deep social responsibility to protect that. Through us all, Jack marches on. Borrow his intelligence, share his drive, feel his passion, burn with his anger, and extinguish hatred with his kindness. Never give up his fight.'

This was printed in *The Guardian* on 3 December 2019, five days after his murder. Jack was working in the field of prisoner rehabilitation and was attending the same workshop as his killer.

This was a lesson for me, a call for a clear intention to work towards lessening hatred. Sometimes that might mean just a pause while I notice that my first reaction is aversion. This time of divisiveness, when our politics and our mood, in this and many other countries, becomes more and more hateful. A time when an intention to soften hatred by non-hatred is crucial. This does not mean compliance with or resignation to the hateful. I hope to challenge it where I can without escalation. To turn it round for myself. It is easy to react with anger and vitriol when people are disagreeing or disagreeable but how to soften this tendency is the ongoing challenge and one that Jack Merritt and the other victim Saskia Jones were living by. It is an ancient premise. This quote from *The Dhammapada*, ascribed to The Buddha, speaks to this:

'Hatred is never appeased by hatred in this world. By non-hatred alone is hatred appeased. This is a law eternal.'

There were tens of thousands of refugees from Cambodia in the time of the Khmer Rouge under Pol Pot. People lived through countless horrors and terrible tragedies. Maya Gosananda, a Buddhist monk, addressed these refugees in their camp in Thailand by chanting over and over:

'Hatred never ceases by hatred; but by love alone is healed. This is an ancient and eternal law.'

This brought relief and weeping, and some extraordinary healing in the face of deep trauma. In Maya Ghosananda's book, *Step by Step* (1992) he wrote this poem:

Cambodia has suffered deeply.

From deep suffering comes deep compassion.

From deep compassion comes a peaceful heart.

From a peaceful heart comes a peaceful person.

From a peaceful person comes a peaceful family and community.

From peaceful communities comes a peaceful nation.

From peaceful nations come a peaceful world.

At the heart of the American Civil Rights movement, Martin Luther King spoke out against violence:

'Darkness cannot drive out darkness; only light can do that. Hate cannot drive out hate; only love can do that.'

Some people who work to make the world a better place are activists. Such is their struggle against all odds that they suffer burnout. More than ever there is a need for the resources of mindfulness training to remain robust in this burning world.

See: https://www.themindfulnessinitiative.org/uk

https://mindfulnessandsocialchange.org/uk

https://www.themindfulnessinitiative.org/mindful-nation-report

How do we act in times of difficulty, especially in the overwhelming threat of climate emergency? The government of Wales has declared a climate emergency. But what can I do?

Sometimes I can feel so powerless in the face of the climate emergency, but my family are trying to do our bit: planting trees (Bastin *et al*, 2019), changing our heating system away from oil and gas to ground source heating, and demonstrating. My two poems below show action in the face of difficulty.

The Children's Strike

It's so big –

And the children so small.

A line of enormous

London bobbies tower above you.

With tangled long yellow hair

You scurry past.

Eleven years old,

Striking from school

Is it worth the teachers' anger, Cai,

Right now?

It's your future.

You have the courage to stand.

Your world is disappearing

glaciers melt,
crash into the sea
Right now

Horror... as the walrus
can't find a beach
to rest on, to give birth on.
She struggles out of the sea
Climbs the cliff.
Right now

Sea creature,
How will she get back?
By tumbling down over the cliff
falling, bouncing,
on jagged rock – on ragged flesh.
Bloody.
Right now.

'It's our future'.
Fourteen-year-old, Robyn,
Speaks on the megaphone in north Wales:
'The teachers say striking isn't going to help
I think a big crowd always helps'.
Right now

Sylvie, she's only 10,
Sings to the crowd:
'Our world is hot right now,
Our world is warming up,
Gonna stop it
Right now'.

Hearing of mass extinctions
The children are crying.
No more tiger, lion and polar bear?
Iola paints them bright
She will stand, will fight
for climate justice
Right now

– Annee Griffiths

Indra's net

The god of fire, Indra, has a net.
A net of jewels each one mirroring the other
Like glittering stars infinitely
Reflecting each and every one of us.
The blaze too bright for our imagination.
Each one of us a sun.
The warmth in the chest an intimation of our fire,
The quiver in the heart is a mere glimmer.

Star-like, still we operate like planets with orbits
Interconnected with one another.
Fire powers our centre
Whilst on the surface each one
has our own weather system
Constantly changing the atmosphere.

Recently, the jet stream, winding in air ribbons
High above the North Atlantic Ocean,
Has shifted, bringing extreme weather conditions.
In the southern hemisphere El Nino,
A warm current in the Pacific Ocean,
affects the winds of the planet,

changing our life far away in the north
as well devastating its own near neighbours.

Here in North Wales, we have had too much rain.
Flooding
And further south
Too much sun.
Land dries up, crops fail.

Affected by the moods of oceans and winds
Thousands of miles away,
Refugees flee weather and war.
No water, no food. Nothing to share.

Yet hands reach out to lift survivors out of rickety boats.
Here and there, victims of the flood and fire
are embraced, befriended.

A smile begets a smile.
Kindness reverberates.
I smile and you are friendly.
We reflect each other.
Like the spider's web in autumn
Silver silks cover the fields.
As sun shines on the tiny drops of dew
The webs catch the light.

Polish the jewel, our own jewel in Indra's net.
Let the net gleam.
Golden.

– Annee Griffiths

Chapter 8: Gratitude

'I find ecstasy in living, the mere sense of living is
joy enough'

– Emily Dickinson (1870)

'Piglet noticed that even though he had a very small heart, it could
hold a rather large amount of gratitude.'

– A.A. Milne, 'Winnie the Pooh'

Grateful people are happy people. We can intentionally cultivate gratitude
in a way that helps us to realise the goodness in our lives and even to share
this goodness out.

There is a fairy story called 'The Three Wishes', told in many cultures in
different forms. Here is a version from my culture.

'There was once a woodcutter who was about to cut down a big oak tree in the forest. A fairy flew down from the crown of the tree and begged the woodman not to cut the tree down. "This is my home," she said "Please don't cut my tree down." The woodcutter agreed and, out of gratitude, the fairy granted him three wishes. He rushed home to tell his wife and they planned all the things they could possibly wish for. The wife said it would be a good thing to be out of poverty and the husband said it would be better to wish for health. They argued between themselves for a while and in a moment of carelessness his wife said "It's a lovely fire, I wish we had a nice string of sausages to cook on it." Just as soon as she said that some sausages appeared in a pan on the fire. In a fit of fury, seeing that his wife had wasted a wish, the husband said: "I wish those sausages were stuck to your nose".

All of a sudden, the sausages flew up and stuck to her nose. She cried and cried, trying with all her might to pull the sausages off her nose. There was nothing for it but to wish she had her nose back to normal. He wished that she returned to her own lovely self. The couple were so grateful to be back to normal that they decided that their life was right just as it was. And they lived gratefully ever after!'

Maybe, sometimes, we have to experience a loss or a near miss in order to see that the life we are living is the life that is possible for us right now. We can influence this life by appropriate action.

> JULES said he was grateful for his meditation practice because of the transformation he had experienced over time: 'It is difficult to explain to anyone who hasn't experienced it, the paradox that seems to be at the centre of mindfulness practice... accepting however things are in me moment to moment, and within that acceptance finding a releasing of the hold of a strong emotion... so, for example, that loneliness that was so much part of me, it has gone – where and when did it go? Where has it gone? When all I did was totally accept it, be curious about it'.

The attitudes of trust and acceptance are the precursors of gratitude. Sometimes we fail at interview to get a job we think was meant for us or the love of our life breaks our heart and the relationship ends. Maybe it was impossible to be grateful at the time, or even to trust and accept that things would be alright. But later on we may realise that the earlier heartache was necessary. We may look back and say, 'Yes, it was meant to be – this has set me on a different path and it's the right path'. 'Clearing you out for some new delight', as Rumi says in *The Guest House*.

Sometimes, we experience great pain or suffering; at these times gratitude or appreciation of our life is not our primary concern. The pain, whether physical or emotional, can overwhelm us, and our lives may be miserable.

Yet even in these times it is worth considering what is positive in our lives at this moment. This may help us to find some small goodness to shift the balance even a little.

Once we get what we want – a relationship, a family, some possessions – we may begin to take them for granted and become critical of any imperfections. How do we continue to savour the joy that we once had for that newness? We may try to cultivate an attitude of recognising and celebrating our good fortune. If this proves difficult, we might add another layer by being self-critical. Realising that it is not our fault when we are critical of ourselves because it is a deep habit allows us to soften towards ourselves.

It can be easy to take some aspects of our life for granted and even find them burdensome. Take a garden for instance. We have quite an unruly garden – there are always jobs to do. If it's dry it needs water, when it's wet the weeds grow with vigour and need to be controlled to protect the more tender plants. It is easy to complain about never-ending jobs or walk into the garden and see only jobs. For me, it is a practice to walk into my garden and appreciate the life that is there, to celebrate the colour and rejoice in the changes. We can think of gratitude as breathing in, accepting the nourishment of the air. The act of taking in and appreciating the good things.

'Gratitude is not only the greatest of virtues, but the parent of all others.'

– Marcus Tullius Cicero

Meditation on appreciation

This meditation is an opportunity to contemplate the good things in your life.

Grounding. Scan your body for any tension. Are there any areas where you are clenching, tightening? What's here in this moment? Feeling your feet on the floor, your bottom on the seat. Experiencing a sense of being rooted, secure, held by the seat and by the floor, held by the earth itself.

Noticing your breath moving in and out and paying particular attention to the out-breath. A sense of exhaling into spaciousness. Your out-breath mingling with air, the space around you. Resting in a sense of openness and space.

Asking yourself the question: 'What little inconsequential thing do I appreciate in my life today?' Perhaps remembering a pleasant sensation, an enjoyable experience. This could be your morning coffee or an enjoyable drink or seeing sunlight at the window or a person's smile. Finding one thing you appreciated in your day. Just choosing something small. →

Noticing how the body feels while recollecting this special moment.

Now asking the question: 'Who do I appreciate in my life?' This can be a person or an animal. Reflecting on the positive aspects of your relationship with this someone. Be specific. Finding a couple of specific things that you notice. This could be the colour of their eyes, their spontaneity or their seriousness, the way they move, their sound.

Appreciating them, checking into the sensations in the body no matter how subtle. Maybe saying to yourself: 'I am grateful you are in my life'.

Now asking yourself the question: 'What do I appreciate about my life as a whole?' This could be where you live, your work, your freedom, your family, your friends, your pastime or project, your mobility, your hands, something in your life you appreciate. Just choosing one and leaving the others for another day. If there is nothing at this moment, maybe experimenting with finding one thing you could appreciate if this was a better time. Then when you have chosen, be specific about finding one or two aspects of that one thing. Saying to yourself: 'I am grateful for... [this aspect of my life].'

Notice any feelings that you have in your body no matter how slight.

Now asking yourself the question: 'What do I appreciate about myself?' Be specific about this too and pinpoint one or two things that you appreciate about yourself. Taking in the good. Circumventing that tendency to be self-critical and instead appreciating something about ourselves.

Saying to yourself: 'I am grateful for my life'. Again, noticing any feelings that you have in your body no matter how slight.

Ways to cultivate gratitude

Be specific about what we are grateful for. To describe what we like about someone's friendship or our experience in the moment. This may include one or more of our senses. 'I like it that you make such tasty bread'.

To say thank you for the small things (and the big things) can help us not take things for granted.

- Beware of feeling entitled, that life owes us something. Our inner teenager may feel that life isn't fair, that we are entitled to have exactly what we want.

- Turn impediments into opportunities. A problem is a challenge. We may not like it but we can attempt to make the best of it and be grateful for our resilience.

- Turn 'I wish I was better at this' to 'I am having a go and I am grateful for the opportunity.'

- One way of not taking life for granted is to remember that we are mortal. We will eventually lose life and all we love.

Counting your blessings

Ram Das, a well-known meditation teacher, struggled with being dependent on others after becoming severely disabled after a stroke. At first, he was very resentful of his dependence, 'I've gone from being the helper to the helpee'. The dependency was so hard for him because he was a 'super-independent' person as a leader and a guru. Also, as an American, he saw how his culture valued independence and was shamed by dependence. After some time he realised that 'It was my vulnerability which opened me up to my humanity.' He wrote in his book *Still Here*: 'What a gift the stroke has given me.' The suffering caused by the stroke helped him to see that he was surrounded by love, 'The stroke created more love than I had ever seen before'.

Cindy Cooper, a dear friend and fellow teacher at the Centre for Mindfulness, Research and Practice in Bangor, said a similar thing about her terminal illness.

'And one other major thing that my illness has taught me is gratitude. What a gift this illness has been in the outpouring of people's love and concern, and how that opens my heart and it opens their hearts too. I remember feeling quite early in the diagnosis that this is something quite magnificently beautiful. We really meet each other in these deeply human places. It is so clear people want to give and to help. Interestingly, this has added another layer of practice for me – how do I open to letting people help me. This can be very difficult actually.'

– Cindy died two years after this interview, which is reproduced in full in Chapter 10.

A dialogue of self and soul

I am content to follow to its source

Every event in action or in thought.

Measure the lot; forgive myself the lot!

When such as I cast out remorse

So great a sweetness flows into the breast

We must laugh and we must sing,

We are blest by everything,

Everything we look upon is blest.

– W. B. Yeats

Blest by everything? There is a story in Rachel Remen's *My Grandfather's Blessings* that gives 'counting your chickens' a different slant.

RACHEL's mother was near death. Rachel wanted her to meditate with her because she thought that it would help her mother face her death more readily. Yet whenever Rachel opened her eyes her mother appeared to be just looking at her and not doing the meditation that Rachel wanted her to do.

Then one day she was lying quietly with her eyes closed. Rachel knew she was not sleeping and thought that at last her mother was cooperating with her. When Rachel asked her what she was doing she said, 'I was counting my chickens'. Rachel asked her what she meant, and she said that she had chicken once or twice a week for dinner most of her life. She was counting the weeks of her life. She worked out that about 8,500 chickens had sustained her over her life. She tried to imagine what this would look like.

'All that innocent life' she said. 'Was I worthy of it? So, I reviewed my life. I have tried to be kind and generous whenever I could and I have tried not to harm any person deliberately.' On reflection she felt she had lived a good life and that the chickens had helped by sustaining her.

Negative aspects of gratitude practice

Gratitude work comes with a warning. It doesn't help a depressed person to tell them to count their blessings or to tell them that they have everything they need, that they should be grateful. This could cause unnecessary harm.

Gratitude for the love and care of parents and or partners can be so rich for some people. But for others, for example, people who have experienced abuse either physically or emotionally, it is wise to distance themselves from the abusive one for their own preservation and wellbeing. Giving the perpetrator of abuse gratitude or appreciation is not likely to change their tendency towards abuse.

AMMA was doing a gratitude practice in class. The teacher invited her to be grateful for her parents. This was extremely upsetting for her; she burst into tears and then expressed her anger. 'I cannot be grateful to my parents. They are not worthy of it. I have spent many years trying to forgive them but I can't. Now I have my little Ella, my own baby, I am even more aware of their neglect and abuse.' She didn't tell us any details. The teacher emphasised that she did not have to force a feeling of gratitude – just to acknowledge her feelings here was enough. After a three-step breathing space Amma told us how she loved her own little girl and how grateful she was to be given a chance to love unconditionally.

Some things are impossible to come to terms with. The effects of war, cruelty, accidents and the death of a loved one may leave us devastated. But if we can find something to be grateful for, even in these difficult times, it may help us find a path through them. How much do we take for granted?

To be grateful is not to be in denial of the negative but to see the negative and the good in the situation at the same time, if possible – in this way, readdressing the balance as best one can. Nor is gratitude a stick with which to hit oneself or another. Don't say: *'I know I should be grateful'*, but try saying: *'Things are bad at the moment and... I still have these things to be grateful for'*.

For example, ageing fills one with contradictory thoughts. On one hand it is difficult to lose mobility of body and mind. It is hard to be grateful for this. On the other hand, for most of us, it is better to grow old than to die young. If growing old means loss, it may also mean the richness of the experience of a long life. Wrinkles and grey hair may seem to be frivolous examples. But many people, particularly women, in our culture will pay good money to be rid of them. Wrinkles are the map of our lives. Can we be grateful for them? After a certain age many old people do become proud of their age – 'I'm 90!' they declare, their eyes glowing with pride.

Resistance to gratitude meditation

Practise this when you are not feeling very appreciative of either your meditation or your life.

Breathing in, I am grateful for this in-breath that keeps me alive. Breathing in oxygen.

Breathing out, letting go of this breath, giving it out into the world. Breathing out for the trees and plants... giving them carbon dioxide.

Asking yourself: 'What blocks me from feeling happy, from feeling gratitude in my life?'

Being here, now, in the moment. Feeling the sense of aliveness in your hands, in your chest as it moves in time to the breath right now in this moment.

Breathing in, breathing out. Noticing whenever your mind wanders. Taking note of where your mind goes.

Hearing sounds; being grateful for the sense of hearing and distinguishing the sounds of your environment. The natural sounds of birds or the wind, perhaps the rain. The sounds of human activity. Hearing sounds as part of your world, feeling connected, feeling grateful. Taking in the full soundscape whether it be quiet and subtle or a cacophony.

Bringing a curiosity to what blocks you from feeling gratitude in this moment. Maybe this moment is not enough? Maybe you want something more? Maybe you are searching for some kind of entertainment, some drama. So being curious about what it is that takes us away from being present. This can be an intention or a theme in your practice for the moment. ➔

Do you want a peaceful, happy state from your meditation? Do you say to yourself: 'I will be happy when I have...'? Can you sense how this feeling of wanting, grasping, clinging feels in the body?

Does this wanting or not wanting overwhelm this moment? What is happening right now? Not grabbing on to it or trying to make it go away. Feeling the space around it.

Recognising the block, allowing it to be here – by fully acknowledging it. Investigating how the body reacts to each distraction from the moment. This can be the practice, to notice what pulls us away. This too we can be grateful for. This too is telling you about yourself and about what is present for you in the moment.

Saying to yourself 'This is enough. This moment is enough.'

Checking into the body, is there a pleasant sensation somewhere in the body? Perhaps just sitting, perhaps feeling your hands on your body, the breath breathing. Maybe sensing light or hearing a sound that pleases you.

What is pleasant in this moment? Is it possible to find something in this moment to be grateful for? Your body that is alive, your environment, your situation.

If you feel yourself resisting being grateful for your life because it is not how you want it right now, honouring this feeling. However, you are feeling in this moment, asking yourself 'is it possible to bring a gentleness to this?' If there is judging, noticing the judging, if there is warmth noticing warmth, if cold noticing coldness.

How would it be to bring an intention of kindliness to this moment?

Saying to yourself: *'I am doing my best at this moment, I am aware of obstacles, I am aware of resistance to this practice and yet I am here. I have shown up, I can meet this moment with compassion, I can be caring, kind to myself in this moment.'*

If this doesn't feel possible, saying to yourself *'This is hard for you'*, and breathing into your heart area and breathing out from your heart area.

There is no right way to feel, just acknowledging how you are in this moment and having an intention to be gentle and caring towards yourself and to others who are sharing in your experience in this moment. Again and again, remembering to be aware in this moment. This moment is the only moment in which to experience your life.

Is it possible to feel appreciation towards yourself? Consider the work you have done to get here, the practice you have worked with, the effort you have made.

Breathing-in in appreciation, breathing-out a thank you for all the people and circumstances that have helped you to arrive here to this place in your life.

If this feels right wishing yourself well maybe using these phrases or others of your own choosing:

'May I be grateful.'

'May I appreciate my life.'

'May I be free in the midst of barriers and difficulties.'

'May I be thankful.'

'And wishing the same for others in your world.'   →

Or saying to yourself:

'Grateful for the breath.'

'Appreciating my life.'

'Thankful for all the tiny moments.'

If you would like to, you can set an intention to be generous, to give to others in your world, in the wider world. You can set an intention of generosity to listen to others, to pay attention to them by considering their needs and caring for them as best you can. Thanking them in your heart and wishing them well.

The world needs our awareness, our care.

Gratitude on 10 fingers

This is a short meditation that is useful to do every day, perhaps just before bed.

Sitting or lying quietly with your hands together. Now feeling the thumb of your right hand, as you trace the side of your thumb with a finger of your other hand recalling something you are grateful for. It can be the smallest thing like the comfort of sitting or lying here. Or you could think of someone or thing that is precious to you. When you have finished the movement of your left-hand finger on your right thumb, slowly move your left finger to your right index finger and think of someone or something else to be grateful for. (If this brings up sorrow or any aversive emotion, stop to be with this with a RAIN meditation.)

Continue tracing the outline of all fingers on the right hand and on each finger finding someone or thing to be grateful for.

Now change hands and with the other hand finger trace the left thumb recalling or visualising anything you are grateful for. It could be as simple as the sound of the birds or a gentle breeze in summer. Continue tracing on each finger on the left hand, finding some small or big thing to be grateful for.

Research on gratitude practice

In recent years there have been several scientific studies into the effect of gratitude practice. It has been found to be useful for wellbeing and for physical health problems, including heart conditions.

Amie Gordon has undertaken many studies of positive appreciation and gratitude practice within romantic relationships. The studies found that appreciating your partner has mutual benefits, that the appreciation is often reciprocated. The couples who demonstrated appreciation responded to each other with hugs when they were feeling troubled and when they were feeling good. The research found these relationships are more likely to be long-lasting (Gordon *et al*, 2012).

Research studies have been undertaken on the value of keeping a **regular gratitude journal**. Writing down on a regular basis what we are grateful for may well be a beneficial and enjoyable practice for some people, whatever their physical or mental health. *'It seems that a more grateful heart is indeed a healthier heart, and that gratitude journaling is an easy way to support cardiac health,'* said Paul J Mills, Professor at the University of California, San Diego, who conducted a gratitude and journaling study (Mills *et al*, 2015).

As well as better heart health, their research found that the subjects experienced improved sleep and mood. The study was undertaken with 186 people who had asymptomatic (Stage B) heart failure for at least three months. Some of the group were asked by the researchers to write down three things for which they were grateful. They were to do this most days for eight weeks. These patients showed improved heart health and had improved wellbeing. They had better sleep, less depression and less fatigue than the control group.

Emmons and McCullough's 2003 research was a 10-week experiment with people who were all asked to write a weekly report. One group wrote about what they were grateful for. Another group wrote down things they found irritating or didn't like. The third group wrote down things that made an impression on them, either negative or positive.

The results showed that the gratitude group reported being happier and healthier than the people in the other two groups.

Participants in this group wrote down at the end of the day any positive events which made them happy. This activity apparently helped them sleep at night as they reported feeling calmer. It also lowered their self-reported stress levels.

Emmons, a Professor at the University of California, said this about keeping a gratitude journal:

> *'Writing helps to organize thoughts, facilitate integration, and helps you accept your own experiences and put them in context.'*

He says that there is no right way to do it but it helps if you make a conscious decision to be more grateful. *'Motivation to become happier plays a role in the efficacy of this journaling,'* says Emmons.

However, gratitude journals don't always work. Some studies show benefits, others do not.

Keeping a gratitude journal

The act of writing things down enables you to emphasise the importance of the event or person you feel gratitude towards, but simply reliving the experience and giving it some attention can be also effective. Therefore, it may be equally effective to do a gratitude meditation before bedtime.

There is a body of research showing that writing a gratitude journal does have an impact upon personal happiness. Being specific about what you are grateful for and drawing out detail also have been shown to be beneficial. If it is difficult to fit in a daily diary, writing once a week rather than every day may be more realistic as you can pick and choose the most important aspects of your life.

You can buy specific gratitude journals and find templates online. You can choose a beautiful notebook or just a cheap jotter. You can use your computer. If you are artistically inclined you can illustrate your journal with pictures. Some people blog their gratitude diaries on Instagram.

A gratitude journal is a physical intention to nurture gratitude. You begin to look for gratitude inducing things.

To make the most of your gratitude journal:

- Stay focused. Remember it is a journal about gratitude not your disappointments or your wishes.

- Consciously practise being more grateful and look out for opportunities to be grateful.

- Write in depth and give details.

- Be grateful for people not things.

- Be aware of the unexpected.

- Reflect on what you love and what you would miss if it wasn't there.

- Don't rush it. Enjoy it.

A writing exercise on gratitude and celebration

Oneself

Spend a little time reflecting on your life. Quickly without censor write down some of your good qualities. Qualities you are grateful to have. Maybe it's a good sense of humour, a good appetite and an appreciation of food. It could be you are kind-hearted and generous. Maybe you love to run or to sing. List what you are grateful for in your life. Showering praise on yourself as if you were speaking at your own funeral or maybe writing a blurb for your autobiography.

A loved one

Contemplate some of the good qualities of a loved one. A tribute to this person at the moment. If there is nobody that springs to mind choose a pet or favourite place. Write down what makes you feel grateful when you think about them. Again, imagine you are speaking at their funeral or writing a reference or a blurb for the back page of their autobiography. →

A neutral person

Bringing to mind now a person who you see regularly but who is just an acquaintance. What good qualities can you bring to mind about this person. Maybe their smile, their sense of humour, their kindness. Finding something to commend them. Write it down. Being grateful just for their very existence in the world.

Someone you don't like or find a little tricky

Now here's a challenge. Reflecting that this person too has good points. Imagining how you can celebrate their life. Finding some good qualities to applaud and appreciate. Noticing how you want to focus on the negative aspects of this person and allowing yourself generosity of spirit. Checking into the body to see how this feels. Then write down their good points as if you really mean it. Try to see what their own loved ones see in them. Again, seeing it as a tribute or commendation.

Now imagining all four of them together in one room. They each say one word about themselves. What one word do you choose for each person?

Gratitude and generosity

This meditation is a practice in giving back. Acknowledging what you are grateful for and practising saying thank you. We can practise this quietly to ourselves and then we may decide to say thank you in person to express our gratitude.

Breathing in gratitude – for the nourishment of the air. For life.

Breathing out generosity – a wish to give out.

First, bring to mind a person in your world who has been giving to you. Remember how it felt to receive their kindness. As best you can, stay with this feeling in your heart. Feeling gratitude for their giving to you. Saying thank you in your mind or out loud if it is appropriate. Thank you for your kind attention. Thank you for your care.

Now recall someone or maybe a pet you care about. Remembering how he or she looked. Remembering an expression on his or her face. Noticing the feeling in your body when you think of him or her.

Letting the feeling of love be here and the arising of the feeling of warmth or other feelings. Allowing a sense of tenderness. Feeling grateful that this person or animal is in your life. Giving out a sense of gratitude, a thanking. Saying thank you to them in your mind. Having an intention to thank them in some way when you are able.

Now recall someone you feel you could be more generous towards. Noticing judgement, the 'I should be kinder, more attentive' when you think of them. Bringing a sense of forgiveness to yourself for your previous lack and having an intention to extend some generosity towards them when you are able.

Now staying with your own body and heart. Breathing-in in gratitude for this life-giving oxygen received from the plants.

Now, on the out-breath, having a sense of giving out, as you breathe out carbon dioxide as a gift to the plants.

Breathing in gratitude for your lungs breathing it in, for your heart pumping blood. This wonderful body. Being grateful for your life. →

Breathing out letting go, giving out a sense of generosity. A sense of giving out.

Continue breathing in and breathing out for the rest of your day. For the rest of your life.

A 'catalogue of merits' journal

Buddhist teacher Ayya Khema suggested keeping a diary that was called a 'catalogue of merits'. This journal is to note your good deeds or positive actions. This to many of us feels big-headed and 'counterintuitive'. I practised this for several months some years ago and it felt strange to write down any good deeds in a journal. The fact that it was a private journal was essential.

I did, however, share some of the entries with my friend and colleague Judith Soulsby, who was also working with this practice. It was an interesting and intimate connection. The onus and privilege of this endeavour meant I took it seriously. I enjoyed writing it and still have the journal with its beautiful purple silk cover. It felt very different to a CV, which is also a practice of enhancing your profile!

Prayer

Traditionally, many religious and cultural traditions have ritual gratitude practices. There have been several academic studies on gratitude and prayer. Lambert et al (2009) found that student athletes who were randomly assigned prayer practice daily showed more gratitude after four weeks.

Research by Adler and Fagley (2005) found that rituals and prayer reminded people to be thankful. They surmised that the repetitive aspect of prayer acted as a reminder to be aware of gratitude in their lives.

Muslims and Christians have prayers that acknowledge the blessings in their lives. First Nation people in North and South America bow in appreciation to Father Sky and Mother Earth. The indigenous peoples of New Zealand and Australia also show a deep respect and gratitude to nature. Buddhists have gratitude chants.

Tibetan Buddhists have gratitude prayers even for the suffering in their life. They believe that their suffering helps them to become more compassionate. One expression of this is the prayerful: *'Grant that I might have enough suffering to awaken in the deepest possible compassion and wisdom.'*

The Dalai Lama tells a story about a Tibetan monk imprisoned in Communist China. He felt grateful to his tormentors because he had an opportunity to practise forgiveness and compassion. By bearing his suffering and forgiving his tormentors he was transformed into a more compassionate human being.

The Buddha said:

'These two people are hard to find in the world. "Which two?" we ask. "The one who is first to do a kindness, and the one who is grateful and thankful for a kindness done."

'If the only prayer you said was thank you, that would be enough.'

– Meister Eckhart

In my 60s I went to the Himalayas with my husband John and a group of four friends and a trekking company called 'Beyond the Limits' (I should have been warned!) It was hard work, but the beauty of the Himalayas truly compensated for aching legs, blisters and uncomfortable conditions. It was heavenly. So much pleasure, so much freedom. Just walking under vast skies in the sunshine. It was easy to be in the moment, the senses so alive.

But a story usually needs a dark side, or an element of risk and this one is no exception. In my case we arrived rather too quickly at high altitude and I had difficulty breathing and in fact moving at all. To go down as advised in the manual would take another six hours, which was impossible as we had taken all day to arrive at our night stop – the only habitation was within a day's journey. So we crawled into the village after dark, our hands and faces freezing.

Fortunately, we were met by a Tibetan woman who held my hands to warm them and took us into her kitchen where she was cooking on a wood fire. I loved that woman.

I had heard stories of people dying in their sleep at high altitudes so I slept in all my clothes with the window open to get as much oxygen as I could. It was so cold. And yet, miserable as I was, I noticed how many stars there were and how bright. At dawn (awake because it was so cold) I saw a beautiful sunrise over the iconic fishtail mountain (Machhapuchare).

After a day or two we had somewhat acclimatised and we set off even higher. After resting for a few days in Nar (a remote village with no access by road only by footpath), we set off on ponies to trek over the Kang-la pass, 5,322 metres high. Even the ponies struggled at this altitude. Then the puffing ponies went home and left us to ascend to the very top on foot. It was impossible to walk at a normal pace – we shuffled up, such was the effect of altitude. It was even slower than mindfulness walking.

Short of breath, I struggled up to the top – the top of the world. I could see the whole of the Annapurna range all around me. But for once I did not want to linger and appreciate. I felt awful physically. I was also terrified. Following my breath, which was short and painful, was my only option. Heart pounding, limbs barely able to move, this was one of the few truly life-threatening moments I have experienced.

I inched down the other side of the mountain. At my lowest point I sat by the guide and cried. 'I am dying', I thought. On top of the physical discomfort there were the extra emotional layers. I felt a failure, the deep shame of being mortal! The shame of being weak and not making it! I sat there on the barren scree slope and felt disappointment that I wasn't 'cool' about facing death. Where was the self-compassion now?

Is it the culture or is it just me that feels shame around illness and, in this case, my own death on a lonely mountain? In that moment I was still alive, but my energy, my head space was taken up with self-doubt, anxiety, disappointment and, yes, anger. I was angry with my companions who had sped off to a more comfortable breathing space. I felt abandoned and unloved. This story didn't end in my death so I can't know what my thoughts would have been had I been truly dying.

It is interesting how many emotions were present in this life and death situation. So many thoughts about who I am. The main ones were 'I don't want to die here. I want to see my children, grandchildren and friends again. Not this now.' This sense of loss and sadness was the strongest feeling. This longing to see my loved ones again has left me with a lasting sense of gratitude that they are in my life.

Gradually, I began to notice these thoughts as negative thoughts, extra and unnecessary. The fear, the shame, the disappointment, the anger all wrapped up in the 'story' of me'. I was able to bring some compassion to myself, and an absolute appreciation for that which I had taken so long for granted, my breath. This in- and this out-breath and then oh joy, this inbreath again, no matter how short. I joined my friends whose love and concern was overwhelming. Someone took my bag. John hugged me and with their help, I made it down that very steep mountain. Again, more gratitude!

We are mortal. It is humbling. And we must make the most of it while we can.

For the rest of the trek I felt enormous gratitude; so glad to be alive, so in love with the beauty of the Himalayan people and landscape, so appreciative of my friends and family and my companions on the trek.

Six short gratitude practices

1 A walk of appreciation

Decide to walk mindfully for a short time. Five to ten minutes at first. Using the five senses, consciously take in and appreciate what you perceive sense by sense. When your mind wanders bring it back to the senses you are experiencing in this moment.

2 A walk of gratitude

Ask yourself as you walk along 'What am I grateful for?' and reply with 'I'm grateful for…'. Then ask yourself again 'and what else are you grateful for?' Continue to do this for a set time or a set distance.   →

3 The five senses sitting or lying meditation

Choose to sit or lie down with an intention to stay for five to ten minutes, being aware of your five senses and appreciating what you perceive.

4 Notice what you take for granted

Spend a few moments each day noticing what you take for granted and savour them.

5 Thank people

Get into a habit of noticing what people do for you. Thank them and be specific. 'Thank you for the way you… Thank you for including me… Thank you for phoning'. Sometimes a little thank you gift or email may be highly significant.

6 Contemplate death and loss, yours or a dear one (when you feel able)

This contemplation may be included in a sitting meditation. It may cause anxiety or upset so it is necessary only to do this for as long as feels right for you in this moment. Maybe just to touch on it for a moment and be grateful for your own or another's life. If that person or beloved pet has died is it possible to be grateful that he or she was once in your life?

You could also do this if you are suffering a loss of status or possessions.

18 Simple Steps to Appreciating Your Garden in the Spring

1. Find a time when you're not fully awake and no one else is around.
2. Make some tea or coffee in your favourite cup.
3. Put on appropriate clothing.
4. Wander out into your garden (or yard or nearby park).
5. Walk naturally and without purpose, as if you did this all the time.
6. Imagine that you are at home here – that the garden may be greeting you even as you greet the garden.
7. Notice what attracts your attention and move towards it.
8. Get close and look closely.
9. Touch it gently as if you were shaking a tiny hand.
10. Look to see what is next to it and what it might be doing.
11. Continue wandering and noticing without purpose.
12. Gently see what you haven't seen before.
13. After some time, find a place to sit and rest for just a few minutes.
14. Receive whatever comes – through your eyes and ears, through your nose and skin, through your mind and imagination.
15. Consider that you may be here simply to appreciate.

16. After some time, take your cup and go inside.

17. Don't try to talk about what you experienced in the garden.

18. Let whatever happened or didn't happen be enough.

– David Rynick

Wonder

'This too is wonder'
Were her last words.
What was the wonder?

This breath, this last breath
In this tiny old lady's chest
Breath filling the world
and emptying again.

The full high tide
Followed by low tide
As the sea recedes
Leaving the way clear.

The last moment of wonder
What was it?
Gratitude
For her lived-in life?

Or for this moment
Wondered at now?
Or a glimpse
Beyond breath?

We shall never know.

– Annee Griffiths

Chapter 9:
Continuing to Practise –
Keeping It Alive

Rivers know this: there's no hurry. We shall get there one day.

A.A. Milne, 'Winnie the Pooh'

One day a woman was walking in the mountains. The path narrowed to a ledge winding round the edge of a cliff. Suddenly a tiger came around the corner. He was too close to run back the way she had come. So she scrambled down the cliff as fast as she could and took hold of a creeper. The tiger stood looking down at her from the top of the cliff. No way back up. She looked down and saw more tigers waiting at the bottom. Tigers above, tigers below. What to do? She held on to the vine desperately. Then she noticed two mice nibbling the vine at the top. It was hanging by a thread. She looked to her right and saw a wild strawberry. Swinging out to reach it she plucked it and ate it. Oh, so sweet!

This well-known Zen story resonates with me when I feel like a rabbit in the headlights. Which way to go? What to do? So useful is that mindful pause, when we can just to stop and breathe and take in the moment.

We need to be here for our moments. Many people have told me that, although they find it difficult and find excuses not to practise, mindfulness meditation does benefit them, and it helps when they are having difficulties. They appreciate Jon Kabat-Zinn's encouragement 'to weave the parachute before you jump out of the plane', however, they have many strategies for avoiding sitting in formal meditation.

Nevertheless, we may find it easy occasionally to sit simply with or without a cup of tea and watch the birds in the garden or the clouds out of the window. A natural meditation may be standing by a fast mountain stream listening to the sounds or sitting on the beach noticing waves lapping or bashing the shore. Watching or listening to raindrops on a windowpane or cloud-gazing can be prompts to anchor us into the present moment. This relaxed way of being does not register as meditation for most of us and yet this could give us a necessary break from a mind that wishes to be busy, busy, busy. These are all informal meditation practices and when we recognise this it may help us to realise that we do practice. The next step is to create the conditions for a more formal intentional practice where we mark out a time and place for meditation practice.

> You will not find the boundaries of psyche
>
> by travelling in any direction, so deep
>
> is the measure of it

– Heraclitus

A hunter goes into a forest. He wanders around for days and does not catch anything. But his time is not wasted for he has learned the paths and habits of the forest. In the same way we are learning about the forest of our minds, its ways and habits, whether or not we capture that coveted experience. It is the journey, not the arrival. When we let go of a perceived goal, we are the richer.

> *'After you practice for a while, you will realize that it is not possible to make rapid, extraordinary progress. Even though you try very hard, the progress you make is always little by little'*

– Suzuki: Zen Mind Beginner's Mind

Suzuki compares meditation practice to going out in a mist. You gradually get wet without noticing. Practising meditation is not like going out in a storm and getting soaked. It is an accumulation of experience. Drop by drop. Practice is how you master it.

To explore and experiment with practice is to keep it alive and allow more spaciousness in our lives. On every Staying Mindful course there are several participants who notice how they have treated their practice as yet another chore and have been harsh with themselves for not doing it regularly. This can take the form of chiding themselves with the threat of becoming unwell again with stress-related illnesses. Their attitude to practice changes with the realisation that they do not have to be stiff around their practice, they can be creative and exploratory. They connect to the fact that it is a heart practice and that we must find our own way to make it relevant to each one of us as we are unique.

Present

Out in late afternoon light
after days of rain, seeking

a gratuitous moment and finding one:
a flight of white birds, silent as angels,
that come and come, carried on the wind,
in drifts towards the west

white seabirds, flying low
towards the Irish sea

sailing past, above me, not that high
for minutes, more and more,
as if blown towards the sunset

and the halfmoon hangs in the blue
and the puffball clouds scud on

– Fiona Owen

SUKI was very struck with the metaphor of the practice being like a bird with two wings: the wing of mindfulness and the wing of compassion. She said she'd been a one-winged bird striving to be more concentrated and to be aware in the present moment without bringing her heart to the practice. She was struck by the realisation that mindfulness is a Western translation of the more eastern approach of heartfulness. This realisation that the practice has both wisdom and love can give us wings to freedom.

Bird Wings

Your grief for what you've lost lifts a mirror

up to where you are bravely working.

Expecting the worst, you look, and instead,

here's the joyful face you've been wanting to see.

Your hand opens and closes and opens and closes.

If it were always a fist or always stretched open,

you would be paralysed.

Your deepest presence is in every small contracting and expanding,

the two as beautifully balanced and coordinated

as birdwings.

– Rumi, translated by Coleman Barks

KATERINA felt her practice nurtured the vulnerable part of herself. Like a chick in the nest this tender part could not be hurried to heal but needed a period of time being nurtured and fed until she too was ready to fly independently.

Above all, be patient with your practice and with yourself. Sometimes the work can feel slow, yet all you need to do is to focus on bringing more awareness into your life little by little and you will notice the difference. Often people notice the difference more in everyday life than in their meditation practice.

Everyone needs support for practice. Communicating with other like-minded people is supportive. You can seek out specific groups or friends and arrange to meet to practise together. Your teacher or others from an eight-week course may set up a follow-up group in your area. Also, there may be an opportunity to join with the all-day of practice, which is included in the eight-week course. This gives you a flavour of a retreat and the luxury of practising for a longer period with others.

YouTube videos are a valuable resource, and nothing quite beats a book. Inspirational reading of mindfulness or meditation books may well inspire and further your practice. There is a reading list at the end of this book. Meditation apps have become popular in recent years. More information on these later in the chapter.

You could also consider going away on retreat for a few days. It is quite an experience. There are plenty of retreat centres around the country and abroad.

Meditation retreats

What does going on retreat mean for most of us? It is usually a chance to step out of our everyday preoccupations, recharge our batteries and find inspiration and new meaning in our lives. For some it is a spiritual journey, for others it is a chance to experience the unique opportunity to be in silence with others in a beautiful environment. It is about self-discovery. For some it is to find out experientially what meditation is really about and for others it is to explore and deepen an existing meditation practice.

Sharon Salzberg, a leading meditation teacher in the United States, suggests that we could see a retreat as an experiment. An experiment in happiness. It gives us plenty of time and space to get into the weave and warp of our lives and to explore the territory that is ourselves. A retreat is intensive and the work we do here invaluable. We learn more about who we are so that we can act more skilfully in our life. Those of us who have done the eight-week MBSR or MBCT course may be familiar with the all-day of practice. Many people who first come to this all day do so reluctantly, apprehensive of a day in silence, saying: 'I can't be silent for a day, it's impossible' and their friends and relations will all agree. They are often surprised both because they managed to be quiet and that they learnt so much. This all-day is a unique opportunity to pay attention moment by moment and to discover and explore new layers of experience that are easily missed in our everyday lives.

A retreat, especially a silent one dedicated to mindfulness practice, extends the experience of the all-day. The opportunity to be with many states of mind allows us to notice how experience changes moment by moment as we practice cultivating patience and compassion. Our personal stories will absorb us for some of the time, but given plenty of time and space, we begin to foster a different relationship to our stories or obsessions. We may notice where we hold these in the body and in time learn to let go or at least be able to step back from them, so that these stories of who we think we are don't take over our experience so readily. At times we can see that we are more than just our stories, obsessions and personality and we experience a release from their hold on us. We may experience moments of profound peacefulness and spaciousness.

Retreats are often held in places of great beauty and the silence means that we can have a different relationship with nature; our senses are enhanced as we awaken to the beauty around us. Silence also invites us to experience a different relationship with others in the group. Even though people may not be talking to each other in the usual way there is often a sense of togetherness and support from other members. A sense of common endeavour. As the group practise together in silence there is a growing deep connection.

*'We can make our minds so like still water that beings gather about
us that they may see, it may be, their own images, and so live for
a moment with a clearer, perhaps even with a fiercer life because
of our quiet.'*

– W.B. Yeats

The main emphasis on a silent retreat is on doing sitting (or lying)
meditation, alternating with walking meditation and some movement
practice. The teacher or teachers are not completely silent as there is
some meditation guidance, particularly at the beginning. There are also
opportunities for short individual sessions with the teacher or teachers
and the possibility of group discussion at some point and especially at the
beginning and the end of the retreat. There are usually daily talks and poems
given by the teacher to further enhance the learning, develop insight and
inspire and deepen the retreat experience.

The Mindfulness Network offer several different retreats. Some are suitable
for beginners and some for people with more meditation experience. I teach
some of the meditations and exercises from this book on the Staying Mindful
Retreat. This retreat differs from many other retreats offered for meditation
practice. It aims to remind and further the participants' relationship to
the familiar practices while developing a deeper understanding of practice
in general. There is a group discussion and a few interactive practices.
It is useful for anyone wishing to enhance their meditation experience, to
improve motivation and inspiration to practise and for mindfulness teachers
wishing to run their own follow up courses.

Here are some participants' comments about the silent retreats they have
taken with us:

*'I was quite frightened at the idea of being silent and just being with myself.
I found it quite amazing, a completely new experience; there were tears at
times but more times when I found myself smiling and completely in the
moment.'*

'I learned a lot about myself; it wasn't always pleasant, but it was useful.'

*'I was surprised by how many moments of beauty there were. At one point
I wanted to hug a tree and I'm just not like that... and the food... it was
incredible. I could really taste it. I felt so alive.'*

'I feel refreshed and rejuvenated.'

*'The retreat provided a very good transition from eight-week courses and
structured practices to a deeper underlying mindfulness practice.'*

The following poem is written by Lindsey Tossell, a Staying Mindful student,
after a silent retreat:

In the Silence

In the silence

I see I am welcome

and the one who welcomes

this human flesh and blood into existence

In the silence

I see I am the flesh and blood

And the unfathomable timeless space

out of which this human existence arises

Born, welcomed again

over and over

into each moment

fresh, new, unknown

In the silence

I can feel my heart beating in my chest

My breath coming in

and going out

And I can see my thoughts are not entirely believable

and my emotions will ebb and flow

like the tide, ceaselessly touching my heart

like the roar of pebbles, under the oceans heave

In the silence

the blurry picture of my life comes more into focus

Choices emerge

I am not a victim

When the light

of kindness sheds its warm glow

over my existence

I see that I'm already at home

I have been all along

but I didn't know it

– Lindsey Tossell

The following poem is by Vicki Thomas who participated in a retreat I led with Sarah Millband in Trigonos in Snowdonia.

Silence is enough

17 people sit in silence
By a shimmering lake
And vast mountains in solid stillness

17 people walk very slowly in silence
Hearing the rushing brook, sensing foot touching earth.

17 people eat in silence
Tasting mouth-watering, home-grown food
Taking time to eat, the echoing sound of steel on plates

17 people sleep in silence
Gentle wind and rain on waking at night

17 people listen as the tinkling bell rings
Time to walk silently to the next cup of tea...
To hear the crunch of feet on gravel
The rustle of cloth as coats are removed

17 people lie in silence
Bringing presence
To their soft, breathing bodies
Sensing their feet, their arms, their faces.

17 people stand silently in awe, one last evening
Watching as the full moon slides out in its silver glory
From behind the vast dark shape of the mountain.

17 people being together for four long stretched-out days

Like the silent lake outside, connecting deeply.

No words are needed in these still waters.

Silence is enough.

Oh how the world needs this silence…

– Vicki Thomas

Meditation apps

At the time of writing I found a few useful apps that some of my friends found invaluable. There are many other apps on the market. Search for mindfulness apps on the web to find the most suitable for you.

The Oxford MBCT app: This is an excellent resource. It has several guided meditations from teachers from the Oxford Mindfulness Centre and the Centre for Mindfulness Research and Practice. It includes other useful resources including talks from the teachers. The app is to support people going through MBCT and beyond the eight-week course. It is freely available at: http://mbctapp.oxfordmindfulness.org/

The Centre for Mindfulness, Research and Practice has audio downloads at:

https://www.bangor.ac.uk/mindfulness/audio/index.php.en

Headspace is an extremely popular app which is recommended by many health professionals and is very engaging. It has over 36 million members across 190 countries. It doesn't use jargon and offers bite-sized chunks of meditation. It has made meditation accessible for many people who would not or could not attend a class. It is excellent for beginners.

The **ZenFriend** app is user-friendly. There are a number of choices. One, two or three bells for starting and ending the meditation and interval bells to remind you that you are meditating. You can select the length of your sit. You have a choice of about 14 (at the last count) sounds. A range of pretty bell sounds, some meditation bowl sounds including a deep Tibetan gong, a Japanese style woodblock and even a higher sound bell called Energy. There is one called 'waterdrop', which can be used intermittently during the meditation. The timer will inform you how many times you have used the app in the last month and since you first downloaded it. You can be told how many days in a row you have meditated and if you miss a day it goes back to zero, this is an incentive for some people. At the end of the meditation there is an inspirational quote and space for journaling. You can also see how many people are meditating at the same time as you and even connect with friends. On this app there are guided meditations by meditation teachers.

Insight Timer also has a wonderful collection of guided meditations and community links including a map which shows how many people are meditating worldwide. It has a choice of seven beautiful Tibetan bell sounds and all the features of the ZenFriend. Both these apps are a great aid to those who have smart phones and can be downloaded onto personal commuters, tablets, iPads and iPods.

Calm has a lot of variety and uses Stephen Fry and Matthew McConaughey as engaging voices. It uses 10-minute videos of movement practice that many find helpful.

Short practices

Short practices are useful aids to maintaining a mindful life. We learn on the eight-week course to do the three-step breathing practice and the three-step coping practice. Many people find these short practices to be a life-saver and for some people it becomes their main practice.

The following meditations are very short, but we can have an intention to choose one or a different one of them week by week.

1. Have an intention to notice the first breath in the morning and the last breath at night.

2. Be there for each cup of tea or coffee you drink. Taste your cup of tea, really being there for it.

3. Take a mindful pause, capturing the moment you are in right now. Taking a snapshot of what you are seeing, or a sound shot of what you are hearing.

4. Take a mindful breath in between one work assignment and another.

5. Be mindful of the steps as you walk to a pre-chosen area in the house or garden or office. The walk from the bus or the car to work or school/nursery, the purposeful journey.

6. Be aware every time you walk up the stairs.

7. Stepping outside the door and taking a breath of fresh air, looking about you, perhaps choosing one thing to focus on the sky or a flower.

The Five Senses Meditation

This short practice brings you into the present moment immediately.

Closing the eyes

Hearing: listening to sounds inside you, inside the room and outside.

Then move to the sense of seeing, opening the eyes. ➔

Seeing: what's just in front of you. Seeing a wider view. Practising using a wide-angle vision and then focusing in close. Noticing something at hand and seeing shapes, colours, textures, shades.

Smelling: sniffing and noticing if there is a smell or seeking out a smell.

Tasting: is there a taste in your mouth perhaps toothpaste or tea/coffee, maybe neutral?

Touching: feeling your feet on the floor, your bottom on the seat, your hands with whatever they are touching. Feeling the sense of clothes on your body, the air on your face.

Bringing a sense of gratitude to each of the senses one by one.

Letting go of focusing on a particular sense and allowing awareness to whatever sense arises in your consciousness moment by moment.

When conditions are right this Five Senses Meditation can be a source of wonder. The beauty of the world we live in sensed and savoured moment by moment. How wonderful to enjoy the senses, to be conscious.

'One touch of nature makes the whole world kin.'
– **Shakespeare,** *Troilus and Cressida***, Act 3, Scene 3**

Zen Koan practice

David Rynick and Melissa Blacker are teachers in the Zen tradition. Both have taught mindfulness classes in the past. They are an inspiration for my own meditation practice. Some years ago, I decided I wanted to study koans in order to keep my practice fresh and hinder my tendency to fix or conceptualise what my practice was about. I mention it here as a further option for keeping the practice alive. There are many other inspirational ways such as different religious traditions and cultural adaptions, but I may not be so familiar with them. It is for everyone to find their own path. The path with heart.

Koans are often tricky stories that make no sense at all to the rational mind. But when the stories are meditated on, they may provide insights into a different way of seeing the world. The most famous of these koans is 'the sound of one hand clapping'. Koan study is undertaken with a teacher who follows a tradition that goes back to the 8th century in China. It is not a practice that suits everyone. It can seem esoteric as the stories are about people from another time and culture. Nevertheless, they are just as human as we are and the universality of the truth behind the story can be quite enlightening. The encouragement to 'practise like your hair is on fire' that Jon Kabat-Zinn uses is from the Koan tradition. *The Gateless Barrier* is a collection of koans compiled in the early 13th century in China. The paradox within the title is continued throughout the 48 stories and commentaries within the book.

Gateless is the Great Tao,

There are thousands of ways to it,

If you pass through this barrier,

You may walk freely in the universe.

– Mumon

'*The barrier is something we encounter when we imagine that the life we're presently living is somehow lacking – that this life is not a life of practice. Passing through means seeing through a construction of our own making.*'

– Melissa Blacker

Snowdrops

As the snow retreats

they surprise me every year

in the same place.

– David Rynick

Anne Frank innately knew that people can be 'good at heart'. She lived her life under extraordinary circumstances and wrote an astonishing testimony that despite terrible life experiences we can believe in the goodness of humanity. Anne hid from the Nazis in an attic in the Netherlands from 1941–1944 and died in a Nazi concentration camp aged 15. To me it is worth considering that 'in spite of everything' we can intend to believe in the basic goodness of humankind and to contribute to our own world.

In spite of everything, I still believe

That people are really good at heart.

I simply can't build up my hopes on a foundation

Consisting of confusion, misery and death.

I see the world gradually being turned into a wilderness,

I hear the ever-approaching thunder, which will destroy us, too,

I can feel the suffering of millions, and yet,

If I look up into the heavens

I think that it will all come right,

That this cruelty will end,

And that peace and tranquillity will return again.

This brings me back full circle to the first chapter when we reflected on the value of remembering our intention to practise and reminding ourselves why we practise. No matter how bad it gets there is always hope. The intention to practise being aware, being kind, being compassionate is a way of life.

On a lighter note, my granddaughter Iola is, at this time, almost the same age as Anne Frank and happily living in a different age. She gave me a 'Be Happy Jar' for my birthday. It is full of small pieces of paper with mood brightening phrases and her personal illustrations. The one I picked up today is funny and relevant.

'Be a pineapple. Stand tall, wear a crown and be sweet on the inside.'
(with acknowledgement to Kat Gaskin)

I also picked these two:

You owe yourself the love that you so freely give to others.

Hope = the only thing stronger than fear.

Hope is the thing with feathers
That perches in the soul,
And sings the tune without the words,
And never stops at all

– Emily Dickinson

It may be helpful to have a daily resource of inspirational words to refresh our practice. To keep hold of the thread of practice.

Flamingos

There are moments which gleam
Like jewels in a dark coronet.
Many are snapshots,
A delicious titbit lingering on the tongue.
A solitary tree lit up
Defying the approaching dusk.
A track of silver
Through the turquoise sea.
Or a view through the mist,
Houses stacked one on top of the other,
Like a labyrinthine wedding cake.

There was one afternoon
When we were quite young,
Yet old enough to sit still
In the sun by a lake,
Where we stared at 16 or 17 birds
All standing on one leg.
Their necks long, heads at right angles
Croquet sticks of the Red Queen.
From time to time
One would stretch out a pink wing,
A ballerina pirouetting.

Her backcloth a straw-yellow reed bed,
Where skulked the Kingfisher
Senor of the waters
In a flash of blue
Sifting the shallows.

We too were fishing
For sunlight and silence
We too landed
A peculiar peace
On that shore.

– Annee Griffiths

Chapter 10: Personal Stories

There is so much to be gleaned from others' experience – their stories can help us see things more clearly in our own lives and inspire us to keep trying, to stay mindful. This chapter contains six personal stories about how people used mindfulness to help with addiction, grief, illness, pain and other life challenges. There is also a moving conversation at the end of the chapter with Cindy Cooper talking to Rebecca Crane about coping with the last stages of cancer and continuing to practise and teach mindfulness. This was first published in the Centre for Mindfulness Newsletter.

Rosie's story

Rosie Seymour: After her father's sudden death when she was still a fresher at university, Rosie Seymour was traumatised and tried to resolve her emotional difficulties with alcohol. Although her stay at a recovery centre helped a little, it was only her ongoing practice of mindfulness that led to her recovery. She is now training to be a medical herbalist.

'I first came across meditation in a treatment centre in Spain. I was there due to a variety of addictions I'd developed to cope with the sudden death of my dad when I was 19. There was a meditation hut in the garden, full of beads, prayers on the wall, and a simple white cushion on a stool. I can still picture it now! I felt drawn to that hut, and the peace it offered, even though I had no clue what meditation was. I used to sit on the stool, and that was it really. I just sat, for once giving myself the opportunity to just be. I'd watch the light change on the wall, listen to the insects, and feel sensations in my body. It felt like a decompression. A way to start redressing the balance of years of self-destructive behaviour.

I stayed in that centre for four months, and when I came home studied the eight-week MBSR course with Annee one-to-one. I was so grateful for that opportunity, and we spent many hours in Annee's living room in North Wales doing body scans, sitting, stretching, and mindfully walking around the garden. Although the practise was often difficult, with intrusive thoughts, pain, restlessness, I noticed I always felt more grounded afterwards.

After years of suppressing I had a lot of feeling to do, and mindfulness gave me a reassuring and empowering way to do that. There was a list of core emotions on the wall at the treatment centre. We had a "process group" each morning that started with a check in. I remember staring at that list as I waited for my turn, trying very hard to pinpoint what I was feeling.

Was I angry? Scared? I had no idea! Sitting gave me a way to be with and explore my emotions. Get to know them. What does sadness feel like? How about anger? I'd often be unaware of how I was feeling until I sat down. I'd start thinking I was fine, and suddenly tears were rolling down my cheeks. Or I'd be wound up and expecting a "difficult" meditation and be quickly drawn into feelings of calm. I could never predict what was going to happen, the moment is full of surprises! However, I did start noticing certain patterns, for example, if I feel anxious and numb, it's likely there is suppression happening, and I need to create space to feel. I've learned that I'm an introvert and need plenty of alone time to feel energised and balanced. Now I take care to plan things around the reality of who I am, knowing that's OK.

Mindfulness has helped my relationships with other people – particularly family. We've been through a tough time together and grief can appear as many things – anger, strained relations. I've become much less reactive as now I have time to breathe and consider my responses to people and situations. It gives me the chance to unhook from old patterns and be present without the lens of the past. It doesn't *work every single time of course, I'm human, but it's so much better than it was; and this aspect of being human is important too.*

I'd never heard the term self-compassion before mindfulness, but boy did I need it! Self-kindness, loving kindness, maitri, I needed it all in spades! I'd spent so long treating myself badly and feeling ashamed of myself. It took a lot of work to even start feeling more kindly, and forgiving, but it has been an essential part of me learning to accept myself and has revolutionised how I relate with emotions and feeling states I once deemed negative such as anger, and shame. It also helps me to extend this compassion to others, recognising that we're all just doing our best.

I was too young when I went to treatment to accept the fact that I had to stop drinking for ever. I was convinced it was life event related, rather than a combination of trauma and genetics. So I tried many times to drink "normally". Meditation has been there throughout this journey, along with counselling, somatic experiencing therapy, and the support of friends and family. In December 2018 I finally realised that my life was indeed better off without alcohol.

This was also the time I started to come to terms with my fertility issues. Infertility is full of grief, uncertainty, and loss. Despite this, I'm more grounded than I've ever been. Being open about it helps, as do mindful activities such as long walks with my dog, running, and cold-water swimming. I was listening to an interview with Francis Weller recently and he asked, 'How big can you be? How large can you become in this moment? To get your arms around the most difficult things that life has thrown at you?' Mindfulness helps me create that expansiveness he's talking about. It gives me the space, kindness, and compassion to hold all of these immensely difficult things in a way that makes me feel acutely, and gratefully alive.'

– **Rosie Seymour**

Hannah's story

Hannah Griffiths is an environmentalist. She was a former activist with Friends of the Earth and then became a manager at the World Development Movement NGO when she became ill with ME. She writes poignantly of the difficulties in accepting a more passive role and of the support staying mindful has given her in starting a new career as a writer.

'Before I had Myalgic Encephomyelitis (ME/CFS) I thought I knew what "tiredness" was. I'd had two babies who didn't play by the sleep rule books. I was a driven environmental and social justice campaigner and

was working in a stressful, senior management role. I was busy and tired but motoring on through regardless even though I was often ill, normally with some viral thing which didn't help my seemingly endless sinusitis. I thought this was normal. I was having it all – a great career and being a hands-on Mum – and I thought feeling exhausted was the price you paid.

ME/CFS often has a sudden onset after a trigger like a viral illness. Mine, however, was gradual onset. I gradually wore myself down until my body forced me to listen. This is like burnout with knobs on: intense fatigue, brain fog, aching body and post-exertional malaise.

Conventional medicine can't help much with ME/CFS so I launched into a quest to educate myself as much as possible, to take back control, to cure myself. These are some of the things I've tried, with varying levels of success: supplements, sinus surgery, acupuncture, cognitive behavioural therapy, emotional freedom technique, graded exercise therapy, neurolinguistic programming, sleep training, restricted diets. And mindfulness.

Some of these things have cured some people, but realistically most people with ME do not fully recover. We aim for long periods of remission and wellness and we manage our lives with the goal of nurturing and supporting our bodies as much as possible so that healing can take place. Mindfulness has been fundamental in helping me to do this.

I did my first eight-week MBCT course on the NHS in Hackney, London, after being referred by the GP to a psychologist. At this time, I was in the middle of a staged return to work after four months' sick leave. I'd had my sinus surgery and my sinuses were much improved, but my fatigue was still phenomenal. I would work one day and need to stay in bed the next. I felt useless and slow-witted at work and guiltily absent at home.

I was obsessed with questions like "When am I going to be better?" and "What else should I be doing to get myself better?" I like to be in control and ME/CFS was thwarting me, maybe mindfulness would help me to take back control of my health and life?

The course did help me to feel more on top of things. It helped me to notice when I was fatigued (all the time!) and what I was feeling about my illness (frustrated, angry, failing). It helped me to understand myself in a different way and to plot my course forward. But it did not help with my symptoms, I was as fatigued and foggy as ever. And without fail I fell asleep in the body scan!

After the course I had one-to-one CBT sessions with the course leader who encouraged me to use mindfulness at times of intense tiredness and fogginess to be present with those feelings, instead of fighting against them. He would say, "If you can bring awareness to how and where you feel the fatigue in your body, you might find that the feeling is not so bad". I would want to shout, "That's not the point! The point is that this is ruining my life," but I would go away resolved to try anyway. I found it impossible to practise in times of intense fatigue, and I still do.

But I have slowly come to understand that he was right – the feelings of fatigue, fogginess and pain are not actually always that bad in their own right. They are not pleasant, but they are not always unpleasant either. A lot of the horridness arises from my brain's response to them, which typically goes something like this. "Oh, ****, I feel awful, I need to sleep and not to think, but oh no I'm meant to be doing X". Where the X can be any task or commitment – the kids are due home from school, I'm meant to be meeting a friend or going food shopping, the dinner isn't cooked, etc. This is followed by panic and guilty feelings, which use up more energy and stop me from resting.

I learnt a lot about this in a second eight-week course, Mindfulness for Health*, for people with chronic illness and pain. We looked at different dimensions of pain and illness: the physical feelings – called the primary suffering – and the emotional reactions to those feelings – the secondary suffering. This includes all the thoughts and emotions that we have about the pain like anxiety, tension, depression, fear, anger and worry. The secondary suffering can come to be more unbearable and debilitating than the primary suffering and may even make the primary pain worse through lack of sleep and increased tension. Awareness of secondary suffering, through mindfulness, can help it to dissolve.

By observing the thoughts and emotions arising in response to my physical symptoms I have been able to modify my behaviour and thoughts when I am feeling ill and tired. I strain and rail less against those symptoms and find it easier to take them as they come. The mind chatter of "I should be able to stop this from happening," or "This isn't fair," is easier to observe from a little distance and therefore to keep in its place. I think this is called acceptance, or something approaching it! This is very freeing – it's like there's still a brick wall there but I am no longer banging my head on it and I may even have discovered a door through it.

Because I now panic less and feel less guilt when I'm too ill or tired to function, I am now more likely to give my body the mental and physical rest it needs when my symptoms flare up. This has contributed to my flare-ups being less frequent, less intense and shorter-lasting. My body no longer crashes and burns in the same way it used to and I think mindfulness is a big part of why.

Mindfulness has also helped me a lot with sleeping. I used to suffer from insomnia and although other things have helped me enormously with this (mainly sleep hygiene and nebulised magnesium) I have also noticed that if I don't do any mindfulness practise for a few days then my sleep is likely to start going off kilter.'

Staying mindful

'Why is it at times so very hard to keep up with my mindfulness practice even when I know how much difference it makes? Sometimes my practice can be steady, for months and months. Yet at other times I neglect it or like a rebellious teenager I reject it. I can't be bothered, I'm a genius at making up excuses as to why I can't do a practice right now and a master of procrastination. As I no longer work and the kids are out all day, it's not normally that I don't have the time – time is one thing I do have. I eat consistently well; I very rarely skip brushing my teeth and yet this other element of self-care is much easier to neglect.

Staying mindful for me requires a combination of self-discipline and external help. The external help can come in many guises. A reminder on my phone. A set time of day. A retreat. A practice with friends. Talking about it to others. Reading about mindfulness. Teaching mindfulness to kids (I trained to do that! And I volunteer at my children's school).

The self-discipline can be harder to get a handle on. I know I can be very disciplined; I am certainly very achievement-focused and that helps, but it is still easier when there is some degree of external accountability. Simply deciding "I will re-start my mindfulness practice" does not work and other things need to kick me into action. Insomnia certainly does the trick – a sleepless night or two and I am back on that meditation stool before you can say "self-compassion". But I need to build other things into my life that will give me the impetus I need. The things that seem to work best for me are attending a regular group, having a regular practice with a friend or two, going on a retreat. Unfortunately, all these things are hardest to achieve when my health is bad, which is the time I need them most.

However, despite the hurdles, mindfulness is helping me with the most challenging thing I have faced in life and it has helped me to have less regret about my health and more appreciation of the fact that, whatever tomorrow may bring or yesterday held, today now is often actually pretty good. From a mindfulness perspective, and from many other perspectives too, there is indeed more right with me than wrong with me.'

*The book that goes along with this course is called *Mindfulness for Health: a practical guide to relieving pain, reducing stress and restoring wellbeing* by Vidyamala Burch and Danny Penman (2013) published by Piatkus in Great Britain.

– Hannah Griffiths

Tara's story

Tara Dew was an active GP who had to retire because of ill health. She found mindfulness to be extremely helpful both in accepting her new life and in managing a chronic illness. She now teaches mindfulness and has a role as an assistant to the main teacher at the Hermitage in Criccieth, North Wales

My journey with pain

'All was going according to plan until my body just gave up on me. I was 32 years old, a healthy fit doctor enjoying many interests including a trekking trip in the Himalayas. It was on this trip that a combination of hardships and infections challenged my health to the degree that for whatever reason I didn't recover. Then followed 10 years of chronic fatigue syndrome that left me, at my worst, bed-bound and barely able to speak. My body was also exhibiting all kinds of strange symptoms that defied medical definition and treatment and were often painful. My energy levels were about five per cent of my normal healthy self.

I was incredibly fortunate to have really supportive friends and teachers who could guide me through this time or simply be alongside me. I was also incredibly fortunate to already have an established meditation practice before I got ill. I needed it! One of the helpful phrases I would remember was "Don't make more of it than it is". This encouraged me to become as simple as possible with my experience of pain and illness, sifting out all the fears and stories from the raw physical sensations. Fear could escalate my pain rapidly, and the story of "It's been like this for so long and it will always be like this" could tip me into despair. If I could notice these thoughts and added emotions I could become more interested in what was actually present in my body without adding to it.

I tried very hard to be a good meditator and always turn towards my pain and other symptoms and be curious about them. I think I was too "good". I realised later on that I was actually being pretty hard on myself and denying myself painkillers as I thought I should look directly at my pain and not give in to medication. This required a lot of will power which I do seem to have. It's not always helpful though! Another phrase I treasure is: "Acceptance has nothing to do with will power!"

All this endurance was actually not coming from a place of kindness and gentleness. I gradually learnt to give attention not only to the pain but to the one in pain. This one was suffering and lonely and scared and hopeless at times. I thought I had to be strong to get through the tough times and yet I was gripping on to some sense of being in control. The idea of turning towards all the sadness and fear in myself felt like I would lose control and just drown. It didn't feel like a fruitful place to go. Yet I have another phrase that continues to help me now, which is "Give up without giving up". In other words, it is a letting go of the struggle without dropping into resignation and despair. Both the struggling against pain and the resignation involve being stuck in worlds of thinking. The giving up without giving up is like dropping out of all these worlds into something completely different. It feels very tender, alive, poignant and connected, not just with me but with all beings. A heartfelt place. Perhaps this is what acceptance means?

Another practice I have found invaluable over the years is asking myself "What else is here?" Pain is very sticky. It draws you in and your awareness becomes narrowed and glued to the intense sensations. You forget to notice all the other many aspects of your experience including the pleasant, the beautiful and the simply OK aspects. I now make sure that I balance my practice with plenty of "taking in the good", really noticing and appreciating goodness however it manifests.

I continue to live with a degree of chronic pain and tension and continue to value bringing a kindly awareness to my experience. I ask myself, "What exactly is this experience?" and "Is it possible to meet this?" The answer may be no – not yet anyway. It may be wise to do some mindful distraction, to notice the good around me, to access resources, to take medication… If the answer is "yes" then I ask myself, "How would it be to meet this experience as if I was meeting a good friend?" Sometimes, I find myself bringing to mind a sense of sharing a joke with a friend and feeling the warmth of that connection soaking into me. I then open to the pain with this inner warmth and smile. Occasionally I find myself playing with bringing the vibration of a laugh into parts of my body that are hurting. It can be surprising! Warmth, friendship and laughter are perhaps some of the best medicines!'

– Tara Anne Dew

Tim's story

Tim Clark worked in further education as a lecturer and an Inspector for The Office for Standards in Education, Children's Services and Skills (Ofsted). After retiring Tim became a funeral celebrant. He recognised that he needed something to support his encounters with grieving people. He took the Staying Mindful course in 2010 and acknowledges how useful it has been in helping him live with an understanding of mortality – his own as well as that of others.

'When I started working as a funeral celebrant, I was woefully under-prepared. I had, of course, been trained and mentored, and all that. The preparation I lacked was interior work on my own understanding of mortality: its iniquitousness and its inevitability. Talking to grieving people and staring at coffins every now and then will naturally tend to make one think of an absolute truth: I will die, one day, sooner or later.

This didn't depress me in any obvious way, and at first it didn't make me anxious about possible threats to my continued existence. (I've never enjoyed walking under ladders, in any case...)

But you need, I think, a lot of empathy to be of any use to a grieving family, and that is a two-way traffic. There was also a sudden realisation of the absoluteness of death – he went to the paper shop and he never came back, and now he's a name on my work schedule and I'm talking to his grieving family. He was here and now he doesn't exist, as himself.

After a while I felt an uncomfortable mix: a sort of background lowering of the spirits, a glumness; a worry that I didn't really know what I thought or felt about mortality; a low-level rumble behind the day-to-day consciousness. More obviously, I was feeling the anxieties caused by doing something which had to be right first time every time. It wasn't a high-level anxiety, or a crushing depression, but it worried me. I felt I should do something about it.

I was interested in meditation in my youth, in a fairly disorganised and ignorant way, and that was also part of my motivation, though a minor one. I was surprised and pleased to find that Bangor University, just down the road, was an international centre for teaching mindfulness meditation, so I applied.

In the pre-course phone chat – invaluable – I said to Judith that I was concerned that I'd be taking up a place that could go to someone with a much more urgent need – someone clinically depressed, desperately anxious or suffering from chronic pain. She reassured me, with the idea that you don't wait till the plane's on fire before you start sewing the parachute (Jon Kabat-Zinn), and that people tend to find their way to mindfulness when they need to. I needed to.

That was six years ago now. I was asked more than once, "Did mindfulness change your life?" (We do love a slogan, don't we?) My response was that it was changing my life – life always changes anyway, and it was enormously helpful to make the eight-week course part of the changes. It wasn't a single revelation.

At the practical level, the course helped with funerals. If I'm feeling tense whilst I'm waiting by the coffin, with people filing in, music playing, then a couple of minutes focusing on my breath, feeling my feet on the floor, being in the moment, is really helpful. I am certain I am better at this work than I would have been had I not taken mindfulness courses.

What about any deeper levels? Once I'd got beyond the idea that meditating would result in a blinding moment of enlightenment that made everything different (Saint Paul on the road to Damascus syndrome) and I realised that it doesn't work like that, I could feel how meditation seeps into the rest of my life.

Working on not striving, on choiceless being with whatever is happening, on acceptance – I think all this has helped me deal not only with funeral work but with my own fears about death and dying. The cliché that death is part of life began to feel true – or perhaps death is part of life is part of death, is etc.

This isn't just a matter of concepts and intellectual understanding; it has to be felt and lived with, and that's what meditation is helping me to do.

But my own practice fell away, became spasmodic and occasional. So I took the six-week course. This opened more doors out of the basic structures of mindfulness practice. It helped me to consider why I wasn't doing more regularly something I actually liked doing. (I think the answer to this problem has to be found individually.)

I began to meditate more often, I began to encourage and value "informal practice" such as a few moments of present momentness when out walking, or just sitting around. I began to feel more strongly the links between sitting meditation and being in the present moment wherever I was.

I also understood more fully the importance of not striving, of not being dissatisfied with a half-hour sitting meditation that "didn't go well". I understood that what happens in a meditation is what happens in a meditation; that slipping back into the narrative flow of thought ("running scripts" is my slogan for it) and bringing the attention back to the breath, to the present, is the meditation. A talk by John Peacock gave me the "unhooking" concept, along with much else.

'There was also some work on kindness, and compassion for self and others. My own view is that it grows out of meditation, out of acceptance of oneself, not from seeking explicitly to develop it – but that's only my own preference.

'I went on Annee's introductory retreat a year or so after completing the six-week Staying Mindful course, and I found that a rich and deeply helpful experience, which I shall look to repeat from time to time.

'After this I decided to find support for my practice by organising a local group of people who had done the eight-week course and who would sit and meditate together from time to time. And talk about their practice. Or something like!

'At present, I am in a sense trying to gently disengage from seeing mindfulness meditation as a set of pre-formed exercises and approaches, with its own slogans, and let it be simply: meditation. Part of life itself, not an extra. Mindfulness tuition establishes it for us, helps us with methodologies, and then we take it forward each in our own way. I'm deeply grateful to the Centre for Mindfulness at Bangor University for setting me going.

'An Iranian friend, a Muslim much influenced by Sufi who took the eight-week course with me, said he found it valuable chiefly for the doors it opened into so much else. I'm busy opening a few doors right now.

'One of those opening doors lets me see that this narrative is deceptively well-ordered and coherent. The ego doesn't let go easily, does it?'

– Tim Clark

Hedwig's story

Hedwig Du Jardin is a mindfulness teacher and therapist who lives in Belgium. After meeting at mindfulness conferences and training events we decided to do the Staying Mindful course as a one-to-one virtual course. In this piece her description of a body scan shows how much we can learn from just one practice. Hedwig has severe arthrosis and long-term family problems. She found that a regular practice helped her to take care of herself.

'I didn't like the body scan when I began the staying mindful course, it made me uncomfortable, grumpy, frustrated and very disappointed in myself that I could not do it after 10 years of mindfulness practice.

It was only when I reflected on my bad mood after a couple of scans, in fact had written about it in my diary, that I discovered that I could learn from it. I reflected that it was my expectations, wanting things to 'work', self-criticism and lack of compassion that made it so painful.

'I realised I needed to bring a different attitude to the practice. I checked into myself asking myself how I was. What's going on physically and mentally? (Self-care and kindness.) Then I stretched, noticed where I had tension and deliberately grounded myself. That is, I noticed which parts of the body were in contact with the ground. I took several deep sighs and then I noticed that suddenly, in a flash, my whole body was there: pleasant, delightful, warm, sandwiched between the two blankets, I felt comfortable carried by the ground. I realised that I expect a body scan to be relaxing and awakening.

'It is very difficult for me to accept discomfort and stiffness; I have a feeling of having failed in that case. Nevertheless, in spite of noticing that, I have a better feeling about it because it allowed me to relax. I wrote in my diary: I hope someday to be less judgemental, to be able to permit myself to "not get it right" and not be disappointed in myself.

'The intention to do this body scan with compassion made me cry a little, and I remembered my son who had problems again. I felt grief about my son. I wondered if this crying – remembering my intention to let it be compassionate - was self-compassion or self-pity. And then I became aware that I was being self-critical, or self-suspicious again – and I remembered that self-pity isolates whereas self-compassion connects. I felt that my son and I are both suffering, struggling at the same time.

'I was determined to bring an intention of Beginner's Mind to the practice. I listened to the recording of the body scan three times and then did the practice guiding myself through the body. I was very happy with my practice. I found that it took longer. I came back to the same place where I had lost attention. The first time I did it I spent most of my time just scanning the legs. Instead of berating myself for not doing it properly I enjoyed the practice because I was able to let go of my preoccupation with doing it right and bring a kindness to my mind wandering. The second time, although it still took longer to do the scan, I visited more parts of my body. I noted that I was learning to be more experimental, curious about my mind as well as my body and notice a painful habitual reaction around self-judgement. I was aware of the softening effect of kindness. My mother was very strict with me as a child and I carried this judgemental voice in my head, which I recognised as my mother's.

'I then practised without the CD. I didn't miss any body parts (which makes me feel sorry when practising with CD), I just went back to the place where I lost attention. My body itself was calling me back from *mind wandering and I was able to bring a different attitude to my painful sensations. Disadvantage – after 40 minutes I did only the lower body!*

'When I write this, realising that even today, deep down I think that "I'm bad"! This is like I felt when I was a child (and the black sheep of the family). I thought I had got over that when I was 24 when I had my first baby and felt so much love for him that I thought: "Feeling so much love I cannot be so bad!" But no, today I discovered that the feeling of guilt and worthlessness of being so "bad" is still there. Perhaps I'm punishing myself by self-sabotage; perhaps this is one of the reasons it was so difficult to persist in a regular meditation practice. Important recognition, isn't it?

'I doubt myself; I don't trust myself and this is why I couldn't have a regular practice. And now I am prepared.'

– Hedwig Du Jardin

Maureen's story

Maureen O Callaghan: In her sixties she decided to do a MSc in Mindfulness-Based Approaches at Bangor University. Maureen then set up a social enterprise providing mindfulness-based interventions tailored to the needs of the most disadvantaged, e.g. young offenders, care givers, and the unemployed. Currently she provides businesses and organisations with mindfulness-based training, mentoring and retreats. She is now writing a PhD at Lincoln University looking at mindfulness in the development of self-mastery and social responsibility.

Reflections on movement practice

'Looking back at my mindfulness journey it seems that I have experienced a number of challenges when it came to paying attention to my body. There were times I found the body scan either frustrating or distressing because there were areas of my body where I felt no sensation at all. Although the teachers on the Master's Foundation Module repeatedly explained that it was OK not to experience sensations, I still felt disconnected from my body. It was those times when an element of striving would take over as I tried hard to feel something... anything. The harder I tried the more disconnected I felt. It wasn't until I learned to let go and to accept that this was just how things are that I REALLY allowed the numbness to be part of my experience. Gradually, as the weeks passed and I persevered with the practice, I started to feel sensations where previously it had been numbness.

'My next challenge was Mindful Movement. My body, which was now in its early 60s, was not as strong or as supple as it used to be. It also carried some extra weight, which didn't help! I was conscious of the discomfort I experienced as I tried to get into certain postures, how difficult it was to maintain my balance and how hard I found it to coordinate movement and breathing. Memories of my childhood when I struggled with gymnastics would come to the surface. I could do Mindful Walking but I struggled with Tai Chi or Yoga postures so I stuck with the Mindful Walking and enjoyed the feeling of massaging the earth with my feet.

'When I embarked on the Teacher Training modules as part of an MSc in Mindfulness-Based Approaches it was with a sense of unease. How could I possibly teach Mindful Movement if I struggled with the postures, keeping my balance and coordinating my breathing? Looking back, I realise that I didn't really understand what it meant to be a mindfulness teacher. I thought I needed to be the "expert" to be able to teach other people. "How can I teach other people if I can't do it myself?" I remember asking my supervisor. With her help I came to understand that in struggling with Mindful Movement I had invaluable insights that I could share with learners, insights that those who found Mindful Movement easy may not have. And so I began to teach Mindful Movement as part of the eight-week course and I got some very positive feedback from learners despite what I still saw as significant failings.

'It was this feedback that gave me the confidence to attend a Yoga and Tai Chi retreat where I was able to access personal tuition and where with support and encouragement I began to fully connect with my body. I learned a series of simple Yoga postures and Tai Chi moves that now form part of a daily 20-minute morning practice. I also learned to listen to what my body needs and as a result I eat when I am hungry, drink when I am thirsty and rest when I need to.

'Learning how to treat my body with kindness and respect has led to improvements in a number of physical health problems. I am now looking to incorporate what I have learned into a Mindfulness for Health programme for older and less mobile people, combining the learning from the experiences of struggling with Mindful Movement and the more recent experiences of learning how to work with my body.'

– Maureen O'Callaghan (www.mocallaghan.co.uk)

Cindy Cooper talking to Becca Crane

Cindy Cooper was a mindfulness teacher and trainer in the Centre for Mindfulness Research and Practice (CMRP). Cindy died on 2 March 2017. She was greatly loved. This conversation was originally printed in the CMRP newsletter. I asked permission from both Cindy and Becca to reproduce the conversation in this book. I include it because I found it helpful and inspiring to read about Cindy's reflection on mindfulness practice when she was suffering from multiple myeloma and in great pain.

BECCA: So, would you begin by sharing about your illness and the challenges that you are facing through it?

CINDY: Yes – a little over a year ago I was diagnosed with multiple myeloma, which is a cancer of the bone marrow and blood. It's not curable. Until recently you'd die from it pretty quickly but there are chemo drugs now that can prolong life for a year or two. I began chemo last year but had such very bad reactions to the main myeloma drug that we had to stop it early. I did continue with the other chemo drugs, and they have had a reasonably good effect on my blood counts.

Myeloma affects and weakens bones and it has affected my spine particularly badly. Eight or nine vertebrae have totally collapsed. I've had an operation to inject cement right into some of the vertebrae, so they are a little more stable now, but they are still very painful.

So, what has been most challenging? It has been the chemo side-effects, it has been the pain, it has been the uncertainty of how long I'm going to live, and the uncertainty of how much I'm going to be able to do. Presently I'm actually functioning fairly well. We are in a waiting stage right now, waiting until my blood gets really bad again. Then I will be offered a new chemo drug, which again may prolong life for a little bit but won't cure me. I may or may not decide to take this further chemo depending on its side-effects and how I tolerate it.

BECCA: How has your mindfulness practice unfolded through this time?

CINDY: It has been really interesting because the mindfulness practice has just taken over. The practice is incredibly practical in something like this. I'm not doing as much formal practice as I have in the past – largely because I haven't been able to sit as long as I could before, but every minute of every day I am doing my mindfulness practice – with the pain but also with the illness and the uncertainty. It's interesting, people often ask me about my "battle against cancer", and it is so funny because I am not fighting. That is the last thing on this earth that I am doing.

Fighting against it would make it a lot worse. So, it is more about learning to be with it, which is what mindfulness is all about. And especially with pain. It is not about struggling and fighting it and trying to get rid of it. It is realising that that struggle is what causes the suffering. So, it's more about, "Can I relate to it? Can I be with it?"

BECCA: So – is it very moment by moment?

CINDY: Very moment by moment. Coming back to this moment again and again and not jumping ahead to all those worries – "Will I be able to do this, that and the other?". It is right now, just here. It is an ever-changing constant. And this moment is manageable.

BECCA: Do you get the sense of the work that you have put in over your life with your practice? How has this bank of practice had an influence?

CINDY: Oh yes. Oh, very definitely. I don't know what it would be like if I had not had that bank, but it felt very natural when I was first diagnosed: "OK, here we are, now we are with this." In fact, I really do find it interesting. That is one of the things that I teach most in terms of mindfulness – "Can we get curious and interested in what is going on?"

I am actually quite fascinated by this illness, about what it does to me and what it does to my life and how I can play with it. My doctors are always astonished. They really don't know what to make of my approach to my illness!

BECCA: So you have in part answered this question, but I will ask it anyway to see if there are other areas you might want to go. What is the illness teaching you about your practice, and what is the practice teaching you about your illness?

CINDY: My illness has been teaching me in a very intense way what the practice is – so I have really been learning about coming back to being present and living in the moment.

One of the practices that one of my teachers has given me is three sayings: "Whatever happens, let it happen", "Wherever it goes, let it go" and "There is no purpose anyway". These are pretty strong things, and it wasn't until I worked with them with the myeloma that I really understood them.

I remember one day walking down the street. It was in the bad phase of chemo and I could barely walk. I kept falling down and cutting my face. I was walking down the street trying to keep my muscles going and thinking, "Oh, damn, I am going to fall on my face again" and "Oh, it is going to be horrible". Then I just remembered, "Whatever happens, let it happen" and "Wherever it goes, let it go", and suddenly it got through to me in a much deeper way.

I suddenly realised in that moment that the sun was shining. It was a beautiful day, which I hadn't noticed in all my worry. And it became clear that "there is no purpose anyway" is about how 'purpose' is a kind of future thing, and all I have is right now. And it is sunny.

So – a deepening or intensifying of that understanding of really being here in the moment.

And one other major thing that my illness has taught me is gratitude.

What a gift this illness has been in the outpouring of people's love and concern, and how that opens my heart and it opens their hearts too.
I remember feeling quite early in the diagnosis that this is something quite magnificently beautiful. We really meet each other in these deeply human places. It is so clear people want to give and to help. Interestingly, this has added another layer of practice for me – "How do I open to letting people help me?". This can be very difficult actually.

BECCA: How have you navigated being a teacher and a supervisor through this time?

CINDY: I was committed to teach a Teacher Training Course and an eight-week MBSR course when I started chemo and I wasn't in very good physical shape. I did have co-teachers that I could depend on which was invaluable, but I felt at that point that what was really important was that I was open and honest about this illness, not trying to hide it, and that in my role as a teacher it was important for me to model what mindfulness is about. Can I somehow be steady with the difficult? I wasn't sure I could be.

In particular, with the teacher training group over 8-weeks, I felt it was important to model both that we can be steady with the difficult and also that there are times when we shouldn't be teaching. So I was very open with them about my process.

At the start of each training day I checked in with them and said: "Yes, right now I feel I can be steady and grounded enough with myself and with you, so I am here." But on one day I felt awful and I remember thinking: "I really have to go and tell them why I can't teach today." So I came to them and said: "I am not going to be with you today because I don't feel steady enough to hold myself – so I can't hold all you either." I felt that it was important to model that.

So that was kind of easy but in terms of how I've navigated other relationships, especially with my supervisees, it's lot trickier – never knowing how much I should share with them in terms of my health.

Cancer and death and loss are scary. It became clear that some people really wanted to know what was going on with me and others really didn't.

And it changes over time. And I get it wrong sometimes. This is all about relationships, so hopefully there's always the sense 'we can work with that too'. But it is tricky, very tricky.

BECCA: So, no rules – is it an in-the-moment process?

CINDY: Yes, and recognising that in some ways this illness is easier on me than on others. I can really see that and understand that. It is mine and

I can live with it, but for people around me, especially if they care, it is a lot harder – so honouring that is really important too.

BECCA: Staying with this theme of your teaching – how has the learning from this time informed your teaching practice?

CINDY: This is a very interesting one. I think that my teaching has always been about the human condition, but I think that that has been intensified with this bigger issue of life and death, which is of course fully human.

I don't know that I teach in any different way, but I have had feedback from some of my participants that they come out of the teaching with a much greater sense of how big this course is – not how big it is, but how big are the things that it works with. I'm not sure how that works – but people tend to see that their own problems are maybe not the biggest thing in their lives. But I think you would have to ask them about this.

BECCA: You spoke at the beginning about navigating the uncertainty of all this – and I wondered if you have some words with how you are playing with that, with the not knowing?

CINDY: Boy, "play" is the word. In some sense this is the hardest thing, hardest in a very practical way even – particularly in work with CMRP. We have to plan a year to two years in advance. I don't know if I am going to be around. Maybe I will, maybe I won't. So it's very hard on that practical level to know how to work with it.

On a more personal level, this is just what we teach. When I am panicking about not knowing where this is going… Well, it is here. Just come back to here.

BECCA: There is this dynamic of having to plan so that you can respond to that?

CINDY: Yes, and that is tricky. I am conscious that I am living on my own so I need to plan what is going to happen when I can no longer live on my own. So, some kind of planning has to come in – I don't know what it is or when it will happen – so there is planning and also letting go of that.

BECCA: Are there any areas that you feel are important that we haven't spoken about yet?

CINDY: All this can sound very Pollyanna-ish. I want to make it clear that there is also very definitely loneliness, despair, fear, anger and sadness in the mix. When I take the time and energy to explore my anger, I touch into the deep aloneness and fear. And underneath the fear I touch into the sadness. But when I really open to the sadness I touch into the tenderness and poignancy of my heart, which connects me immediately back to others – to all beings. So each of these emotions has some kind of meaning and beauty. It's very scary sometimes and incredibly painful – emotionally as well as physically and mentally. But it all feels that this is part of life and this is workable.

My palliative care pain specialist is always trying very hard for me to have no pain, but I'm finding that when that happens there is no joy either, so really needing to balance those two. I need both. The sadness, the happiness, the joy, the pain. The Full Catastrophe. And maybe it isn't a catastrophe.

I also want to reiterate how important and how magnificent this mindfulness programme is. I have always loved it and I have worked with difficulties within it in the past, but I see other people in the hospital – and I see the doctors who are treating me, who are utterly baffled by my being OK with this illness and this pain. And it isn't a gritting my teeth kind of OK.

This is really fine, this is life. This isn't death, it is actually life. And just how privileged I feel that I have been given the tools and the understanding to be able to relate to all aspects of life – and hopefully death – this way, which is something that most people out there don't have. So, there is something really important about this.

A great deal of gratitude.

Chapter 11:
Course Session Plans

Note: it is highly important that you don't use this material in a group session without mindfulness training.

Overall aims of the Staying Mindful course:

To encourage and inspire people to develop and or restart their mindfulness practice by enquiry into experience, motivation and common barriers to practice

To introduce new mindfulness practices

To support mindfulness teachers in teaching beyond the eight-week mindfulness courses

Objectives:

To enhance wellbeing by refining and deepening mindfulness practice and understanding by:

■ exploring how to be more awake and aware in our lives →

- clarifying and increasing motivation to practise and exploring the role of intention in strengthening mindfulness practice
- examining barriers to an effective mindfulness practice
- introducing new practices for working with difficulty and stress in daily life
- presenting practices to enhance appreciation and gratitude.

To share developmental activities and ideas with practitioners, students and teachers by:

- exploring mindful communications in relationships
- cultivating a compassionate attitude to ourselves and others
- considering ways of being more socially aware
- exploring how to work with emotions
- suggesting ways to sustain and nourish mindfulness practice.

To provide resources for teachers to run mindfulness follow-up courses by:

- providing session plans with activities
- offering guided meditations
- presenting materials suitable for handouts.

Session 1: Intention

Aims of session 1

- To introduce teacher and course participants
- To explore what you want from the course
- To explore intention and motivation in mindfulness practice

Notes for the teacher

Gathering: Settle the group by ringing the bells to formalise the start of the session and sit quietly for a few moments.

Introduce guidelines for the course: Confidentiality, mutual respect and mindful listening. (Write on board.)

Icebreaker

Ask people to talk to the person next to them to introduce themselves. Asking the three Ws: Who are you? (Your name?) Where do you live? Why are you here?

Go round the whole group with introductions. 'Say your name and something else which you feel relevant to the group.' (It could be why you are here or how you are feeling right now.)

The 'Pebble in well' Meditation Activity (see Chapter 1)

What brings you here – what do you really, really want?

Teacher to start a go-round group: 'Please say your name and one word to sum up the exercise.'

Intention for the course

Notes for the teacher

Distribute Post-It notes and paper and pens.

Ask each person to write intention for the course on the Post-It note and to put on it on the board or flip chart.

Read out everyone's intention. (Rationale: Everyone hears their intention – and that of others – from the teacher, which saves embarrassment.)

Sharing Fears exercise

Notes for the teacher

Hand out two small pieces of paper (half A4) and pens

Ask group: What are your fears or concerns about the course?

Pass a hat or a wastepaper bin around the group. 'Post-box'. 'Post your fears in this.'

Collect at the end of circle and pass around again, asking each member of the group to pull out a piece of paper.

Ask participants to read out someone else's 'fear'.

Discuss common themes with group. Acknowledge all the fears by mentioning them.

Rationale: Reading someone else's fear is less exposing and helps with connection and empathy. This builds a collaborative group that is able to share the beginnings of trust and intimacy.

Themes of the course

Notes for the teacher

On the board draw a triangle of the three axioms of mindfulness: intention, paying attention, attitudes.

Week 1, 2, 3 – the three axioms of mindfulness: intention, paying attention, attitudes.

Week 4 – the theme is working with difficulty and how to work with anxiety. This is followed by self-compassion and befriending practices.

Week 5 – we will cover mindful communications.

Week 6 – the last week will be a summing up, a review and a looking forward analysis.

Aims of course

Notes for the teacher

Draw from and include aspects mentioned in their introductions.

WRITE ON BOARD
- To deepen our experience with practice
- To increase motivation to practise and look at what gets in the way of being present
- To explore working with emotions
- To cultivate a compassionate attitude to ourselves and others

Meditation Activity 45 minutes

Teacher-led body scan practice including appreciation at some points of the body.

Teacher-led enquiry into the experience of the movement practice to the whole group.

Read poem

Home Practice

Notes for the teacher

Teacher to photocopy home practice instructions and hand out to group.

Teacher to read out home practice instructions.

During the week do the body scan at least once guided by a CD and once without a CD

Practise a meditation every day, deciding and experimenting with length of practice and time you practise

Remember to set an intention each time you meditate

Photograph or draw or note down five things you have noticed with fresh eyes or ears

Reflect on what is meaningful for you. What are you good at? What do you enjoy?

Engage the five senses to appreciate your life in as many moments as you can.

Teacher rings bells to finish the class

Session 2: Paying attention

Aims of session 2
- To explore how we pay attention
- To consider what are the obstacles to practise and within a practice

Notes for the teacher

Bells to start the session

Signpost what the session involves

Go-round the groups each person saying their name and one word how you are feeling

Movement practice – teacher-led

Move the participants into pairs to talk about their experience of the practice.

Teacher-led enquiry into the experience of the movement practice to the whole group.

Home practice review

Notes for the teacher

Invite the group to talk about home practice in pairs for 10 minutes

On the board highlight questions they can ask each other:
- What gets in the way?
- If it was different, how was it different?
- Was working with an intention useful? How did you work with setting an intention?
- Are you reminding yourself why you are practising?
- Are you able to practise every day, even if that means you have adapted the practice to fit in with your life for this day?

Bring group together for whole group enquiry

Whole group to put mats away. Chairs back in a circle.

Choice of activities

Activity 1: Sea of reactions

Notes for the teacher

Notes for the teacher

1. Give out A4 paper and coloured pens or highlighters.

2. Say to the group:

Close your eyes and connect with the feeling you most get when you think about fitting practice in that day.

The excuses you make to yourself not to do it now.

Remembering an occasion or occasions when, and how, you reacted to the idea that you 'should' do it. Connect into the feeling in the body around resistance to practice.

3. Teacher to ring bells.

4. Ask them to write down the words that related to the feelings or impulses that came up on A4 paper and pens.

5. Collect and scatter them around the room on the floor.

6. Ask them to: walk through the sea of reactions – with an emphasis on noticing what draws you, what resonates. This could be a word that you have written, or it could be something someone else has written.

7. Say: 'Stand on the word that seemed to best capture your experience. And to notice who is standing near you'.

8. Guide three-step breathing space.

9. Divide into pairs to explore how we can work with the chosen barrier with a gentle awareness. Can this enable us to come to our practice from a different place?

10. Whole group sharing and enquiry.

Write hindrances on board with a brief explanation after activity.

If time divide into different pairs to ask what hindrances came up in the earlier paired discussion. Identify your common obstacles.

Teacher-led enquiry

Mats away. Chairs back to edges of room

Read poem

Notes for the teacher

1. Explain how the activity will work. Divide participants into pairs, and ask them to identify themselves as 'A' and 'B'.

A asks B: 'How does your practice serve you?' B answers with one word. A says: 'Thank you'. A asks B: 'How does your practice serve you?' B answers with one word. A says thank you. This continues even when B has nothing to say. When this happens B just connects with the body sensations. A allows the pause, B can say nothing. After a moment or two A asks again. B says whatever comes into his/her head.

2. After around three to five minutes, ring the bells and ask participants to change partners.

This is good for more experienced groups or alternatively can be done on the last night of the course as a reminder.

3. Chime the bells to bring the activity to an end.

Activity 2: How does your practice serve you. (An Alternative to Activity 1)

Home practice

Teacher to photocopy home practice instructions and hand out to group.

Teacher to read out home practice instructions.

- Focus on doing some movement practice every day. Be creative around this. Sometimes listen to a movement tape, do slow walking and fast walking, walking in nature and dancing.
- This week go for at least one longer walk outside. Pay attention to how your body feels. Use all your senses.
- Notice these five obstacles to practice as they come and go. One may turn up or be stronger than the others. Focus on this one and see how you are with it. Experiment with ways to work with it. How do you react when it shows up? What can you learn from it? Experiment with strategy.
- What surprises you this week? Note it down.

Ring bells to finish session

Session 3: Working with attitude

Notes for the teacher

Bells to settle to start the session. Two minutes

Signpost what the session involves.

Go around the groups, with each person saying their name and one word about how they are feeling.

Activity 1: Qualities of a good friend

Teacher to lead the following brief contemplation:
- Think about a good friend. What are their special qualities? What qualities would you like in a good friend when you are in need? What quality can you best give yourself when you are in need?
- Group to discuss in pairs then teacher to ask them to share their response by pop corning out qualities of a good friend. Teacher puts answers on the board.
- Alternatively participants put their reflections in brief on a post it note and participants put post its notes on board
- Teacher writes down any remaining attitudes from Chapter 3 on board

Sitting meditation – Teacher-led

Emphasise:

Paying attention to what pulls you away (remember the hindrances from last week) and what attitudes you notice are here in this meditation.

What attitudes can we bring to practice and therefore life to soften our resistance to being present each moment? For example: non-judgement or patience, acceptance, gentleness, friendliness etc.

What are our counter-attitudes? For example: self-critical, judgemental, impatience, lack of trust, boredom versus Beginner's Mind, non-acceptance.

Notice what comes up in the practice.

Teacher-led enquiry into the sitting practice

Home practice enquiry

Ask: How did the movement practice go? What did you notice about obstacles to practice?

'Focusing on the Positive' Meditation

Grounding: feel into whatever is supporting you. This could be your feet on the floor, your bottom on the seat. If you are lying you can feel the back of your body making contact with the floor. Feel into this contact with the ground, allowing the earth to hold you.

Breathing: feel the breath in the body.

Recognising: recognise something positive in your life by bringing to mind one or more of the following:

Something pleasant about your experience in the present moment

A pleasant moment from your day or yesterday

Something you like or love in your life. It could be the warm sunshine, a pet, a child

Find something good in your situation, something you are glad about

Think about things that make you feel one or more of these: grateful, calm and peaceful, loving, loved, happy.

Choose one thing and stay with it awhile.

Acknowledging and Absorbing:

Once a positive feeling comes to the front of your awareness, staying with and re-imagine the story around it. Picturing it. Hearing it. Using your senses.

Investigating:

Where are you feeling it? Where in the body? Acknowledge the pleasure or the delight you feel by staying with it, lingering with it. Are you feeling a sense of warmth or maybe coolness? Lightness or heaviness?

Nurturing:

Stay with this feeling and nurture it. It's OK to be here. Enjoy it. If any judgemental thoughts come up, accept them too in the moment and soothe with kindness. There is this judgement and also this positive feeling. I'm OK and it's OK to feel the way I do.

A meditative pause when things are difficult: STOP

STOP MEDITATION

Stop slow down,

Take a few deep breaths,

Observe thoughts emotions body sensations,

Proceed with awareness and curiosity.

Home practice

Notes for the teacher

Teacher to photocopy home practice instructions and hand out to group.

Teacher to read out home practice instructions.

Do sitting practice every day. Have an intention to do at least 20 minutes; however, do at least two 45-minute practices between now and next week

Remember to walk mindfully when the opportunity arises. Have an intention to make it happen

Note what attitude you feel most drawn to on a daily basis. Does this change from day to day or are you developing one in particular?

What body sensations do you notice while you are practising? What links are there between body sensations, thoughts and emotions when you are practising?

Practise STOP if possible once a day or more

Session 4: Working with difficulty and cultivating compassion

Aims

To consider fight, flight and freeze reactions.

To explore working with the difficulty and emotional reactions, particularly fear.

To investigate our reactions a little deeper, in order to understand ourselves better.

To consider self-compassion.

Notes for the trainer

Themes from Chapter 4 Working with difficulty and cultivating compassion

Highlight 'Fight flight freeze' mechanisms. Ask them what they normally notice

Site Davidson's research on long term meditators (Chapter 6 compassion)

Read 'The Guesthouse' by Rumi

Highlight the importance of self-compassion

Meditation Activity

Either RAIN meditation or Fear Meditation or Yes/No Meditation (Chapters 4 and 5)

Activity: Work with someone you haven't yet in pairs or groups of three to discuss where you felt sensations, if they changed, were too much, overwhelming, you felt nothing, numbed out, you thought about something else. Do not talk about your story.

What did it feel like if you didn't do it? Check in now notice how it feels in the body

Notice any fear arising as you talk in the group. Where are you feeling it in the body?

Teacher-led enquiry to whole group.

Home practice review.

Teach self-compassion break (Chapter 6)

Self-compassion break

A useful short practice to come to when you are feeling distressed.

1. Say to yourself: **This is a moment of suffering**. (Mindfulness)

Bringing mindfulness to this: What are the thoughts? The feelings and emotions? The body sensations?

2. Say to yourself: **This is part of life** (Connection) This links you with others / common humanity.

Imagine all the other beings in the world who are feeling like this at this time.

3. **Put your hands on your heart or both hands on opposite arms, or just one hand on the opposite arm, give yourself a self-hug or just rub your arm gently.** (Soothing yourself or self-compassion).

Feel the warmth of your hands, or feeling under the hands the breath moving in the chest.

You could say words of your own choosing to bring some kindness to yourself.

Or 'May I be kind to myself.' 'May I accept myself just as I am'.

Created by Kristen Neff

Befriending or loving kindness meditation

Divide into small groups

Teacher-led enquiry: whole group

Home Practice

Notes for the teacher

Teacher to photocopy home practice instructions and hand out to group.

Teacher to read out home practice instructions.

Meditate every day.

Practise with the guided sitting meditation once, practise the same sequence without the tape at least once.

Do one choiceless awareness practice being aware of what ever arises in the moment.

Do at least one self-compassion or befriending practice with yourself in mind.

Or do a movement befriending practice. Mix and match these practices depending on what you need day by day.

■ Do self-compassion break whenever you need it.

■ Work with exploring strong emotional reactions

Say some positive affirmations to yourself at least once a day. For example: 'I am doing the best I can'. 'In this moment I accept myself just as I am' or whatever feels right for you.

Bells to finish

Session 5: Mindful communications

Aims

To consider how to be mindfully aware in relation to others.

To practice mindful communication and listening.

Activity 1: Mindfulness communications

Notes for the teacher

Lead a short meditation to ground participants.

Then straight into a contemplation on a difficult communication they had in the last week.

Move into RAIN meditation.

Ring Bells to finish.

Teacher says:

1 'In your pairs decide who will be A and who B. There is no need to share anything you don't want to. What you say will be at your own discretion. The invitation will be to focus on the body sensations and feelings (emotions) that arise during the contemplation rather than the story'.

2. This is a Talking and Listening Paired Activity.

A will talk. B will listen without commenting or sharing. Give full attention to your partner. Partner A will talk about the feelings and body sensations you noticed during the exercise if you didn't notice anything then talk about how that feels. Partner B job is to notice body language, facial expression and to report back what you can remember all in the service of A.

A will talk for 4 minutes. Notice what it feels like to be listened to in this way.

B your job is to mindfully listen and then reflect what you heard, not interpreting or advising or fixing, instead saying 'this is what I heard'. I noticed that you frowned or smiled for example. I noticed such and such body language.

Teacher rings bell and times four minutes rings bell again to finish A's talking.

Teacher says:

B feedback what you heard, body language etc, without providing any advice or solutions (2 minutes).

Teacher ring bell

A clarifies to B what she/he initially said (1 minute).

Teacher ring bell

Change over. B talks A listens and observes body language (4 minutes).

Teacher ring bell

A reflects and feedbacks what they heard, body language etc, without providing any advice or solutions (2 minutes).

Teacher ring bell B clarifies to A what they initially communicated.

Teacher ring bell

Then the pairs talk about the experience in normal conversation first one then the other for five minutes.

Bells

Thank partner.

Finish pairs and pull together in whole group for enquiry and discussion.

Befriending or loving kindness meditation
Brief enquiry

Home Practice

Choose one meditation to work with on a daily basis. Find a pattern that's doable for you with a fine balance between commitment (intention, motivation) and flexibility. Spend a few moments before you practice deciding what you need in this moment, this particular day or time in your life. Allow for creativity but also for stability.

Think of 2 or 3 relationships that are important to you. How would you like to be in those relationships? More open or more private/ More direct or more allowing? Consider what kind of support would you like from others and what kind of support you can give.

Next week is the last week of the course, review what you have learned on the course and how you can support yourself in this practice in the future.

Bells to finish

Alternative exercises to Mindful Communications exercise

Stones and Buttons Exercise

An exercise to do in class or on your own.

Contemplation

Think of a difficulty you are having in a relationship. It is important to focus on the little things and to make it clear that you don't have to share with the group if it is uncomfortable for you. Identify a situation and the people involved.

Pause, breathe and then act without too much deliberation.

Several stones and buttons are placed in a bowl. Without giving it much thought, each person picks one to represent oneself, significant others, or whoever comes to mind and then positions them in some sort of group on the table or floor in front of them. Size/shape/colour/texture etc may on reflection be significant, as can the spacing and distances of the objects. Choose stones or objects quite quickly, without too much conscious thought.

The exercise could be done in pairs or threes and then shared with the whole group if it is appropriate for some members.

Teacher to ask the group open-ended type questions to get them going on the idea of self in relation to other people in their lives. Then the teacher asks them to explain to the pair or others in small group, why they choose that stone for that person and this one for themselves.

One person said: 'the big, dark, rough stone is my father, that little, smooth white one my mother, and she is hiding behind that stone, which is me'.

This may be more relevant in a therapeutic setting, so choose your group well. Relate have been using the stone exercise for years. Sometimes it allows people to work more unconsciously.

Thanks to Mary McIntyre for this exercise.

'Who are you?' Exercise

(This can be done on your own into a mirror, if you are not too self-conscious.)

Divide into pairs. Decide who is A and who is B. Set up the exercise saying that A will be the questioner first and B the answerer.

A asks B: 'Who are you?' B answers and then A asks again.

Be sensitive with your partner: sometimes asking quickly, sometimes leaving a space.

B can answer with the first thing that comes into his/her head or close the eyes and contemplate for a few moments. There are no right answers and your partner takes a non-judgemental stance. If you notice self-consciousness or judgemental thoughts coming up, stop and notice where you are feeling this. After observing this you could include it in your answer to your partner. Remember there is nowhere to get to. Nothing to prove. (Three minutes.)

Stretch and change questioner and answerer. (Three minutes.)

Thank your partner and talk about how it felt, first together then in the whole group.

Mindful walking communication exercise

The teacher's spoken guidance is in italics.

First lead a walking meditation slowly for ten minutes.

Being aware of soles of feet etc

Now the second part of the walking communication exercise:

Walk at a normal pace.

Then move into hurry mode. 'I need to catch a bus, get to a meeting'. Faster and faster. 'Get out of my way' Be aggressive and self-serving.

Ring bells.

Stand still pause and breathe.

Start walking slowly again. Paying attention to the walking and the breathing.

Now walking like 'I don't want to see anyone.' Passive, not wanting the others to be there, not connecting, feeling that they are in your way, but you can avoid them.

Ring bells.

Stand still pause and breathe.

Walking mindfully. Coming back to the moment, feeling your feet on the floor. The experience of walking.

Ring bells.

Stand still pause and breathe.

Walking mindfully. Compassionate and befriending walking, allowing yourself to feel connected to the others as part of this group, making eye contact as you pass if this feels OK.

Ring bells.

Stand still pause and breathe.

Explore with the group how this felt.

An alternative to the exercise is to divide the group into four.

One group has a piece of paper with the 'I'm in a hurry, feeling aggressive' instructions on it. The second group has instructions to be passive, apologetic for being there. Say or whisper 'sorry' throughout the exercise.

The third group has instructions to walk mindfully connecting with the body and not making eye contact.

The fourth group has instructions to walk making eye-contact and feeling connected.

Then each group swops pieces of paper until they have all experienced the four ways of walking.

Finish with a class discussion. This exercise is quite powerful, and it is necessary to assess whether your group will benefit. If people are sensitive at the time of starting the class, are suffering from anxiety or depression it may be not be suitable for them.

Moving communication exercise

Stand up. Get into pairs Decide who will be A who B.

A places finger on B's hand A leads by moving his/her finger. B follows. (Two minutes.)

Change over. B now leads A (2 minutes).

Then A and B put finger to finger. Now A and B move fingers. No is one leading. (Two minutes.)

Thank partner.

Chinese Finger-Trap

A Chinese finger-trap is a woven piece of bamboo like a stick, but hollow and open at both ends. These are cheap and easily found on the internet.

When you put your finger into the finger-trap and then try to pull it out you find you are struck. How to escape? Usually the victim pulls harder and gets more stuck. The secret is to let go of the resistance, stop the strain by moving towards the stuckness and not pulling away from it. This is an analogy that really works well in mindfulness training.

Take emotional pain: We can try many strategies to rid ourselves of it and yet the strategies don't work. When we push it away by saying to ourselves 'stop thinking and feeling this', we find ourselves still ruminating. If we judge ourselves for this, we feel more pain. If we try to fix or understand it, problem-solving and analysing can often make us more stuck. However, if we practise turning towards the pain and don't try so hard to get rid of it, we don't get stuck. The metaphor of the Chinese finger-trap works well particularly in relationship to others.

Instead of fighting our own corner so relentlessly, we might find some common ground. We can use questions and statements like:

'How do you see this working out?'

'How do you feel about this and what is your expectation of my feelings here?'

'This is very difficult for me; I am not feeling heard.'

'You make a good point.'

'I hear you and I hadn't seen it in that way.'

Chinese finger-traps can be a useful exercise if done with a group. After dividing into pairs, each person puts one on his or her finger and his or her partner tries to get it off. They work together until they work it out or someone tells them how it works.

Aikido Exercise

(I have found this exercise very effective in some groups.)

See *Full Catastrophe Living* by Jon Kabat-Zinn. The Aikido exercise will be found in the Index at the back in any of the editions.

Session 6: Continuing to Stay Mindful

> ## Aims
> To review the course and reflect on what you have learnt and what you will carry forward.

Silent meditation: 45 minutes

Teacher-led enquiry on silent meditation

Activity: Remembering and Looking forward

Hand out paper and pens.

> ## Activity
> Reflect on your intention at beginning of course. Do you feel you remembered your intention? Was it useful? Write down your remembered intention.
>
> What do you need to remember? What was particularly significant in the course?
>
> Did you experience a shift?
>
> Were you moved by anything?
>
> What you have learnt? What has changed?
>
> What do you need to do to support your practice in the future?
>
> Write down any new intention.
>
> Discuss in groups of 3.
>
> Feedback to group as a whole.

Poem

Gratitude meditation or Smile meditation and movement.

Activity: Closing Circle

Notes for the teacher

Ask participants to sit back in a close circle to bring about a sense of closeness.

Go around for the final time, asking each participant to sum up the jewels of their experience or say something to the group about their shared experience.

Alternately this may be facilitated with a bowl of stones. Pass the stones around to the person on the right. Ask them to choose a stone, speak their piece and then pass the stones to the next person. Emphasise: 'Do not pass the stones until you have spoken.'

Include yourself as a member of the group at the end.

Short meditation dedicating our work to all beings or loving kindness meditation.

Bells to finish.

References

Adler MG & Fagley NS (2005) Appreciation: Individual differences in finding value and meaning as a unique predictor of subjective well-being. *Journal of Personality*, **73**, 79–114.

Baker C. House of Commons Library Briefing Paper. London; 2018. NHS website. *Generalised anxiety disorder in adults*. London: Department of Health and Social Care; updated 2018.

Bartley T (2012) *Mindfulness-based Cognitive Therapy for Cancer*. Chichester: Wiley Blackwell.

Bartley T (2016) *Mindfulness: A Kindly Approach to Being with Cancer*. Chichester: Wiley Blackwell.

Bastin JF, Finegold Y, Garcia G, Mollicone M, Renzende M, Routh D, Zohner CM and Crowther TW (2019) The global tree restoration potential. *Science* **365** 6448,76–79.

Batchelor M (2001) *Meditation for Life*. London: Frances Lincoln.

Begley S (2007) *Train Your Mind, Change Your Brain*. New York: Ballantine.

Blacker M & Ford JI (2011) *The Book of Mu*. Boston: Wisdom.

Blake W *Auguries of Innocence* published 1863 posthumously.

Blake W. (1794) *Songs of Innocence and Experience.*

Bowlby J (1969) Attachment. *Attachment and loss: Vol. 1. Loss*. New York: Basic Books.

Brach T (2003) *Radical Acceptance*. London: Rider.

Chodron P (1990) *When Things Fall Apart*. Boston: Shambhala Classics.

Chodrun P (1994) *Start Where You Are: A Guide to Compassionate Living*. Boston: Shambhala Publications.

Chodrun P (1997) *When Things Fall Apart*. Boston: Shambhala Classics.

Chodron P (2001) *The Places That Scare You*. London: Element.

Chodron P (2001) *The Wisdom of No Escape*. London: Shambhala Classics.

Conran T (2015) *Purpose, Three Symphonies*. East Sussex: Agenda Editions.

Crane RS (2009) *Mindfulness-Based Cognitive Therapy, Distinctive Features*. London: Routledge.

Crane C, Crane RS, Eames C, Fennell MJV, Silverton S, Williams JMG & Barnhofer T (2014) The effects of amount of home meditation practice in Mindfulness Based Cognitive Therapy on hazard of relapse to depression in the Staying Well after Depression Trial. *Behaviour Research and Therapy* **63**, 17–24.

Dalai Lama (1998) *Worlds in Harmony*. Berkeley: Parallax Press.

Das R (2000) *Still Here*. London: Hodder & Stoughton.

Davidson RJ, Kabat-Zinn J, Schumacher J, Rosenkranz M, Muller D, Santorelli SF, Urbanowski F, Harrington A, Bonus K & Sheridan JF (2003) Alterations in brain and immune function produced by mindfulness meditation. *Psychosomatic Medicine* **65**, 564–570.

Davies WH (1916) *Leisure from Collected Poems*. London: A.C. Fifield

Dickinson E (1951) *The Complete Poems of Emily Dickinson*. Cambridge, Mass.: The Belknap Press of Harvard University Press.

Donne J (1839) *The Works of John Donne*. vol III. Henry Alford, ed. London: John W. Parker.

Dowling Singh K (2017) *Unbinding. The Grace Beyond Self*. Summerville,MA: Wisdom Publications.

Emmons RA & McCullough M (2003) Counting blessings versus burdens: An experimental investigation of gratitude and subjective well-being in daily life. *Journal of Personality and Social Psychology* **84** (2) 377–389.

Epstein M (2002) *Going on Being: Buddhism and the Way of Change*. London: Thorsons.

Epstein M (1996) *Thoughts Without a Thinker: Psychotherapy from a Buddhist Perspective*. London: Thorsons.

Epstein M (1999) *Going to Pieces Without Falling Apart: A Buddhist Perspective on Wholeness*. London: Thorsons.

Feldman C (2005) *Compassion: Listening to the Cries of the World*. Berkeley: Rodmell Press.

Fredrickson BL & Losada MF (2013). "Positive affect and the complex dynamics of human flourishing": Correction to Fredrickson and Losada (2005). *American Psychologist* **68**(9), 822. https://doi.org/10.1037/a0034435

Frank A (1947) *The Diary of Anne Frank*, London: Pan.

Frankl V (2004) *Man's Search For Meaning*. London: Rider.

Frostadóttir AD (2015) Unpublished Master's degree, Bangor University.

Germer C (2009) *The Mindful Path to Self-Compassion*. New York: Guilford Press.

Gilbert P (Ed.). (2005). *Compassion: Conceptualisations, Research and Use in Psychotherapy*. London & New York: Routledge.

Gilbert P (2009) *The Compassionate Mind: A New Approach to Life's Challenges*. Constable-Robinson. Google Scholar.

Gilbert P (2010) *Compassion-Focused Therapy*. Hove: Routledge.

Ghosananda Maya (1992) *Step by Step*. California: Parallax Press.

Goldstein J (1993) *Insight Meditation: The Practice of Freedom*. Boston: Shambhala.

Goldstein J & Kornfield J (2001) *Seeking the Heart of Wisdom*. London: Shambhala Classics.

Goleman D (Ed) (2003) *Healing Emotions: Conversations with the Dalai Lama on Mindfulness, Emotions and Health*. Boston: Shambala.

Goleman D (Ed) (2004) *Destructive Emotions: A dialogue with the Dalai Lama*. London: Bloomsbury.

Gordon AM, Impett EM, Koga A, Oveis C & Keltner D (2012) To have and to hold: gratitude promotes relationship maintenance in intimate bonds. *Journal of Personality and Social Psychology* **103** (2), 257–274.

Griffiths AE (2008) *Mindfulness-Based Cognitive Therapy and Stress Reduction: Long-term effects and ways to support ongoing mindfulness practice*. School of Education, Bangor University. Unpublished MA thesis.

Gunaratana H (1991) *Mindfulness in Plain English*. Boston: Wisdom Publications.

Hanh TN (1987) *Being Peace*. Berkeley: Parallax Press.

Hanh TN (1991) *The Miracle of Mindfulness*. London: Rider.

Hanh TN (1998) *Teachings on Love*. California: Parallax Press.

Hanson R (2009) *Buddha's Brain*. Oakland CA: New Harbinger Publications.

Hanson R (2013) *Hardwiring Happiness*. London: Rider.

Hopkins V & Kuyken W (2012) Benefits and Barriers to Attending MBCT Reunion Meetings: An Insider Perspective. *Mindfulness* **3**, 139–150. https://doi.org/10. 1007/s12671-012-0088-3

Hope V (2012) 'Mindfulness and Carers'. In: S Silverton (Ed) *The Mindfulness Breakthrough*. London: Watkins Publishing.

Kabat-Zinn J (1990) *Full Catastrophe Living*. New York: Delta.

Kabat-Zinn J (1994) *Wherever You Go There You Are, Mindfulness Meditation in Everyday Life*. New York: Hyperion.

Kabat-Zinn J (2005) *Coming To Our Senses*. London: Piatkus.

Kabat-Zinn (2006) *Mindfulness for Beginners: Reclaiming the Present Moment – And Your Life*. Boulder: Sounds True, Inc.

Kabat-Zinn J, Lipwort L, Burney R & Sellers W (1987) Four-year follow-up of a meditation-based program for the self-regulation of chronic pain: treatment outcomes and compliance. *Clinical Journal of Pain* **2**, 159–173.

Kabat-Zinn J, Massion MD, Kristeller J, Peterson LG, Fletcher KE & Pbert L (1992) Effectiveness of a meditation-based stress reduction program in the treatment of anxiety disorders. *American Journal of Psychiatry* **149**, 936–943.

Kabat-Zinn J, Massion AO, Hebert J & Rosenbaurn E (1998) *A Meditation. Textbook of Psychonocology*. Edited by J Holland. Oxford: Oxford University Press.

Kabat-Zinn J (1999) *Consortium on Integrative Medicine, The Umass Experience, Centre for Mindfulness in *Medicine, Health Care and Society*, unpublished paper.

Kabat-Zinn J (2003) Mindfulness-based Interventions in context: past, present, and future. *American Psychological Association* **D12**, 144–155.

Khema Ayya (1987) *Being Nobody, Going Nowhere*. Massachusetts: Wisdom Publications.

Kornfield J (1994) *Path with Heart*. New York: Bantam Books.

Lambert M, Graham SM, Fincham FD & Stillman TF (2009) A changed perspective: How gratitude can affect sense of coherence through positive reframing. Published online ahead of print: 05 Nov 2009.

Lambert NM, Graham SM & Fincham FD (2009). A prototype analysis of gratitude: Varieties of gratitude experiences. *Personality and Social Psychology Bulletin* **35**, 1,193–1,207. http://dx.doi.org/10.1177/0146167209338071

Lambie A (2016) *'Getting it under your skin': Experiences of monthly mindfulness practice support groups*. MSc in Teaching Mindfulness-Based Courses School of Psychology, Bangor University. Unpublished paper.

Jones J (2019) *Selected Poems*. Bodfan: The Bodfan Press.

Lutz A, Greischar LL, Rawlings NB, Ricard M & Davidson RJ (2004) Long-term meditators self-induce high-amplitude gamma synchrony during mental practice. *Proceedings of the National Academy of Sciences* **101**, 16,369 to 16,373.

Lutz, A, Dunne J & Davidson R (2007) *Meditation and the Neuroscience of Consciousness: An introduction*. Cambridge Handbook of Consciousness

Lutz A, Brefczynski-Lewis J, Johnstone T & Davidson RJ (2008a) Regulation of the neural circuitry of emotion by compassion meditation: effects of meditative expertise. *PLoS One* **3**:e1897.

Mills P J, Dimsdale JE, Natarajan L, Ziegler MG, Maisel A & Greenberg BH (2009). Sleep and health-related quality of life in heart failure. *Congestive Heart Failure* **15**, 228–233. http://dx.doi.org/10.1111/j.1751-7133.2009.00106.

Mandela N (1994) *Long Walk to Freedom*. London: Little Brown & Co.

Miller JJ, Fletcher K & Kabat-Zinn J (1995) Three-year follow-up and clinical implications of a mindfulness mediation-based stress reduction in the treatment of anxiety disorders. *General Hospital Psychiatry* **17**, 192–200.

Mindfulness All-Party Parliamentary Group (MAPPG) (2015) *Mindful Nation UK*. London: MAPPG.

Nairn R (2001) *Diamond Mind*. Boston & London: Shambala.

National Institute for Clinical Excellence. (2004). *Depression: Management of Depression in Primary and Secondary Care. Clinical Guideline 23*. London: NICE.

Neff K (2011) *Self-Compassion*. New York: HarperCollins.

Neff K and Germer C (2018) *The Mindful Self-Compassion Workbook: A Proven Way to Accept Yourself Build Inner Strength and Thrive*. New York: Guilford Press.

Owen F & Andrea M (2013) *Screen of Brightness*. Gwynedd: Cinnamon Press.

Remen R (1996) *Kitchen Table Wisdom*. London: Pan.

Remen R (2000) *My Grandfather's Blessings*. London: Thorsons.

Rosenberg L (2004) *Breath By Breath – The Liberating Practice of Insight Meditation*. London: Shambala.

Salzberg S (1997) *Loving Kindness the Revolutionary Art of Happiness*. London: Shambhala.

Salzberg S (1997) *Heart As Wide As the World*. Boston: Shambhala Classics.

Santorelli S (1999) *Heal Thy Self*. New York: Random House.

Schore AN (2003) *Affect Dysregulation and Disorders of the Self*. New York, London: W. W. Norton & Company.

Segal ZV, Williams JMG & Teasdale JD (2002) *Mindfulness-based Cognitive Therapy for Depression. A New Approach to Preventing Relapse*. New York: Guilford Press.

Shapiro SL, Carlson LE, Astin JA & Freedman B (2006) Mechanisms of mindfulness. *Journal of Clinical Psychology* **62** (3), 373–386.

Siegel DJ (2007) *The Mindful Brain*. New York, London: W.W. Norton & Company.

Silverton S (2012) *The Mindfulness Breakthrough*. London: Watkins Publishing.

Stafford W (1998) *New and Selected Poems*. Minnesota: Graywolf Press.

Strack F, Martin LL & Stepper S (1988). Inhibiting and facilitating conditions of the human smile: A nonobtrusive test of the facial feedback hypothesis. *Journal of Personality and Social Psychology*, **54**, 768–777. Google Scholar | Crossref | Medline | ISI

Surawy C, Roberts J & Silver A (2005) The effect of mindfulness training on mood and measures of fatigue, activity, and quality of life in patients with chronic fatigue syndrome on a hospital waiting list: a series of exploratory studies. *Behavioural and Cognitive Psychotherapy* **33** (1), 103–109.

Teasdale JD, Segal ZV, Williams JMG, Ridgeway VA, Soulsby JG & Lau MA (2000) Prevention of Relapse/Recurrence in Major Depression by Mindfulness-Based Cognitive Therapy. *Journal of Consulting and Clinical Psychology*, **68**, 615–623.

Thich Nhat Hanh (1991) *The Miracle of Mindfulness*. London: Rider.

Thich Nhat Hanh (1987) *Being Peace*. California: Parallax Press.

Thich Nhat Hanh (1996) *The Long Road Turns to Joy: A Guide to Walking Meditation*. California: Parallax Press.

Wax R (2016) *A Mindfulness Guide for the Frazzled*. London: Penguin.

Welwood J (2002) *Towards a Psychology of Awakening: Buddhism Psychotherapy and the Path of Personal and Spiritual Transformation*. Boston and London: Shambhala.

Williams JMG, Teasdale JD, Segal ZV & Kabat-Zinn J (2007) *The Mindful Way through Depression: Freeing Yourself from Chronic Unhappiness*. New York: Guilford Press.

Williams M & Penman D (2011) *Mindfulness: A Practical Guide to Finding Peace in a Frantic World*. London: Piatkus Books.

Williams W (1997) *The Peacemakers: Selected Poems*. Translated by Tony Conran. Llandysul: Gomer.

Wumen Hui-K'ai (1183–1260)

Yeats WB (1933) "A Dialogue of Self and Soul" from *The Poems of W. B. Yeats: A New Edition*. London: Macmillan.

Yeats WB (1902) *The Celtic Twilight*. London: John W. Parker.

Web links

Centre for Mindfulness Research and Practice – Audio downloads for practices: https://www.bangor.ac.uk/mindfulness/audio/index.php.en

The Oxford MBCT app with Mark Williams, Melanie Fennell, Becca Crane, Chris Cullen, Antonia Sumbundu and Christina Feldman:

http://mbctapp.oxfordmindfulness.org/ (Mental Health in Wales: Fundamental Facts 2016)

www.mindandlife.org

http://themindfulnessinitiative.org.uk/images/reports/Mindfulness-APPG-Report_Mindful-Nation-UK_Oct2015.pdf`

http://www.themindfulnessinitiative.org.uk/about/who-we-are

http://greatergood.berkeley.edu/article/item/how_mindfulness_can_defeat_racial_bias

Mental Health Foundation Evidence & Research: http://bemindful.co.uk/evidence-research/

There is a wonderful YouTube video of the *Nine Attitudes from Jon Kabat-Zinn*: https://www.youtube.com/watch?v = 2n7FOBFMvXg

Recommended reading

Barks C (1995) *The Essential Rumi*. Translated by Coleman Barks with John Moyne and A J Arberry. London: Penguin Classics.

Brach T (2003) *Radical Acceptance*. London: Rider.

Burch V and Penman D (2013) *Mindfulness for Health: A practical guide to relieving pain, reducing stress and restoring wellbeing*. London: Piatkus.

Chodrun P (1990, 1997) *When Things Fall Apart*. Boston: Shambhala Classics.

Chodrun P (1994) *Start Where You Are: A Guide to Compassionate Living*. Boston: Shambhala Publications.

Chodrun P (2001) *The Places That Scare You*. London: Element.

Chodrun P (2001) *The Wisdom of No Escape*. London: Shambhala Classics.

Dhammapada Shambhala Classics

Feldman C (2005) *Compassion: Listening to the Cries of the World*. London: Rodmell Press.

Frankl V (1959) *Man's Search of Meaning*. London: Rider.

Frank A (1947) *Anne Frank's Diary*. London: Pan.

Hanson R (2013) *Hardwiring Happiness*. London: Random House.

Kabat Zinn J (1994) *Wherever You Go There You Are: Mindfulness Meditation in Everyday Life*. New York: Hyperion.

Ram Das (2000) *Still Here*. London: Hodder & Stoughton.

Remen R (1996) *Kitchen Table Wisdom*. London: Pan, Macmillan.

Remen R (2000) *My Grandfather's Blessings*. London: Thorsons.

Rumi translated by Coleman Barks (1995) *The Essential Rumi*. London: Penguin

Silverton S (2012) *The Mindfulness Breakthrough*. London: Watkins Publishing.

Williams M & Penman D (2011) *Mindfulness: A Practical Guide to Finding Peace in a Frantic World*. London: Piatkus Books.

Wax R (2016) *A Mindfulness Guide for the Frazzled*. London: Penguin.

Rynick D (2012) *This Truth Never Fails*. Boston: Wisdom Publications.

Salzberg S (1997) *Loving Kindness: The Revolutionary Art of Happiness*. London: Shambhala Classics.

Salzberg S (1997) *Heart as Wide as the World*. Boston: London: Shambhala Classics.